THE REFRACTIVE THINKER®

AN ANTHOLOGY OF DOCTORAL WRITERS

VOLUME VII
Social Responsibility

Edited by **Dr. Cheryl A. Lentz**

THE REFRACTIVE THINKER® PRESS

The Refractive Thinker®: An Anthology of Higher Learning
Vol VII: Social Responsibility

The Refractive Thinker® Press
9065 Big Plantation Avenue
Las Vegas, NV 89143-5440   USA

info@refractivethinker.com
www.refractivethinker.com
blog: http://www.dissertationpublishing.com

Books are available through The Refractive Thinker® Press at special discounts for bulk purchases for the purpose of sales promotion, seminar attendance, or educational purposes. Special volumes can be created for specific purposes and to organizational specifications. Please contact us for further details.

Orders placed on www.refractivethinker.com for students and military receive a 15% discount.

Please visit us on Facebook and like our Fan page. www.facebook.com/refractivethinker

Copyright © 2012 by The Refractive Thinker® Press
Managing Editor: Dr. Cheryl A. Lentz

Library of Congress Control Number: 2012909551

Volume ISBNs   Soft Cover   978-0-9840054-2-0
                E-book/PDF   978-0-9840054-6-8
                *Kindle and electronic versions available

Refractive Thinker® logo by Joey Root; The Refractive Thinker® Press logo design by Jacqueline Teng; cover design by Peri Poloni-Gabriel, Knockout Design, www.knockoutbooks.com; final production by Gary A. Rosenberg, www.thebookcouple.com.

Printed in the United States of America

10   9   8   7   6   5   4   3   2   1

Contents

"Be the change you want to see in the world."
—MAHATMA GANDHI

Foreword

For the past 25 years, I have enjoyed the great fortune and unique privilege of working to build some of the United States' most effective nonprofits. I have asked a lot of people for a whole lot of money; millions for education, tens of millions for hunger relief, and so on. But in 2007, as I led a group of leaders in Southern Nevada to build a national model food bank, a prospective corporate donor asked me a question that—even now—still guides me. "Why do we have "to" feed all these damn people?"

At the time, I was horrified that someone would think like that. But as I thought more, I realized what he actually meant was "what's in it for me?" And that, I think, is in an entirely reasonable question. In part, we give of ourselves because it is an innate, unique part of the American experience. Unlike many countries and communities in the world, where there is little civil society— either because (sadly) no freedom exists or because local government supplants the need for philanthropy—our cities and neighborhoods are strengthened by the people who call them home. Simply put, we are a country where neighbors help neighbors and strangers help strangers. Moreover, we give of ourselves because even when the tangible value cannot be identified, doing so simply feels good.

Still, philanthropy has changed in the 120 years since Andrew Carnegie formed his influential foundation; people, corporations, and associations are increasingly strategic and coordinated in using their resources. Funders are moving from the notion of *giving* to *investing* and are looking for return on investments (ROI). In short, funders are treating philanthropy as they do a business.

The rise of strategic philanthropy and especially the increased collaboration among funders is good for communities. For example, Michael is an African American high school student who received desperately required assistance from Southern Nevada's social sector. What makes Michael a paradigm of modern philanthropy is that he received coordinated assistance that met his unique spectrum of needs—food from our food bank, social services from our partners, and financial assistance for college from a funder we all had in common. As a result, Michael is transcending the odds of his peers and his neighborhood.

As funders continue to explore methods to maximize the impact of resources, *and* as we, as a nation, seek progress in our most grinding challenges, it is more important than ever to work more intelligently in concert. Indeed, we are most impactful when we a) engage with other funders and across the private and public sectors, and b) insist that our philanthropy be passionately driven and bolstered by a crystal-clear vision.

We collectively have the ability to make our communities vibrant places, where exceptional education is accessible to all, quality of life indicators soar, and businesses thrive.

What my friend did not understand when he asked about why the food bank should help people, is that all people in a community are tied to one another—our communities are more like ecosystems than fragmented individual pieces. When communities are strengthened, everyone benefits. So, if nothing else, that is why have "to feed those damn people." This edition of the Refractive Thinker is full of stories regarding *corporate social responsibility* that, in one way or another, answers the question of *what's in it for me.* Why do we give of ourselves, our companies, and why do we expect others to do the same? Read on to find more answers.

Julie A. Murray
President & CEO, Moonridge Group

Preface

I *think* therefore I am.
—RENEE DESCARTES

I *critically think* to be.
I *refractively think* to change the world.
Welcome to *The Refractive Thinker® Vol VII: Social Responsibility*

Thank you for joining us for the Spring 2012 edition as we continue to celebrate the accomplishments of doctoral educators affiliated with many phenomenal institutions of higher learning. The purpose of this next offering within the anthology series is to share current research from these participating authors, specifically on the topic of social responsibility. Our goal is to add to our quest as refractive thinkers, and to ask the question: *what is the purpose of the doctoral scholar?* In this edition of the award-winning series, we offer many answers for contemplative thought.

This peer-reviewed resource provides a framework to discuss social responsibility from the perspective of the doctoral scholar. Topics for discussion include an expectation of the lifelong learner, challenges for empowering women, influence of women leaders and entrepreneurs, generational conflict, value of innovative leadership practices, succession planning, public trust, the role of elite athletes, the role of stakeholders, the role of technology and social irresponsibly from the perspective of sustainability. Further, these topics reflect the construct of the refractive thinker where each author challenged the conventional wisdom and expanded beyond traditional boundaries. These authors dared to think not only *outside* of the box, but also beyond. Instead, the discussion continues to evolve, exploring entirely new ideas for construction of 'the box.'

In addition to exploring various aspects of social responsibility, the purpose of *The Refractive Thinker®* is to serve the tenets of leadership. This is not simply a concept outside of the self, but comes from within, defining our very essence. The search becomes a personal journey of the lifelong learner, not yet a finite destination.

The Refractive Thinker® is an intimate expression of who we are—the ability to think beyond the traditional boundaries of thinking and critical thinking. Instead of mere reflection and evaluation, one challenges the very boundaries of the constructs itself. If thinking is *inside* the box, and critical thinking is *outside* the box, we add the next step of refractive thinking, *beyond* the box. Perhaps the need exists to dissolve the box completely. As in our first six volumes, the authors within these pages are on a mission to change the world through scholarly research. Refractive thinkers are never satisfied or quite content with *what is* or asking *why;* instead these authors intentionally strive to push and test the limits to ask *why not.*

Join us on this next adventure of *The Refractive Thinker®* where this edition of Volume VII continues the discussion. Remember not only do we offer seven volumes (one with two editions) for your consideration in research choices, but 71 individual e-chapters are also available should you desire to select your favorites.

Please contact The Refractive Thinker® Press for further information regarding these authors and the works contained within these pages. Perhaps you or your organization may be looking for their expertise to incorporate as part of your annual corporate meetings as a keynote or guest speaker(s), or to offer individual or group seminars, coaching, or consultation.

We look forward to your interest in discussing future opportunities. Let this collection of authors continue our journey, which began with volume I. Come join us in our quest to further develop our skills as refractive thinkers and add your wisdom to the collective. We look forward to your stories.

Acknowledgments

The foundation of leadership embraces the art of asking questions—to validate and affirm *what* we do and *why*. Leaders often challenge this status quo, to offer alternatives and new directions, to dare to try something that has not yet been done as again proved true in this case with our Volume VII. This publication required the continued leap of faith and belief in this new publishing model by those willing to continue forward on this journey. As a result, please let me express my gratitude for the help of the many that made this project possible.

First, let me offer a special thank you to Trish Hladek for her unwavering support and belief that traversing unchartered waters is worthy of the journey. My gratitude extends to our Peer Review Editors, Dr. Laura Grandgenett, Dr, Judy Fisher-Blando, and Dr. Freda Turner, our Board of Directors to include: Dr. Judy Fisher-Blando, Dr. Tom Woodruff, (and myself), and our Author Advisory Board: Dr. Sheila Embry. In addition, let me offer a well-deserved thank you to our production specialist, Gary Rosenberg; Refractive Thinker® logo designer, Joey Root; and our cover designer, Peri Poloni-Gabriel, Knockout Design, and companion website designer, Jacqueline Teng, maintained by AJ Shope.

Let me also extend my sincere gratitude to all participating authors within The Refractive Thinker® series who continue to believe in this project as we continue to expand our program. We appreciate their commitment to leadership and to the concept of what it means to be a refractive thinker.

Dr. Cheryl A. Lentz
Managing Editor
Las Vegas, NV
August 2012

CHAPTER 1

Social Responsibility of Doctoral Scholars

Dr. Tom Woodruff & Dr. Cheryl A. Lentz

One of the aims for *The Refractive Thinker®* Series is to offer a forum for doctoral scholars to share the results of their dissertation and doctorate studies research with those who may benefit from this advancement in academic knowledge. We believe more is at stake than simply a quest in the pursuit of post-secondary education that culminates in the achievement of the coveted doctor title of the individual. Instead, our goal for this next edition in the series is to look deeply at the role and responsibility of the doctoral scholar to share their knowledge to make a difference in the world they serve.

To Whom Much Is Given

> "For everyone to whom much is given,
> of him shall much be required."
> —LUKE 12:48

When one thinks of a doctoral scholar, one often thinks of those who advance knowledge for the betterment of society, following the tenets of social responsible leadership. Perhaps this leadership follows the path of protecting human rights, the environment as well as protecting the rights of animals, social justice, corporate social responsibility, and responsible corporate governance. The question to ponder is the nexus of societal needs with business imperatives—what denotes good citizenship and to be a good steward of one's environment? What role does the doctoral scholar play because of their education as part of this equation?

According to Roome and Bergin (2006),

> Responsible leaders are defined as people of the highest integrity and deep understanding of difficult concepts such as sustainable development, committed to building enduring organizations in association with others, leaders who have a deep sense of purpose and are true to their core values. (as cited in D'Amato, Henderson, & Florence, 2009, p. 9)

Society demands that the doctoral scholar move beyond their individual economic prosperity and contribute to the greater whole.

Leadership can be many things to many people, from transformational to situational to serving those one leads (servant leadership). Instead of traditional leadership recognized in grand gestures and big moments, such as the image of strength and charismas such as in the General Patton's and Winston Churchill's of history, what of the simple, the subtle, the quiet leadership from the pen of the doctoral scholar? What if leadership simply came softly? Is there a moral responsibility and expectation of the scholar regarding their leadership role upon completion of their doctoral journey? Is there an expectation related to what the scholar needs to do with the results of their research? What responsibility does the scholar owe to society? What does the community expect?

According to D'Amato, Henderson, and Florence (2009), "Responsible leaders are concerned with reconciling and aligning the demands, needs, interests, and values of employees, customers, suppliers, communities, shareholders, nongovernmental organizations (NGOs), the environment, and society at large" (p. 6). The question before us is to ask, what is the expectation of the doctoral scholar? What is their social responsibility? With doctoral scholars being such a small part of society—less than 1% of the population (Purdue University, n.d.)—is there a role and responsibility that the doctoral scholar has beyond their individual achievement? Is there perhaps a leadership imperative for which moral exemplars would apply? Our goal is to dig deeper in search of the rights and responsibilities of the highest scholars within post-secondary education regarding society's need to educate leaders whose role is to make a difference in the world through the means of social responsibility.

Metacognition and Doctoral Scholars

The personal actions of a leader should match his or her words to be considered authentic (Higgs, 2003). Cashman (2003) suggested that a leader should also be authentic to his or her "unrealized potential" (p. 248). The meaning of life is different for each of us and for many this means sharing ourselves with others (Cashman, 2003). The ability of a leader to achieve this potential may start with fully knowing his or her body of beliefs. Metacognition is one such tool that can be implemented to expand the use of our brains, to develop our stream of consciousness, to synthesize learning in all aspects of our life, and to break down perceived physical or spiritual barriers. A basic definition of metacognition is thinking about thinking (Hofer & Sinatra, 2010). Understanding the relationship between epistemological beliefs and metacognition may help explain how two intelligent doctoral scholars can view the current environment and derive unique conclusions regarding the most significant needs of society and their role to play.

According to Desoete and Ozsoy (2009), metacognition has three unique components including metacognitive knowledge, metacognitive experiences, and metacognitive skills. Metacognitive *knowledge* in its most basic form exists as the storehouse of our formal knowledge (Desoete & Ozsoy, 2009). Metacognitive *experiences* relate more to our personal emotions and feelings about certain activities (Desoete & Ozsoy, 2009). Metacognitive *skills* relate to our ability to control our thought processes (Desoete & Ozsoy, 2009). Examining all three components may provide the key to identifying the full range of epistemological beliefs.

Mason and Bromme (2010) analyzed the relationship between epistemological beliefs and metacognition. The authors also considered three specific areas regarding metacognition the physical organization of our mind in relationship to knowledge (how knowledge is stored and accessed); the type of relationship that exists between knowledge and learning; and why a relationship exists between these beliefs and learning. The overriding focus was the effect these areas have on self-regulated learning and the adult learner.

Every adult learner to include the doctoral scholar has a unique toolkit of experience and education that collectively produces the attitudes, beliefs, and approaches he or she has toward the attainment of knowledge (Hofer & Pintrich, 2002; Pintrich, 2002). Much of this knowledge and belief system is entrenched in adult learners and requires a modification of personal epistemology to open the door to active learning (Murphy & Mason, 2006). Hofer and Pintrich (2002) maintained that the more knowledgeable and mature an adult is about the beliefs they hold, the more success they will have in educational and other pursuits. This same concept applies to leadership, as well, as the better, we understand ourselves, the more likely we will lead with an open mind (Bennis, 2001).

How Doctoral Scholars aka Lifelong Learners Can Make a Difference

In 1952, Knowles and Bradford recognized changes in society that suggested adult participation in groups promoted additional learning. Knowles (1978) later demonstrated that andragogy (adult learning) was, in fact, different from pedagogy (the traditional teaching method refers to how children learn). Andragogy is the theory and process of adult learning (Knowles, 1978). The origin of the term is credited to Alexander Kapp, a German schoolteacher, who posited in 1833 that adult learning differed significantly with learning by children (Knowles, 1978). According to research cited by Knowles, the term was discredited and fell out of use until the next century. Knowles cited Eduard C. Lindeman and his focus on the "artistic stream, which seeks to discover knowledge through intuition and the analysis of experience" (p. 10) that laid the foundation for the evolution of Andragogy. Knowles formalized the theory of adult education. From a more artistic perspective, Pearsall (2009), in an interesting summary of a keynote speech, noted, "there is no end to learning" (p. 26). This observation suggests the perspective of this commentary where doctoral scholars are lifelong learners because of their very nature of pursuing higher education.

Doctoral scholars are adult learners who motivate themselves; take responsibility for what they study, are active participants in the process; and come from very diverse backgrounds. Adult learners [and the doctoral scholars] prefer to relate new knowledge to their own practical experience and apply this to their personal lives (Brookfield, 2009; Knox, 2009). Knox (2009) also underscored that adult learners desired a praxis-oriented approach to learning that allows the individual to move back and forth between theory and application. This proactive approach creates a fertile field for critical, creative thinking, and refractive thinking that enlivens the learning process. This combination of individual self-direction and team learning is essential to facilitate adult learning and to build individual confidence (Johnson, 2009; Smith, 2008). Ultimately, this individual confidence can lead doctoral scholars to pursue opportunities to make a difference.

Leadership Comes Softly

Leadership offers an opportunity to leave behind one's signature on the world, a permanent legacy as unique as its creator. Conceptually, this legacy offers a commentary on the importance of one's personal and organizational guiding philosophies, built upon core purpose and core values (Crossan, Fry, & Killing, 2005), allowing the leader the ability to transform him or herself and the world in which he or she lives. The purpose of this writing is to examine leadership as a value centric concept in questioning the role and responsibility of the doctoral scholar as part of a strategic value-centric business model, vision, and focus (Bate & Johnson, 2005). Our goal is to examine the lives of those who make an everyday difference in the lives of their followers because of the research they conduct and the results they offer the world.

Leaders are those who are in not only the C-Suite, the boardroom, or the captains of industry with wealth and prestige; sometimes leaders may be the person next to you on the plane or in line at the grocery store, regardless of title, rank, or position. According to Daft (2010), leadership is a function of *influence,* not position. Leadership is the something one *does* or whom one is—wherever one may find themselves within the organization or the community. Leaders earn their place in the annals of history by their stories and the value of the content of their words, their writings, their deeds, and their actions—so too as the role of the doctoral scholar and the benefits of the research they contribute.

This volume of *The Refractive Thinker®* continues the narrative of the doctoral scholar, the silent, sometimes invisible heroes who affect our lives in ways that we cannot always see, yet society benefits from the merits of their scholarly research and refractive thinking. These are the doctoral scholars, the change agents, the leaders for whom leadership comes softly.

Socially Responsible Leadership

Leadership also refers to a broader context of the relationships of humans to each other. Senge (1999) offered a unique concept referred to as conscious oversight, defined as "a discipline of care and nurturing of people and systems with an eye toward the impact on generations who come after them" (p. 545). This piece of the puzzle examines the need for thoughtful planning to consider future consequences of the learning organization within the context of the larger system of society. Perhaps the larger question is how we as scholars measure how our actions benefit the world around us. "When practicing conscious oversight, people focus on insuring congruence and viability of a system larger then themselves, in service of a purpose larger then themselves" (Senge, 1999, p. 546). The tools of the doctoral scholar can offer this alignment.

Part of conscious oversight is the ability to "build and sustain relationships throughout the system' (Senge, 1999, p. 547). This purposeful behavior mirrors the expectations of the community of doctoral scholars—to leave the world a better place than they found it through the efforts of research. Creation of this sense of community is spoken through each of us as members of our respective communities that draws us together regarding fiscal intelligence, social intelligence, and noteic intelligence (capability of thinking and learning in groups) (Senge, 1999). As lifelong learners, our goal is to move the academic football forward, where society as a whole can benefit from the questions our research may ponder, and the advances our research may suggest.

Merrill (2007) developed the "Pebble-in-the-Pond approach to instructional design" (p. 7) that focused on content with the goal of building individual learning from the pebble to subsequent ripples of learning. Step 1 (the pebble) is task centered and focuses on specific concepts. Step 2 activates these new concepts with prior learning. Step 3 demonstrates the relatable skills. Step 4 applies the new skills. And Step 5 integrates the learning into the student's life beyond the classroom. Step 5 of Merrill's (2007) model suggests the position that doctoral scholars are in relation to conscious oversight. Doctoral scholars can be the pebbles in many ponds that forever guide and change our future.

Transformational Leadership: The Role of the Scholar

Transformational leadership also highlights the development and self-actualization of followers, having to balance the needs of the organization with the professional and personal values of employees (Bass, 1990). This school of thought goes beyond merely the traditional view of what is meant to influence followers, preferring motivation to help people mature and reach their full potential. The evidence suggests overwhelmingly that leadership is not a value free concept. Instead, leadership embraces the multiple dimensions of values. Leaders have their own personal interpretations of what they value in people to include individual characteristics, and behaviors based on ethics, morality, and judgment (Cashman, 1998). On a personal and professional level, the purpose of a leader is to identify such values. By living these values by example, both within the walls of the organization and beyond, this experience allows a leader to stay true to their core principles and purpose (Cashman, 1998).

Cashman's (2003) concepts may be an evolution from Peter Drucker (1992). Drucker (1992), a recognized management thinker, believed that the essence of leadership is performance based where "leadership is not by itself good or desirable. Leadership is a means. Leadership is to what end is thus the crucial question" (p. 119). Cashman (2003) suggested that leadership as a legacy provides commentary on whether a leader could use this value creation to make a difference for which he or she wishes to be remembered, having a connection between personal growth and professional effectiveness. Values are not merely words. Instead, values are ethical foundations that are necessary for sustainable business performance and practice. One does not need to sacrifice principles or character for effective business results. Instead, these qualities offer a nexus, a value laden ". . . point of intersection of the soul of the leader" (Cashman, 2003, p. 5).

Leadership, as Who We Are?

According to Toner (1996), "Good leaders do not simply want their followers to *do something;* good leaders want their followers *to be somebody*" (p. 127). The question for this writing is to address the definition for leadership as a noun, a verb, or an outcome of a verb. Toner suggested the latter, believing that definitions of leadership do not go far enough, willing to stop only at the level of action as influenced or inspired by the leader. The entire challenge is this idea of purpose and *intent* of leadership, in which we ask what do we want the result of leadership to look like; conceptually this refers to beyond the perceived outcome of leadership, i.e. *the do something* part. The entire idea of transformational leadership is to acknowledge that a leader's intent as perhaps addressed in the military mantra of duty, honor, country, is the ability to inspire persona, not merely behavior. Again, the true outcome is in the character of the individual for whom leadership is expected, what will they do as leaders in terms of who they are? The physical manifestations of their thinking are only the first step. Is it not enough to be thought of as a good leader simply because of actions, intent, and purpose go to someone's character and the ability to judge one's leadership ability? Toner referred to leadership as genius where "leadership is the ability to inspire appropriate action beyond the expectable" (1996, p. 123). Leadership is not needed in situations where expectations are clear; leadership is needed in the absence of clarity.

Bateman and Snell (2007) added to these definitions of leadership, in which "a leader is one who influences others to attain goals. The greater the number of followers, the greater the influence" (p. 394). Perhaps then, the additional benefit of the doctoral scholar is their rise to the top of the academic pinnacle, establishing more of platform from which to lead and offer their voice of influence?

Doctoral scholars work very hard "to be somebody" (1996, p. 127) in their areas of expertise. With this accomplishment, doctoral scholars have positioned themselves to influence others and to transform the world we see. This is an example of transformational leadership and the social responsibility of doctoral scholar/leaders.

Conclusion

This essay provides a brief discussion of the social responsibility of doctoral scholars to lead by example and to change the world. The ability of a doctoral scholar/leader to achieve this potential may start with fully knowing his or her body of beliefs as well as core principles and values. This combination of individual self-direction and team learning is essential to facilitate adult learning and to build individual confidence (Johnson, 2009; Smith, 2008). Ultimately, this individual confidence can lead doctoral scholars to pursue opportunities to make a difference. Leaders earn their place in the annals of history by their stories and the value of the content of their words, their writings, their deeds, and their actions—so too as the role of the doctoral scholar and the benefits of the research they contribute. Doctoral scholar/leaders have their own personal interpretations of what they value in people to include individual characteristics, and behaviors based on ethics, morality, and judgment (Cashman, 1998). On a personal and professional level, the purpose of a doctoral scholar/leader is to identify such values. Doctoral scholar/leaders can be the pebbles in many ponds that change the future and this is part of our social responsibility.

REFERENCES

Bateman, R. S., & Snell, S. A. (2007). *Management: Leading & collaborating in a competitive world* (7th ed.). New York, NY: McGraw Hill/Irwin.

Bass, B. (1990). *Bass & Stogdill's handbook of leadership: Theory, research, and managerial applications.* New York, NY: The Free Press.

Bennis, W. (2001). *On becoming a leader.* New York, NY: Basic Books.

Brookfield, S. (2009). *Adult learning: An overview.* Retrieved from http://www.nl.edu/academics/cas/ace/facultypapers/StephenBrookfield_AdultLearning.cfm.

Cashman, K. (1998). *Leadership from the inside out.* Minneapolis, MN: TCLG.

Cashman, K. (2003). *Awakening the leader within: A story of transformation.* Hoboken, NJ: John Wiley and Sons.

Crossan, M. M., Fry, J. N., & Killing, J. P. (2005). *Strategic analysis and action* (6th ed.). Toronto, Canada: Prentice-Hall.

Daft, R. (2011). The leadership experience (5th ed.). Mason, OH: South-Western Cengage Learning.

D'Amato, A., Henderson, S., & Florence S. (2009). *Corporate social responsibility and sustainable business practice: A guide to leadership tasks and functions.* Greensboro, NC: Center for Creative Leadership.

Desoete, A., & Ozsoy, G. (2009). Introduction: Metacognition, more than the lognes. *International Electronic Journal of Elementary Education, 2*(1), 1–6. Retrieved from http://www.iejee.com/

Drucker, P. (1992). *Managing for the future: The 1990s and beyond.* New York, NY: Truman Talley.

Higgs, M. (2003). How can we make sense of leadership in the 21st century? *Leadership & Organizational Development Journal, 24*(5/6), 273–284. doi:10.1108/01437730310485798

Hofer, B. K., & Pintrich, P. R. (Eds.). (2002). *Personal epistemology: The psychology of beliefs about knowledge and knowing.* Mahwah, NJ: L Erlbaum Associates.

Hofer, B. K., & Sinatra, G. M. (2010). Epistemology, metacognition, and self-regulation: Musings on an emerging field. *Metacognition Learning, 5,* 113–120. doi:10.1007/s11409-009-9051-7

Johnson, R. G. (2009). The joys of the journey or "hey, who's in charge here?" *American Music Teacher, 59*(2), 23–25. Retrieved from http://www.mtna.org/publications/american-music-teacher/

Knowles, M. S. (1978). Andragogy: Adult learning theory in perspective. *Community College Review* (5), 9–20. Retrieved from SAGE journals online.

Knowles, M. S. (1980). Malcolm Knowles on . . . How do you get people to be self-directed learners? *Training & Development Journal, 34*(5), 96. Retrieved from http://www.traininganddevelopmentjournal.com/

Knowles, M. S., & Bradford, L. P. (1952). Group methods in adult education. *Journal of Social Issues, 8*(2), 11–22. doi:10.1111/j.1540-4560.1952.tb01600.x

Knox, A. (2009). *"What major generalizations about adults as learners are useful to help adults learn and use what they learn? How can educators use such generalizations?"* Interview with Alan Knox: Colorado State University—Global Campus.

Mason, L., & Bromme, R. (2010). Situating and relating epistemological beliefs into metacognition: Studies on beliefs about knowledge and knowing. *Metacognition Learning, 5*, 1–6. doi:10.1007/s11409-009-9050-8

Merrill, M. D. (2007). A task-centered instructional strategy. *Journal of Research on Technology in Education, 40*(1), 5–22. Retrieved from http://www.iste.org

Merrill, M. D., & Gilbert, C. G. (2008). Effective peer interaction in a problem-centered instructional strategy. *Distance Education, 29*(2), 199–207. doi:10.1080/01587910802154996

Murphy, P. K., & Mason, L. (2006). Changing knowledge and beliefs. In P. Alexander & P. Winne (Eds.), *Handbook of educational psychology* (2nd ed.). (pp. 305–324). Mahwah, NJ: Erlbaum.

Pearsall, T. (2009, Oct/Nov). "There is no end to learning" Lifelong education and the joyful learner. *American Music Teacher, 59*(2), 26–29. Retrieved from http://www.mtna.org/publications/american-music-teacher/

Pintrich, P. R. (2002). The role of metacognitive knowledge in learning, teaching, and assessing. *Theory into Practice, 4*(14), 220–225. doi:10.1207/s15430421tip4104_3

Purdue University. College of Science. (n.d.). *Notes on the PhD degree.* Retrieved from http://www.cs.purdue.edu/homes/dec/essay.phd.html

Senge, P. (1990). *The fifth discipline. The art & practice of the learning organization.* New York, NY: Doubleday.

Smith, R. O. (2008,Winter). Adult learning and the emotional self in virtual online contexts. *New Directions for Adult and Continuing Education. 120*, 35–43. doi:10.1002/ace.314

Toner, R. (1996, November 10). Coming home from the revolution. *The New York Times,* p. D1. Retrieved from http://www.newyorktimes.com

About the Authors

Dr. Tom Woodruff

Dr. Tom Woodruff and his beautiful wife, Diane, live in Georgetown, Texas. In addition to his most important jobs as husband, father, and grandfather, Dr. Tom serves as Lead Faculty and Area Chair for the School of Business at University of Phoenix-Austin Campus. In addition, Dr. Tom is a faculty member with Colorado State University-Global Campus and a contributing faculty member with Walden University. Dr. Tom also serves on the board of The Lentz Leadership Institute.

Dr. Tom holds several accredited degrees including Bachelor of Science in Business Administration, University of Missouri-St. Louis; Master of Business Administration, Southern Illinois University-Edwardsville; and Doctor of Management in Organizational Leadership, University of Phoenix-School of Advanced Studies. He also holds a graduate certificate from SW Graduate School of Banking.

Additional published works include: *Ethical leadership is part of globalization* (2010), *Change agents: Building bridges over resistance* (2009), *Change has no conclusion* (2009), and *Normative leadership types and organizational performance: A case for authoritative performance* (2009).

To reach Dr. Tom Woodruff for information on any of these topics, please e-mail: dr.tmwoodruff@gmail.com

Dr. Cheryl A. Lentz

Southern Nevadan internationally published author Dr. Cheryl A. Lentz holds several accredited degrees; a Bachelor of Arts (BA) from the University of Illinois, Urbana-Champaign; a Master of Science in International Relations (MSIR) from Troy University; and a Doctorate of Management (DM) in Organizational Leadership from University of Phoenix School of Advanced Studies.

Dr. Cheryl, affectionately known as 'Doc C' to her students, is a university professor on faculty with Colorado State University-Global, Embry-Riddle University, University of Phoenix, The University of the Rockies, and Walden University. Dr. Cheryl serves as a dissertation committee member, faculty mentor, is a dissertation coach and offers expertise in editing in APA style for graduate thesis and doctoral dissertations. She has earned her Sloan C Certification from Colorado State University—Global as well as her Quality Matters Peer Reviewer (APP/PRC) Certification.

Dr. Cheryl is also an active member of Alpha Sigma Alpha Sorority.

Additional published works include her dissertation: *Strategic Decision Making in Organizational Performance: A Quantitative Study of Employee Inclusiveness, The Golden Palace Theory of Management, Journey Outside the Golden Palace, Effective Study Skills in 5 Simple Steps, The Refractive Thinker®: Vol. I: An Anthology of Doctoral Learners, Vol. II: Research Methodology, Vol. III. Change Management, Vol. IV: Ethics, Leadership, and Globalization, Vol. V: Strategy in Innovation, Vol. VI: Post-Secondary Education.* For additional details, please visit her website: http://www.drcheryllentz.com Please follow her on Facebook, LinkedIn, and Twitter (/drcheryllentz).

To reach Dr. Cheryl Lentz for information on any of these topics, please e-mail: drcheryllentz@gmail.com

CHAPTER 2

Addressing the Challenges of Empowering Rural Women, Can Holistic Leadership and Corporate Social Reasonability Help?

Dr. Beverly D. Carter

In the wake of the devastating effects of poor and unbalanced leadership, evidenced by the near economic collapse of the world economy; greed, genocide, and war, businesses must reconnect with the needs of the people, including the poor, and disenfranchised. The abuse of leadership within many of our organizations around the world has created a demand for more integrated leadership, which is inclusive, transparent, more balanced, and socially responsible. Efforts are in process by some organizations to bridge the gap in the relationship between business and human welfare.

Some of the basic underlying factors of disempowerment faced by women are presented in a review of challenges taken from the perspective of the education of young girls; global literacy and diversity as issues relating to poor and marginalized groups. The purpose of this work is to address the gap in the literature with regard to the challenges to empowering rural women and corporate social responsibility (CSR). "The idea of CSR presupposes that businesses have obligations to society that go beyond profit-making to include helping to solve societal social and ecological problems" (Idemudia, 2011, p. 1). The world stage is set for organizations to be more socially responsible but even with a holistic leadership lens, are business leaders prepared to use CSR to address the heavy burdens of poverty, cultural diversity, and oppression?

The Education of Young Girls

Those among us, who are able, are socially responsible for ensuring the welfare of our children, especially the education of our young girls, who are the key to ending the cycle of marginalized disempowerment. "Every child has rights to a name and a nationality and to live safe from all forms of violence and abuse" (UNICEF Annual Report, 2010, p. 24). Although this sentiment is true, not all children are equally protected. Many children remain vulnerable to injustices or violations for a variety of reasons, such as being poor, disabled, a migrant, or simply female (UNICEF Annual Report, 2010).

> Education speeds human empowerment and transforms society. Without it, the most marginalized children will only fall further behind burdened by shrinking opportunities and reduced productivity that will also weigh heavily on economies and societies. (UNICEF Annual Report, 2010, p. 18)

Among the 67 million children not enrolled in primary school, 43% live in sub-Saharan Africa and 27% live in West and South Asia. Universal primary education while available to many countries is not available to all. Only 53 of 171 countries with reported data can claim to have the same numbers of girls and boys in both primary and secondary schools (UNICEF Annual Report, 2010). Globally, as compared to boys, girls are disproportionately denied their right to an education. For many this is as a result of their gender. Equity, in the form of access to quality education demands recognition of the obstacles faced by different groups of people. These barriers must be addressed directly and deliberately (UNICEF Annual Report, 2010). Investing in girls by confronting the obstacles to their education process is vitally important because according to World Bank, no investment is more effective for a nation achieving its development goals than educating girls (Nmadu et al., 2010).

Challenges to the education of young girls in rural parts of the world are not new and have common roots found in oppression. Disparities in the form of gender discrimination; poverty that demands a child must go to work to survive as opposed to school, and an inadequate school infrastructure unable to provide basics like chalk, books, or chairs (UNICEF Annual Report, 2010). Some additionally identified factors preventing school enrollment for many young girls are early marriage based upon societal beliefs and cultural influences; religious beliefs; teenage pregnancy, and illiteracy within families (Liman, Asraf, & Tajudeen, 2011).

According to the World Development Report (2007), "the percentage of women who gave birth before the age of 15 is significantly higher in the poorest nations" (p. 9). This percentage is supported by "limited economic opportunities, poor access to services and traditional norms surrounding sexual behavior, and parents encouraging marriage at very young ages—even at age 12 or younger for some girls" (World Development Report, 2007, p. 9). There are still some cultures that allow girls to marry grown men as early as 8 years old. This accounts for the extremely high rate of vesico-vaginal fistula (VVF), where the fistulous track of a young girl is compressed during childbirth because her body has not fully developed to deliver a child. This damage to the urinary track causes an involuntary discharge of urine that has a tremendous impact on her physical and emotional wellbeing. Still a child herself, many of these young girls are often cast out of their home by their husbands because of their difficulty maintaining personal hygiene (Liman, Asraf, & Tajudeen, 2011). These are serious challenges to educating young girls and ultimately empowering rural women.

Northern Nigeria

Northern Nigeria is predominantly Muslim in its culture practicing the Islamic tradition. In this ancient society, an ideology exists that suggests young boys are more valuable than girls are. This is because of the belief that boys are more attached and committed to family responsibilities, such as farming, fishing, or carving to support their families. This same ideology suggests that girls, do not require the same degree of development and training and are often sent to work in the marketplace until marriage (UNICEF, 2008).

The concept of Western education in this Islamic region is synonymous with initiation into a world of materialism, dualism, and western culture that is considered a wasteful venture. The cycle of illiteracy in this region remains a powerful, generationally perpetual obstacle. The need of the people to focus on more practical investments that yield immediate results for survival as opposed to the long-term dividends associated with an education is preferred (Liman, Asraf, & Tajudeen, 2011.

Indonesia and Zambia

According to the World Development Report (2007), in Indonesia, the majority of the poorest children complete their primary levels before school enrollments drop dramatically. This trend is similar in Zambia, where girls in particular are left behind with the expansion of primary education. More disturbing, is that vast numbers of children are leaving schools without having learned what they should as per standardized tests for science, technology, and the command of basic skills.

Yemen

The educational opportunities in many developing countries are changing with the help of organizations such as UNICEF, which is helping "countries in all regions establish the national frameworks they need to make education better and more inclusive" (UNICEF

Annual Report, 2010, p. 19). For example, in Yemen, child-friendly schools have been established that have assisted in the "enrollment of girls above the national average of only 73 girls to every 100 boys to 88" (UNICEF Annual Report, 2010, p. 19). The increased enrollment of girls was attributed to sending 1,000 female teachers to rural areas. Apparently, parents in these rural areas were more comfortable sending their girls to school with female teachers (UNICEF Annual Report, 2010).

The benefits to the education our young girls are vast, such as the reduction of child and maternal mortality rates. Educated women are more likely to seek medical care; have fewer but healthier babies; improve child health, as they will ensure their children are immunized; adopt improved sanitation practices; enhance a women's domestic role and political participation; improve economic productivity and growth and are more likely to protect themselves from HIV/AIDS, abuse, and exploitation (Liman, Asraf, & Tajudeen, 2011). In all, education is a powerful tool for reducing girls' vulnerability and building vital human capital.

The Impact of Globalization on Education

The impact of globalization on the world economy has given rise to tremendous advancement. The world economy is driven by an ever-increasing demand for services-based and technology- based industries as well as "a more evolved workforce that is more highly educated than at any other time in history" (Quatro, Waldman, & Galvin, 2007, p. 429). The world is faced with a unique and unprecedented opportunity to invest in our young girls. Educating girls has been shown to "increase income for wage earners and increase productivity for employers, yielding benefits for the community and society" (Liman, Asraf, & Tajudeen, 2011, p. 856) at large.

According to WorldBank (2010), there is no investment more effective for achieving developmental goals than educating girls

(Nmadu et al., 2010). However, the ability of CSR to be applied successfully to the full range of development issues is contingent upon the context CSR is assigned to address. CSR has been analyzed through a range of different instruments, such as localized firm specific initiatives; codes of conduct and global agreements; macro-level policy interventions; a wealth of marginalized groups; resource poor farmers, all cases from private sector businesses around the world. The private sector in these cases included various degrees of state and civil society involvement, and the varied ability of CSR to address a wide range of context driven developmental issues. These examples support the unbalanced global development of the role of CSR (Newell & Frynas, 2007).

Where do business and society meet? If properly harnessed, businesses can use corporate social responsibility to help reduce poverty and marginalization by recognizing their potential to exacerbate poverty if they are irresponsible. Businesses as investors, employers, and taxpayers as opposed to more philanthropic pursuits, adherence to global social standards and codes of conduct can provide new market opportunities to alleviate poverty. However, new business investments and employment opportunities can create both positive and negative influences on social and economic development (Newell & Frynas, 2007).

Literacy

Literacy is conceptualized, developed, and acquired; however, literacy is always socially constructed. The most common view of literacy is limited to forms found in classrooms. Literacy is often linear and measurable with variables that involve both literacy and language development. Another model of literacy involves reciprocity among social participants, such as, the influence that learners have on teachers in a classroom or other setting (Compton-Lilly, Rogers, & Lewis, 2012). A third model of literacy is based upon family literacy goals that include supporting the social and economic growth of families such as learning a skill to earn income (Compton-Lilly, Rogers, & Lewis, 2012).

Literacy involves negotiated groups of social practices that operate within a local and global context, conceptualized differently in diverse environments. Literacies "exist only as part of larger material systems, systems that enable acts of reading or writing" (Brandt, 2001, p. 1) and confer value. For example, there are accounts of rural, Appalachian communities in the United States illustrating how that culture views literacy as women's work. Mountain women were permitted by their husbands to read the Bible aloud to the family in the evenings and write letters on their behalf, and even sign their husbands' name. Mountain women often used these skills as a survival tactic to give themselves a break from the drudgery and difficulty of their lifestyle of hard domestic work (Daniell & Mortensen, 2007).

Another social example of literacy is offered by the Korean comfort women, sex slaves forced into prostitution at military brothels by Japanese soldiers during World War II (Berndt, 1997). They were chosen because of their strong educational background and ability to speak Japanese. Once chosen for this work, they were forbidden to speak a word of Korean for fear of death, until they were liberated. Social status and equality are associated with literacy and languages granting the educated the opportunity to participate in certain social contexts and not others. Education was one variable that made these women more valuable to the Japanese soldiers who enslaved them. Eventually, literacy also provided these women an outlet to their traumatic ordeals, abuses, and oppressions after liberation. By writing down their stories, in Korean, their beloved language, they could share the atrocities of their lives with the world and begin healing (Daniell & Mortensen, 2007).

Certain dynamic aspects to globalization pressure cultures and economies to restructure themselves. This restructuring allows economies to meet the need for global, informational labor through education and the development of diverse literacies. With a shift in the value of material systems of fast emerging capitalist societies to develop " "newer" and "more valuable" forms of life to gain social, political, and economic advantage" (Collin & Apple, 2007, p. 436) have materialized. With the emergence and growth of world economies and the demand for a high technology, service-based culture, economic practices are stressed to support the generation of more intellectually challenging work. Societies around the world are tasked with developing the required human capital to meet the needs unfolding in the processes of globalization.

In the context of globalization, businesses have had unprecedented power to encourage weak governments to place their businesses in areas where the social and environmental regulations are poor (corporate social irresponsibility), encouraging the exploitation of marginalized communities. Finding ways to bridge the divide between accepting the advantages businesses bring to communities and protecting communities from corporate irresponsibility remain a challenge for development practitioners. However, addressing this challenge is responsible for helping to shape the policies of developing countries (Newell & Frynas, 2007).

Literacy in the larger context must be examined based upon the dynamics of globalization and informational labor, shaped by education and requisite literacies to ensure productive and rewarding labor in a global, informational economy. Treating literacy in this manner explains why individuals work hard to achieve literacy and to understand why. "As with any resource of value, organized economic and political interests work to conscript and ration the powers of literacy for their own competitive advantage" (Brandt, 2001, p. 5). The potential of literacy as a tool that can provide new ways of working and understanding can transform identities. This is because literacy and education function together as important global networks (Daniell & Mortensen, 2007).

What is Holistic Leadership?

The holistic leadership model involves skills in four domains, analytical, conceptual, emotional, and, spiritual. Analytically leaders are experts at analyzing the situation at hand (their core dilemma), and conceptualizing the dilemma to give a measured and objective assessment of the situations to be addressed. The emotional domain encourages the acknowledgement of a moral compass, and the spiritual domain addresses the ethical and moral scope of humanity, guided by spiritual masters of different theology (Quatro, Waldman, & Galvin, 2007). The holistic leadership model takes the needs of humanity in consideration as the impact on humanity is referenced in each domain to balance leadership. The focus of this particular style is an inclusive view and approach to leadership that allows everyone to participate.

What is Corporate Social Responsibility (CSR)?

CSR is an approach used by many international development programs given its potential to meet the needs of poor and marginalized groups. Corporate social responsibility began as a public relations instrument used to prevent criticism, involve critics, and take advantage of developing business opportunities linked to the images of virtuousness (Newell & Frynas, 2007). The most inclusive definition of corporate social responsibility is presented according to Blowfield and Frynas (2005),

> as an umbrella term for a variety of theories and practices all of which recognize the following: (a) that companies have a responsibility for their impact on society and the natural environment, sometimes beyond legal compliance and the liability of individuals; (b) that companies have a responsibility for the behavior of others with whom they do business (e.g., within supply chains); and that (c) business needs to manage its relationship with wider

society, whether for reasons of commercial viability, to add value to society. (p. 503)

According to "Milton Friedman and other critics of CSR, 'the business of business is business' and practices that deviate from that goal are misplaced and counter-productive" (Newell & Frynas, 2007, p. 671). Constrained by the logic of capitalistic ideology for production and profitability, businesses will always choose to profit over making meaningful contributions to development (Idemudia, 2011). The idea of CSR presupposes that businesses are obligated to grow beyond the practice of making money alone and address social and ecological issues in the communities they serve (Idemudia, 2011).

Advocates for CSR support an increasingly globalized economy where success is measured by the ability to meet the demands of stakeholders' activism, generate new profits, and maintain a competitive global advantage. The concept of CSR is driven by western societies resulting in a separation between global expectations on how best to contribute to sustainable development and the realities of local priorities, such as, addressing the challenges to empowering rural women or how best to address poverty eradication in developing countries (Idemudia, 2011). "The problems businesses encounter when they attempt to intervene as social development actors in complex development environments" (Newell & Frynas, 2007, p. 671) are challenging and often counterproductive to the bottom line of their natural business model, which is to make a profit.

Diversity

Globalization is responsible for a transformation process encouraging people worldwide to embrace diversity in communities and workplaces. These changes are represented as differences in ideas, beliefs, cultures, race, and religions. Aspects of corporate conduct that impact human rights and other social and environmental issues leave organizations poised to consider how the return on investment in leadership development can be augmented to address challenges to social justice. There is a tacit consensus that CSR will vary from place to place and even within regions of the same places given the diversity among cultures (Idemudia, 2011).

Every society brings its own traditions and cultures, contributing to the diversity of humanity. Values and traditions also allow people to cope with severe poverty without objection (Cahill, 2003). However, within businesses, stakeholder engagement may present challenges in a developing country context that take into account factors such as culture, language, education, and pluralistic views that have an effect on the negotiation and decision-making process. Business has an increasingly important role in world development with the increase of foreign direct investment and private sector development. Agencies such as the United Nations Commission on the Private Sector and Development and the World Business Council for Sustainable Development play a major role in changing the terms of the relationship between business and poverty. Business is presented as a part of the solution to the problems of world poverty with the promotion of free markets and small and medium- sized enterprises in global supply chains. Large companies assist as well with upgrades to their product designs, production and marketing (Prieto-Carron, Lund-Thompsen, Chan, Muro, & Bhushan, 2006).

Conclusion

Women's lives as documented in the literature demonstrate an effort to challenge the nearly ubiquitous domination of women by men and poverty. Gender differences are not merely determined by culture but portrayed and preserved through everyday life practices. Gender identities are created and sustained through culturally coded public acts.

The questions remain, are the voices and the issues of the poor and marginalized (rural women) being heard? Are the challenges to the CSR agenda providing new ways of thinking about the role of business to address sustainable development issues, aside from the old business model of making a profit but to support the obligation of businesses to address the developmental problems in the communities in which they work? Programs raising the status of women for example, challenge the overarching cultural framing and denigration of women trying to build their lives while living in societies divided by class, gender, and ethnic inequalities. Women's lives in context and theory are profoundly shaped by kinship and reproduction, with aspects linked to biology and constructed by culture and power. As social actors, women are inextricably bound by social networks and shaped by cultural orientations, conscious subjects who aim to shape their lives in the face of great obstacles (Orlove, 2005).

On the world stage, CSR is a social actor working out its role in businesses. Continued research, analysis, and discussions about the obvious imbalances in the CSR debate are warranted. The CSR agenda must be set to address the context of business and society. The research must include a link to the worldwide contributions of this ongoing debate. Additional research is also needed to look at the complexities of the relationships that link CSR to sustainable development outcomes. CSR was never created to address societal ills; however, it may offer a plausible framework to do just that with a focus on the people and how cultural, social, political, and economic factors influence business contributions. Integrative and collaborative research methods that address the iniquities of power, participation, and discussion between governments are imperative to the success of the flexible role of businesses to be agents of change. To respond appropriately to sustainable development objectives businesses have to acknowledge that shifting societal expectations demand a high level of social responsibility to address global development concerns.

This edited work was presented at the United Nations Commission on the Status of Women, March 1, 2012 on behalf of the International Affairs Division of the National Association of Negro Business and Professional Women's Clubs, Inc.

REFERENCES

Blowfield, M., & Frynas, J. G. (2005). Setting new agendas: Critical perspectives on corporate social responsibility in the developing world. *International Affairs, 81*(3), 499–513. Retrieved from http://www.blackwellpublishing.com/search.asp

Berndt, C. M. (1997). Popular culture as political protest: Writing the reality of sexual slavery. *Journal of Popular Culture 31*(2), 177–187. Retrieved from http://onlinelibrary.wiley.com/journal/10.1111/%28ISSN%291540-5931

Brandt, D. (2001). *Literacy in American lives.* New York, NY: Cambridge University Press.

Cahill, K. M. (2003). *Traditions, values, and humanitarian action.* New York, NY: Fordham University Press.

Collin, R., & Apple, M. W. (2007). Schooling, literacies, and biopolitics in the global age. *Discourse: Studies in the Cultural Politics of Education, 28*(4), 433–454. Retrieved from http://www.routledge.com/

Compton-Lilly, C., Rogers, R., & Lewis, T. Y. (2012). Analyzing epistemological considerations related to diversity: An integrative critical literature review of family literacy scholarship. *Reading Research Quarterly, 47*(1), 33–60. Retrieved from http://www.reading.org/general/publications/journals/rrq.aspx

Daniell, B., & Mortensen, P. (2007). *Women and literacy: Local and global inquiries for a new century.* New York, NY: Lawrence Erlbaum Associates.

Idemudia, U. (2011). Corporate social responsibility and developing countries: Moving the critical CSR research agenda in Africa forward. *Progress in Development Studies, 11*(1), 1–18. Retrieved from http://pdj.sagepub.com/

Liman, M. A., Asraf, R. M., & Tajudeen, S. A. (2011). Girl-child education in Northern Nigeria: Problems, challenges and solutions. *Interdisciplinary Journal of Contemporary Research in Business, 2*(12) 851–859. Retrieved from http://ijcrb.webs.com/

Newell, P., & Frynas, J. G. (2007). Beyond CSR? Business, poverty, and social justice: an introduction. *Third World Quarterly, 28*(4), 669–681. Retrieved from http://www.routledge.com/

Nmadu, G., Avidime, S., Oguntunde, O., Dashe, V., Abdulkarim, B., & Mandara, M. (2010). Girl child education: Rising to the challenge. *African Journal of Reproductive Health, 14*(3) 107–112. Retrieved from http://www.bioline.org.br/abstract?rh10056

Orlove, B. (2005). Editorial: Placing women's lives in context and in theory. *Current Anthropology, 46*(3), 357–359. Retrieved from http://www.wenner gren.org/

Preto-Carron, M., Lund-Thomsen, P., Chan, A., Muro, A., & Bhushan, C. (2006). Critical perspectives on CSR and development: what we know, what we don't know, and what we need to know. *International Affairs, 82*(5), 977–987. Retrieved from http://www.blackwellpublishing.com/search.asp

Quatro, S. A, Waldman, D. A., & Galvin, B. M. (2007). Developing holistic leaders: Four domains for leadership development and practice. *Human Resource Management Review,* 17, 427–441. Retrieved from http://www.science direct.com/

United Nations Children's Fund (UNICEF). (2008). *Annual report.* New York, NY: UNICEF. Retrieved from http://www.unicef.org/publications/index_49924.html

United Nations Children's Fund (UNICEF). (2011). *Annual report.* New York, NY: UNICEF. Retrieved from http://www.unicef.org/lac/UNICEF_Annual_Report_2010_EN_052711.pdf

World Development Report (2007). *Development and the next generation.* Washington, DC: Worldbank. Retrieved from http://siteresources.worldbank.org/INTWDR2007/Resources/OverviewFull.pdf

About the Author

New York author Dr. Beverly D. Carter holds several accredited degrees; a Bachelor of Arts (BA) in Psychology from Western New England University; a Master of Science (MS) in Adult Education Human Resources Management from Fordham University; and a Doctorate of Management (DM) in Organizational Leadership from University of Phoenix School of Advanced Studies.

Dr. Beverly is a 'corporate physician' serving organizations as a mentor and guide as they shift their organizational paradigms. She has vast experience in the human services field, with program directorships spanning the age spectrum, from preschool to aging. She has a strong international background with extensive world travel including alumnus status with Harvard University's Center for International Development (WorldTeach); medical missions with EJAYES Charities to Nigeria (Nasarawa, Kano, Abuja), Haiti and Kenya. She recently presented at the United Nations Commission on the Status of Women Conference regarding addressing the challenges to empowering rural women from the perspectives of educating young girls, leadership, global literacy, and diversity.

A civil servant, Dr. Beverly led the Older Driver Coalition to winning the 2009 Gold NACO award for exceptional development of a county government program for creating a Roll Call Training for Law Enforcement as "first responders" to caregivers and the growing older driving community. She participated in the development of a County Government Publication: A Guide for Caregivers for which her department won the 2009 Bronze Achievement Award.

Additional published works include her dissertation: *The Impact of Thinking and Leadership Styles on the Advancement of Women, The Refractive Thinker® Vol. IV Ethics, Leadership, and Globalization: Changing the Hegemonic Impact of Leadership Advancement for Women; The Refractive Thinker®: Vol. V: Strategy in Innovation: Change Models and 21st Century Organizations: An Epistemic Journey to Creative Innovation.*

For more information on any of these topics, please e-mail: dr.beverlycarter@yahoo.com

Corporate Social Responsibility: The Influence of Women Leaders and Entrepreneurs

Dr. Gayle Grant & Dr. Judy Fisher-Blando

N oble causes and actions are integral to the corporate social responsibility (CSR) that begins in corporations and communities. Corporate social responsibility was defined by Barnett (2007) as "a discretionary allocation of corporate resources toward improving social welfare that serves as a means of enhancing relationships with key stakeholders" (p. 801). The concept of corporate organizations that donate to charities, save the ecological environment via green initiatives, invest in training and education for those who are poverty stricken, and other magnanimous acts of *do-gooding* have been publicly acknowledged and much rewarded. Well-publicized acts of CSR have raised organizational profiles, consequently attracting a larger and more qualified group of job applicants. Further, with an enhanced positive public image and reputation, these CSR responsive companies have launched new and more diverse products and product lines in expanded market regions (Dowling, 2006). These CSR active firms have shown positive financial performance, greater institutional investing, and increased share pricing. Positive financial gains have also led to greater organizational sustainability (Dowling, 2006).

The general concept of a business with societal responsibility was noted as early as the 1700s in Britain and the United States

(Smith, 2003). The concept of societal obligation evolved with the expansion of business and expectation by society that organizations should embrace social betterment. The specific term, Corporate Social Responsibility (CSR) was not coined and regularly used until the 1960s (Smith, 2003). Several ideas regarding what CSR should encompass have been introduced since. In the United States and Canada, more than 200 hundred universities have established centers, courses, competitions, scholarships, or speakers' series focusing on social responsibility and entrepreneurship (Bornstein, 2007). The goal was to increase social awareness regarding the connection between education and the corporate environment.

Based in part on sociological rearing differences between men and women, women have been shown to be more civic minded and social conscious in a corporate setting (Borkowski & Ugras, 1998; Gilligan, 1982). As more women are promoted into Chief Executive Office (CEO) leadership positions, CSR is increasing. Women who serve on various boards have a positive effect on an organizations' reputation and increased revenues (Bernardi, Bosco, & Columb, 2006), although women remain underrepresented in the boardroom by comparison to their male counterparts ("Catalyst," 2009). Bear, Rahman, and Post (2010) found that the more women directors on boards, the higher the CSR ratings of that organization. Findings also indicated that the more women on corporate boards, the greater the company's reputation ratings from CSR awareness and activities (Bear et al., 2010). These findings should serve as a signal to investors that companies with more women on boards would likely be a driver of increased earnings and resultant profitability . . . all the ultimate goal of any and every organization.

Application of Corporate Social Responsibility

Additional drivers of corporate revenues are the concepts of *social responsibility* and *social entrepreneurship*. The term social responsibility has also been defined as relating to the existence of ethical behavior in the workplace (Carroll, 1991). Ethical behavior in the workplace, in this context is the obligation of organizations to behave in ethical and moral ways as institutions of the broader society (Carroll, 1991). CSR refers to the firms' obligation to its stakeholders and society (Carroll, 1991). CSR is the continuing commitment of the organization to act ethically and contribute to economic development while improving the quality of life of stakeholders and society (London & Morfopoulos, 2009; Ravindran, 2008). Smith (2003) argued that no longer is there a quandary *if* an organization should partake in CSR but rather *how* this might be undertaken. Some examples of opportunities for CSR might be in the case of ethical behavior in the workplace where elements of equality and workplace fairness would be fostered, such as equal pay for equal jobs/productivity, sensitivity to the needs of employees with parenting duties, elder care duties, or extenuating circumstances. Ethical behavior in the workplace could also refer to fair hiring practices, training, and mentorship opportunities as well as fair practices of promoting employees within the organization.

While the concept of CSR has been in place for more than five decades, because of corporate ethical debacles such as scandals at Enron, WorldCom, Tyco, etc. the need for organizational reform and perhaps public reacceptance to heal social ills has perhaps repopularized the concept of social responsibility within the corporate sector (Smith, 2003). Within the ailing corporate sector, perhaps the infusion of more women business leaders offering a heightened CSR presence and responsiveness may be the prescription for organizational recovery, yet corporate boards have not fully embraced this strategy and social advantage.

Ethical behavior in the workplace also extends to the non-exploitation of children in the workplace, the non-use of animal testing in some applicable situations, and other interrelationships between all business counterparts and corporate stakeholders. Also in terms of the management of all business relationships, such as job bidding, pricing, information and data handling and protection of client data, vendor ethics, and adherence to all contractual obligations. Carroll (1991) presented a four-tier definition of CSR in order of responsibility: (a) Economic Responsibilities (profitable to compensate the shareholders), (b) Legal Responsibilities (obeying the law), (c) Ethical Responsibilities (doing what is right), and (d) Philanthropic Activities (voluntary organizational contributions to society) (Carroll, 1991). Carroll proposed that a lack of social responsibility could result in increased government regulations, which could reduce an organization' efficiency and profitability (Wheelan & Hunger, 2008). Women business leaders, given their sociological-edge in the area of increased CSR and Social Entrepreneurship, would likely fuel an organization's positive public relations profile, as well as perhaps accomplishing acts of citizenship, and general community betterment via programs that provide job training, mentorship, and social development.

While much press has been devoted to the topic of CSR and its many purported benefits, in the interest of fair and balanced research and despite all the positive aspects of CSR, that one might think are 'win-win' scenarios with CSR at the helm, some researchers have argued against the inclusion of CSR in corporate strategic plans and activities. This exclusionary view implies that CSR is at worst a costly distraction that reduces the profits for the company and the shareholders, who are viewed as the only relevant stakeholders ("European Commission," 2009). Henderson (2001) and Kapstein (2001) noted a plausible rationale for not implementing projects with CSR. These researchers posited that while company leaders of either gender are queued up to showcase generous personas, there could be significant outlays of monetary resources ultimately owned by the shareholders, to implement CSR that the board might otherwise choose to allocate differently. This view, although not necessarily publicly palatable to some, could be seen as a practical and honest assessment of choosing (or not), to partake in CSR activities in many organizations.

Advantages of Corporate Social Responsibility

As an altruistic endeavor, the concept of both Social Entrepreneurship and CSR offers many facets. Many organizations both public and private donate generously to societal relief efforts, and add resources for the betterment of humankind. Barnett (2007) suggested a somewhat self-serving element or perspective to CSR, whereby organizational donations of money, products, and volunteerism could enhance relationships with stakeholders, business investors and stakeholders. General constituents, stakeholders, and the public at large have a positive image of organizations displaying CSR and Social Entrepreneurship (Cramer & Hirschland, 2006). Fombrun and Gardberg (2000), as well as Vanhamme and Grobben (2009) noted that CSR and Social Entrepreneurship can offset organizational reputational damage from negative publicity that might occur in the event of an emergency or crisis. Human resource leaders have noted that the good reputation of an organization helps attract better quality job applicants. Further, Riordan et al. (1997) noted that a corporate profile is enhanced with an improved reputation, whereby positively affecting employee job satisfaction, and retention. Enhanced organizational branding occurs because of CSR and Social Entrepreneurship, which aids a company's ability to launch new products and expand into new markets allowing greater growth and increased profits (Dowling, 2006).

Results from research suggested a generalized halo effect of companies engaging in CSR and Social Entrepreneurship (Desantis, 2011; Smith & Read, 2010). From a corporate economic standpoint, Fombrun (2006) noted that institutional investors highly regard companies engaging in active corporate philanthropic efforts, which could add 12–14% to their valuation for these well-governed organizations. The 9-11 tragedy in New York in 2001, and in the general area of societal safety and protection in 2002, a survey of 264 Fortune 1000 Chief Financial Officers (CFO) indicated that more than 52% of these leaders believed that companies that exhibit active engagement of CSR are thought to be instrumental in helping thwart terrorist groups and activities (Smith, 2003). As noted in research, developing active and effective CSR and Social Entrepreneurship is viewed as adding to organizational revenues and perceived value. According to Gupta and Pirsh (2008), a growing body of research regarding CSR and Social Entrepreneurship in marketing has shown 'a spillover' or 'halo effect' on otherwise unrelated consumer judgments, such as the evaluation of new products. The "halo effect could also extend beyond product evaluations into non-routine types of judgments such as attributions" (Gupta & Pirsh, 2008, p. 520). For example, when employees are involved in community efforts through a company-sponsored volunteer program, the halo effect can be magnified.

For example, Avon Products, Inc. is an organization that promotes itself as *the company for women* committed by the mission *to do well by doing good.* The core content of Avon's Corporate Responsibility Report represents the three pillars of Avon's corporate mission and the focus of the company's corporate responsibility efforts and achievements: (a) the empowerment of women, (b) sustainability, and (c) philanthropy. Key areas also include the foundation of a good corporate citizen: governance, ethics, stakeholder engagement, public policy efforts, workplace safety, and commitment to diversity ("Avon, the Company for Women,"

2012). Society has benefitted from this corporate philosophy as Avon has been in business since 1886.

In a study conducted at the University of Cincinnati, researchers found that "Men start businesses for the money, women for the social value" (University of Cincinnati, 2012, p. 1). Hechevarria, Ingram, Justo, and Terjesen (2012) found that when starting a company, women are more likely to consider individual responsibility and use business as a vehicle for change. Researchers from this same study posited that "women are 1.17 times more likely than men to create social ventures than economic ventures, and women are 1.23 times more likely to pursue environmental ventures than economic focused ventures" (Hechevarria et al., 2012, p. 45). Data from the study at University of Cincinnati in 2009 was used from the Global Entrepreneurship Monitor, an annual assessment of the entrepreneurial activity across many countries and from different start-up types (economic, social, and environmental) on more than 10,000 individuals from 52 counties (University of Cincinnati, 2012). The findings of this study showed entrepreneurial differences between the sexes and that women are more active in social start-ups than their male counterparts are.

Greater Opportunities to Enhance CSR— Include Women Business Leaders

The way women are socialized, they have a greater sense of CSR with more emphasis on morals, ethics, and positive social relations (Borkowski & Ugras, 1998; Gilligan, 1982). Research conducted by Huse, Hielsen, and Hagen (2009) confirmed that women were more cognizant and supportive of CSR as they are more socially oriented than men, whereas men are more notably driven to elements of money and quantifiable issues with less emphasis on the social nuances of organizations and its members. Women leaders can create and foster an entrepreneurial spirit by instilling values of risk-taking and exploration and by providing the structures and systems to encourage people to explore and implement new ideas (Huse, Hielsen, & Hagen, 2009). Findings by Guse, Hielsen, and Hagen (2009) revealed that women board members offer positive contributions to strategic direction and CSR engagement. Conversely, a reasonable argument could be made for organizations to strive to develop a better positive profile, with more stakeholder support, to raise revenues to diversify board membership to include more women as these women will bring higher levels of CSR. This corporate entrepreneurship could produce a higher than average number of innovations and offer more opportunities to generate higher revenues.

In 2010, Janssen-Selvadurai conducted a study to understand what enabled women to become entrepreneurs and how lived experiences of establishing their own businesses have affected them professionally and personally. Findings present a modern day picture of women who have embraced changes in career development and choice and wanted to create a life that suits their own personal desires (Janssen-Selvadurai, 2010). Themes that emerged from the qualitative study included women who felt that: (a) I am seeking a more meaningful work that accommodates my life, (c) Relationships are paramount to the success of my business, and (b) I want to live my life *my* way. These specific findings highlighted how women entrepreneurs have embraced changes in career development to construct a life that suits their own personal desires.

Kim and Reber (2009) found that women and older practitioners tend to have a more positive attitude toward CSR. Fombrun (2006) indicated that gender diversification by companies can significantly and positively affect board processes, decision-making, improved CSR involvement, thus positively enhancing the corporate profile and reputation of an organization. The conclusion is that Inclusion of women on corporate boards might also cast a signal to investors of the possibility of pending financial growth leading to an increase in institutional confidence and investment, higher financial performance, increased share value, and ultimately lead to increased corporate revenues.

Researchers at Catalyst and Harvard Business School, who conducted the *Gender and Corporate Social Responsibility* study, tracked philanthropic donations in Fortune 500 companies from 1997 to 2007. According to those findings, companies with more women at the top may be better practitioners of corporate social responsibility. Even after controlling for factors that could influence total donations, the presence of women leaders in *Fortune 500* companies still has a significant, positive effect. More women leaders are associated with higher levels of philanthropy (Soares, Marquis, & Lee, 2011).

Gould and Hosey argued (2007) that women are more likely than men are to support environmental causes through voting, activism, and consumer choices. Women clearly have claimed stake in the future of the environment. For example, Habiba Sarabi, the governor of Bamiyan Province and the first female governor in Afghanistan, created the first national park in Afghanistan, Band-e Amir, protecting 220 square miles of pristine lakes and limestone canyons (Hughes & Jennings, 2012). Her work has inspired local communities to join her environmental efforts. The Green Belt Movement was launched Nobel Prize winner Wangari Maathai, which has planted millions of trees in Kenya and transformed women into powerful advocates for their rights, democracy, good governance, and natural resource protection. Mary Mavanza from Tanzania has helped hundreds of Tanzanian women start environmentally sustainable businesses through microcredit loans and by providing training in accounting (Gould & Hosey, 2007).

Findings

Corporate social responsibility has necessitated corporate leaders to initiate steps to increase social accountability. Strategic planning and forecasting of CSR practices are needed. Corporate governance is required to build an atmosphere of mutual trust and responsibility to achieve excellence. CSR and philanthropy enhances reputation among stakeholders, leads to positive coverage in the news media, helps expose organizations to new constituencies, and provides a unique means to differentiate from competitors (Hughes & Jennings, 2012).

Data from the Catalyst, a not-for-profit New York-based women's research organization, showed a change in CSR over the last 10 years. In 2008, women held 15.7% of corporate officer positions at *Fortune* 500 companies; in 2007, this number was 15%. In 2007, women held 6.7% of top earner positions. The number of companies without women corporate officers increased from 74 in 2007 to 75 in 2008. The number of companies with three or more women corporate officers also increased from 203 in 2007 to 206 in 2008 ("Catalyst," 2009). While this increase is progress, at this rate progress would take 40 years for the number of female corporate officers to match the number of male officers. In 2010, women were in charge of 15 Fortune 500 companies; the same number as the previous year (2009), although some of the names have changed. At Xerox, Ursula Burns became the first woman Chief Executive Officer (CEO) to replace a woman, Anne Mulcahy, as a Fortune 500 CEO.

Woman in business are more attuned and conscious of CSR (Borkowski & Ugras, 1998; Gilligan, 1982; Huse, Hielsen, & Hagen, 2009). Companies having solid CSR programs and initiatives are more highly favored by the public as they are labeled with the halo effect and recognition that these civic-minded organizations will be more ethical in business as well as magnanimous to charities and charitable events. Also revealed is that women leaders in business that have greater awareness and involvement in CSR related activities help build and sustain their associated organizations, creating corporate good will and a positive profile that has shown a direct link to increased public support, and resultant higher revenues (Borkowski & Ugras, 1998; Gilligan, 1982; Huse, Hielsen, & Hagen, 2009). Woman positively contributing to a positive corporate profile and helping drive increased revenues would lead one to believe that woman leaders would be highly sought-after by organizations needing a publicity and revenue boost; however, a disparity and disproportion in the number of women exists as compared to men recruited by and hired by organizations. The ultimate and pressing question is why are more women not included at the executive leadership levels, as they appear to enhance organizational image, drive revenues significantly, and certainly create a positive corporate profile where CSR is at the forefront?

Conclusion

Considering the array and volume of corporate ethical debacles, investors, and the public at large highly favor organizations and its leaders who exhibited generosity and social consciousness. Research has shown that women in leadership positions in any organization have brought a higher level of CSR, subsequently driving corporate ratings reputation ratings and resultant increases in higher earnings. While women on boards have proven value, women are still under-represented in the corporate sector. A need for a large-scale adjustment is warranted regarding how women are socialized to consider business as a viable career option, and how woman who are educated and mentored in business can be optimal in the context of driving greater CSR.

REFERENCES

Barnett, M. (2007). Stakeholder influence capacity and the variability of financial returns to corporate social responsibility. *Academy of Management Review, 32*(3), 794–816. doi:10.5465/AMR.2007.25275520

Bear, S., Rahman, N., & Post, C. (2010). The impact of board diversity and gender composition on corporate social responsibility and firm reputation. *Journal of Business Ethics* 97: 207–221. doi:10.1007/s10551–010–0505–2

Bernardi, R., Bosco, S., & Columb, V. L. (2006). Does female representation on boards of directors associate with the most ethical companies list? *Corporate Reputation Review* 12 270–280. doi:10.1057/crr.2009.15

Borkowski, S. C., & Ugras, Y. J. (1998). Business students and ethics: A meta-analysis. *Journal of Business Ethics, 17*, 1117–1127. doi:10.1023/A: 1005748725174

Carroll, A. (1991, July-August). The pyramid of corporate social responsibility: Toward the moral management of organizational stakeholders. *Business Horizons*, 39–48. doi:10.1016/0007–6813(91)90005-G

Catalyst. (2009). *2008 census of women corporate officers and top earners of the Fortune 500*. Retrieved from http://www.catalyst.org/publication/283/2008-catalyst-census-of-women-corporate-officers-and-top-earners-of-the-fortune-500

Cramer, A., & Hirschland, M. (2006, November/December). The socially responsible board. *The Corporate Board*, 20–24. Retrieved from http://business.highbeam.com/412274/article-1G1–154391509/socially-responsible-board

Desantis, B. (2011). Branded-The halo effect: Balancing authenticity and reputation in corporate social responsibilities. *White Paper: New York, NY.*

Dowling, G. (2006). How good corporate reputations create corporate value. *Corporate Reputation Review, 9*, 134–143. doi:10.1057/palgrave.crr.1550017

European Commission. (2009). *Towards greater corporate responsibility: Conclusions of EU-funded research*. Retrieved from http://www.scribd.com/doc/25050562/2009–12-Towards-greater-corporate-responsibility-conclusions-of-EU-funded-research

Fombrun, C. J., & Gardberg, N. A. (2000). Opportunity platforms safety nets: Corporate citizenship and reputational risk. *Business & Society Review, 105*(1), 85–106. doi:10.1111/0045–3609.00066

Fombrun, C. J. (2006). Corporate governance. *Corporate Reputation Review, 8*, 267–271. doi:10.1057/palgrave.crr.1540254

Gilligan, C. (1982). In a different voice. Cambridge, MA: *Harvard University Press.*

Gould, K., & Hosey, L. (2007). *Women in green*. Bainbridge Island, WA: Ecotone Publishing.

Gupta, S., & Pirsch, J. (2008). The influence of a retailers' corporate social responsibility program on conceptualizing store image. *The Journal of Retailing and Consumer Services*. doi:10.1016/j.bbr.2011.03.031

Hechevarria, D., Ingram, D., Justo, R., & Terjesen, S. (2012). *Are women more likely to pursue social and environmental entrepreneurship?* In Global women's entrepreneurship research: Diverse settings, questions, and approaches. Northampton, MA: Edward Elgar Publishing.

Henderson, D. (2001). *Misguided virtue: False notions of corporate social responsibility*. Wellington, New Zealand: New Zealand Business Roundtable.

Hughes, K., & Jennings, J. (2012). *Global women's entrepreneurship research: Diverse settings, questions, and approaches*. Northampton, MA: Edward Elgar Publishing.

Huse, M., Nielsen, S. T., & Hagen, M. I. (2009). Women and employee-elected board members, and their contributions to board control tasks. *Journal of Business Ethics, 89*, 581–597. doi:10.1007/s10551–008–0018–4

Janssen-Selvadurai, C. (2010). *On becoming: The lived learning experiences of female entrepreneurs*. New York University. (UMI 3404541)

Kapstein, E. (2001). The corporate ethics crusade. *Foreign Affairs 80*(5), 105–119. Retrieved from: http://www.foreignaffairs.com/articles/57242/ethan-b-kapstein/the-corporate-ethics-crusade

Kim, S-Y., & Reber, B. H. (2008). Public relations' place in corporate social responsibility: Practitioners define their role. *Public Relations Review, 34*, 337–342. doi:10.1016/j.pubrev.2008.07.003

London, M., & Morfopoulos, R. (2010). *Social entrepreneurship: How to start a successful corporate social responsibility and community-based initiatives for advocacy and change*. New York, NY: Routledge.

Ravindran, N. (2009, January). Community outreach through corporate social responsibility. *Today's Manager, 36*. Retrieved from: http://findarticles.com/p/articles/mi_m1NDC/is_2008_Dec-Jan/ai_n24964174/

Riordan, C. M., Gatewood, R. D., & Bill, J. B. (1997). Corporate image: Employee reactions and implications for managing corporate social performance. *Journal of Business Ethics, 16*, 401–412. Retrieved from: http://academic.research.microsoft.com/Paper/2902674

Soares, R., Marquis, C., & Lee, M. (2011). Gender and corporate social responsibility: It's a matter of sustainability. *Catalyst*. Retrieved from http://www.catalyst.org/file/522/gender_and_corporate_social_responsibility_final.pdf

Smith, C. N., Read, D., & Lopez-Rodrieguex, S. (2010). *Faculty & Research Working Paper: Consumer perceptions of corporate social responsibility: The CSR halo Effect.* Fontenbleau, Cedex, France.

Smith, N. C. (2003). Corporate social responsibility: Not whether, but how? *London Business School: Centre for Marketing,* No. 03–701. Retrieved from http://www.london.edu/facultyandresearch/research/docs/03-701.pdf

University of Cincinnati. (2012, April 3). Men start businesses for the money: Women for the social value. *Science Daily.* Retrieved from http://www.sciencedaily.com /releases/2012/04/120403124404.htm

Vanhamme, J., & Grobben, B. (2009). Too good to be true! The effectiveness of CSR history in countering negative publicity, *Journal of Business Ethics, 85,* 273–283. doi:10.1007/s10551-008-9731-2

Wheelan, T., & Hunger, J. D. (2008) *Strategic management and business policy.* Upper Saddle River, NJ: Pearson Prentice Hall.

About the Authors

Dr. Gayle Grant

Dr. Gayle Grant, a native New Yorker and current Arizona resident holds several accredited degrees, a Bachelor of Arts (BA) from Rutgers University, A Master of Arts (MA) from Kean University, and Doctorate of Management (DM) in Organizational Leadership from the University of Phoenix, School of Advanced Studies.

Dr. Gayle (known to her students as 'Doc') is a university professor in Information Technologies, Business, Leadership, Business Management, Marketing, Quality Processes, and Research with Walden University, Grand Canyon University, University of Phoenix, and City University of Seattle. Dr. Gayle serves as a professor, mentor, dissertation chair, research methodologist, content committee expert, doctoral residency and intensive residency instructor, University Research Reviewer, lead faculty member, and curriculum consultant in her university roles. Further, Dr. Gayle owns dual consulting practices specializing in higher education as well as business management/operations/strategic and tactical planning. 'Doc' is an avid investor and enjoys all things 'entrepreneurial.

Dr. Gayle is currently working on an article relating to dynamic web-enabled doctoral program interfaces for students and faculty. 'Doc' rounds out any remaining time golfing, working out, motorcycling, partaking in various electronic and art related projects as well as sharing her home with her five dogs.

To reach Dr. Gayle Grant for information on any of these topics, please e-mail: gayle.grant@cox.net

Dr. Judy Fisher-Blando

Southern California author Dr. Judy Fisher-Blando holds several accredited degrees: a Bachelor of Science (BS) in Business Management; a Master's of Art (MA) in Organizational Management; and a Doctorate of Management (DM) in Organizational Leadership from the University of Phoenix School of Advanced Studies. She has also obtained her Six Sigma Black Belt certificate.

Dr. Judy an adjunct professor for Walden University and University of Phoenix, teaching classes in organizational behavior and research methodologies.

She is an expert on Workplace Bullying, having written her research dissertation on *Workplace Bullying: Aggressive Behavior and Its Effect on Job Satisfaction and Productivity*. In addition, she is a Life Coach, coaching leaders on how to develop High Performance Organizations, coaching the targets of workplace bullies, and giving presentations on Finding and Measuring your Joy.

To reach Dr. Judy Fisher-Blando for information on any of these topics, and for executive coaching or coaching on workplace bullying, please e-mail judy-blando@gmail.com

CHAPTER 4

Generational Conflict Between Nurses in the Workforce: A Phenomenological Study

Dr. Barbara Welcher

L eaders in health care organizations have a social responsibility to retain nurses in the workplace. In an effort to retain nurses, leaders might not be aware of the impact four generations in the workplace might have toward retention of nurses. The Welcher (2011) study explored generational conflict related to four generations working together and the values, beliefs, and attitudes held by each generation in local hospitals in Georgia. A qualitative, phenomenological study was conducted with 20 registered nurses from a nursing sorority in the city of Georgia, using the modified van Kaam methodology. The 2011 Welcher study investigated the existence of four generations in the current workforce and if conflict existed between the generations. Conflict in health care organizations may cause staff turnover. Leaders may decrease staff turnover by understanding the characteristics, attributes, and experiences that contribute to generational conflict. Hence, leaders have a social responsibility to develop strategies that would benefit four generations working together in the current workforce.

Background of the Problem

A nursing shortage in the United States has existed since the 1980s and with the retirement of Baby Boomers and the decrease in the number of admissions to nursing schools, the shortage continues (Calo, 2008; Kaufman, 2009; Manion, 2004). The focus of this chapter is not on the nursing shortage but on conflict in health care organizations. Conflict in health care organizations may occur for many reasons, but the focus of this paper is the conflict because of four generations working together. Whereas the nursing shortage may not be the cause of conflict in health care organizations, conflict may exist when staffing levels are below minimum (Buchan, 2005). Retention of staff is important to solve the nursing shortage, but may result in conflict because of older and younger generations of staff working together. Laing, Poitier, Ferguson, Carraher, and Ford (2009) suggested the exodus of a large number of Baby Boomers between 2007 and 2022; however, Calo (2008) reported that Baby Boomers are remaining in the workforce longer. The workforce is aging, 50% of registered nurses (RN) in the workforce today are fewer than 10 years away from retirement age but may not retire leaving more of an aging workforce in health care organizations (Bowlby, 2007; Rivers, Tsai, & Munchus, 2005). The increased retirement age, decreased retirement planning and individuals living longer may lead to four generations in the workforce resulting in the potential of more conflict.

Although a large number of RNs will reach retirement age within the next 10 years, many are remaining in the workforce because of two reasons: (a) the age for retirement was increased from 65 to 67 (Calo, 2008), and (b) a decrease in financial planning for retirement (Berger, 2009). Berger (2009) reported some older workers accepted lower paying jobs to meet financial stability in the retirement state. An almost 50% increase in the age of employees over a 20-year span suggesting the average age of an employee in the workforce today is 50 (Doyle, 2008). Four generations are currently employed in the workforce that may lead to generational conflict related to values, beliefs, and attitudes held by each generation. The current workforce encompasses four generations, the Veteran, Baby Boomer, Generation X, and Generation Y or the Millennial Generation (Greene, 2005; Nicholas, 2009; Ro, 2006, Sherman, 2006).

Historically, at least two generations shared the workforce (Giancola, 2006; Wood, 2005). An increase in the retirement age allowed an aging workforce to share a place with a younger workforce (Kiyonaga, 2004). The past retirement age of 53–56 would eliminate the Veteran and many of the Baby Boomers from the current workforce. However, increasing the retirement age to 65 resulted in the Veterans and Baby Boomers remaining in the workforce longer. Kiyonaga (2004) reported that the increasing costs of health care, longevity, decreasing workforce because of Baby Boomers retirement and an age-diverse workforce resulted in generational issues and subsequent conflict.

Kiyonaga (2004) further reported the retirement age for Baby Boomers increased to 65. Increasing the retirement age allows Veterans and Baby Boomers to remain in the workforce longer. Calo (2008) predicted that by 2020 a retirement age of 67 will result in a more age diversified workforce. One report suggested 40.7 as the expected average age of employees in the workforce by 2008 and age 67 as the expected retirement age by 2022 (Fabian, 2007). Fabian further suggested the current 40-year-olds in the workforce could remain in the workforce for another 27 years. Each generation brings with them differences in mores, beliefs, and values (Aro et al., 2005) that may result in generational conflict.

Health care organizations experienced a shortage of health care workers since 1980 but with the changes in retirement laws and an increased length of life expectancy, the environment in health care organization changed as well (Chen & Choi, 2008; Manion, 2004). The previous health care organization had a large number of nurses in the workforce. Cooper (2003) cited "2.5 million nurses (RNs) in the United States in 1998 but suggested by 2020 the supply of RNs will be 20% below the need" (p. 75). Inadequate staff to perform safe and quality care may cause conflict as the workforce decreases but the workload remains stable or increasing. The decrease in supply may cause a problem if a shortage of employees exists in the workforce to perform basic care for the consumer (Dols, Landrum, & Wieck, 2010). While the patient load increases and the staff decreases, staff members will likely struggle personally while providing safe care. The aging and healthier population, increase in retirement age, and inadequate retirement funds have resulted in a paradigm shift in the number of generations in the current health care organization (Goodman, 2005; Lutz & Root, 2007). The Veterans and Baby Boomers are living longer and staying in the workforce longer and the influx of Generation Y in health care organizations resulting in four generations coexisting in the workforce (Kiyonaga, 2004; Ro, 2006).

Methodology

The researcher conducted a qualitative phenomenological research study to understand the phenomenon of four generations working together in the workplace. The researcher also intended to determine if conflict occurs because of the attitudes, values, and beliefs each generation brings to the workplace. The phenomenon included the following questions:

Research Question 1: Do four generations exist in the current workforce?

Research Question 2: What causes generational conflicts in health care organizations?

Research Question 3: What specific worker characteristics, attributes, and experiences contribute to generational conflict?

While leaders in health care organizations try to retain nurses in the workplace, they might not be aware of the impact four generations in the workplace might have toward retention of nurses. Nicholas (2009) suggested conflict among nurses in the workplace is associated with diversity. Kupperschmidt (2006) reported conflict among graduate nurses upon entering the workforce. Often the relationships are strained from the beginning of their work career because older nurses tend to eat their young. Older nurses do not trust the knowledge of the neophyte and this may lead to conflict and may lead to nurses leaving the workforce. Bowles and Candela (2005) reported new graduates leave their job during the first year of employment due to generational conflict. Understanding the attitudes, values and beliefs each generation brings to the workforce may lead to strategies that will decrease or alleviate the conflict. Therefore, it is the social responsibility of leaders to both understand the attitudes, values, and beliefs of each generation and to develop strategies to create a harmonious workplace of each generation.

Research Method and Design Appropriateness

According to Simon (2005), a phenomenological inquiry studies individuals in the lived environment reflecting on the areas of space, body, relationships, and time. A Modified Van Kaam method by Moustakas (1994) using open-ended interview questions allowed an in-depth exploration of nurses lived experiences in the work environment thereby meeting the spatial component. Simon (2005) suggested the best interpreter of the phenomena is the individual living the experience. Individuals sharing the same experiences may share commonality or meaning of the experience (Simon, 2005). Twenty participants were selected for the study. Creswell (2005) and Whitley and Crawford (2005) suggested that a small sample size is appropriate for qualitative studies. Meeting with the nurses to complete the interview in a face-to-face meeting accomplished the body, relationship, and time components. To best understand the relationship among four generations in the workplace, meeting with nurses currently employed in hospitals in the Georgia area allowed an exploration of this phenomenon. A phenomenological method was the best research approach for this type of study.

The qualitative phenomenological method was the best method to use for this study because phenomenological method explored the values held in the relationships between four generations in the current workforce (Welcher, 2011). Each generation may have different needs and expectations because of personal values held within their generation and may oppose another generation for differences in lived experiences from which different values were derived. Because each of four generations in the workforce bring personal values, beliefs, attitudes, work experiences and meaning to the workplace, the employees lived experiences with employees of different generations were gathered, analyzed, and used to report possible conflict. The presence of four generations may be the cause of conflict in the workplace leading to staff dissatisfaction and the furtherance of the nursing shortage (Greene, 2005; Haraway & Haraway, 2005; Ro, 2006). The information gleaned from the lived experiences of the four generations may be used to recognize and improve generational differences in the workforce.

Creswell (2005) suggested qualitative research works best in areas where the researcher is interested in exploring some form of phenomena. The phenomenon explored in this study was how the different values, beliefs, and attitudes of each generation may lead to conflict between generations in the workplace, specifically regarding nurses. Open-ended interview questions allowed participants an opportunity to define values, beliefs, and attitudes within their specific generation. Open-ended questions allowed the participant the option to generate answers from personal lived experiences. The method used for the Welcher 2011 study was qualitative phenomenological.

Population

The targeted population for this study was all registered nurses that serve as members of a local nursing sorority and employed in local health care organizations in the city of Georgia. The sample consisted of twenty registered nurses selected for the study. Volunteers were sought from the estimated membership of approximately 80 members using a letter of introduction via first class mailing.

Sampling Frame

Purposive type sampling was used to select participants for this study. The sample consisted of members of a local nursing sorority working as registered nurses in one of the five major hospitals in Georgia. All registered nurse members of this sorority are over the age of 18 and ages varied. The registered nurse possessed a current nursing license allowing the practice of nursing in health care organizations. Participation was done on a voluntary basis. Participants were selected through a homogenous purposive technique with an aim to have five participants from each age group. Typically, phenomenological studies use small sample sizes to provide a clear picture of the phenomena being studied (Creswell, 2005; Whitley & Crawford, 2005). Purposive sampling allowed choosing participants in each of the four generational age groups. Cooper and Schindler (2006) suggested purposive sampling allows the researcher to select participants based on specifics characteristics.

Data Collection

Data were collected from Registered Nurses who were members of a local nursing sorority on a voluntary basis. Permission to conduct the study with the registered nurses in different organizations was obtained from the individual registered nurse on a voluntary basis. Participants were interviewed on a one-on-one basis and tape-recorded in a pre-identified area for transcribing. Accurate information was obtained through responses from participants answering interview questions.

Instrumentation

The instrument used for this study was developed based on a suggestion by Creswell (2005) that qualitative studies use "self-designed protocols that help us organize information reported by participants to each question" (p. 203). The questions, developed for this study, were designed to explore the phenomena of four generations in the workforce and if the values, beliefs, and attitudes of each generation cause conflict. Creswell suggested that interviews and observations are opportunities to gain information about the experiences, perceptions, and attitudes. Another advantage of one-on-one interview is the response rate of return is immediate, the interviewee and interviewer will have a scheduled meeting time, and the interview will be completed in one setting. The interview questions were open-ended allowing for follow up questions and further inquiry.

Validity and Reliability

Validity is a method of making sure the questions measures what it says it will measure. Neuman (2006) stated that validity "means truthful" and authentic, which means, "giving a fair, honest, and balanced account of social life from the view-point of someone who lives it every day" (p. 185). The questions for this study were designed to measure the truthfulness of the nurses in their lived environment. Two preliminary interviews were conducted with a type of person that represents the potential pool of study participants; this interview allowed the researcher to assess the face validity of the questions asked. The researcher made any necessary adjustments to the interview questions to ensure face validity of the questions was asked.

Data Analysis

Upon completion of data collection, data were analyzed to give meaning. The categories, themes, and patterns that emerged from the data collection were used to produce findings. Denzin and Lincoln, (1998) suggested that no strategy of analysis is better than another but the goal is to find the best method to tell the lived experiences of the participants. The ultimate goal of data analysis is to produce findings (Denzin & Lincoln, 1998). A Modified Van Kaam method was used for data analysis using Moustakas methods for this study. Moustakas (1994) identified a seven-step process of data analysis.

The seven steps in phenomenological data analysis using the Modified Van Kaam Method by Moustakas (1994) list the themes and placed them in groups referred to as "horizonalization" (p. 120). Each expressed idea was listed as an initial theme. The next step was to reduce the irrelevant data to "determine the Invariant Constituents" (p. 120) by testing the expressions for two requirements. "Does it contain a moment of the experience that is a necessary and sufficient constituent for understanding it? Is it possible to abstract and label it? If it can be abstracted and labeled, it is a horizon of the experience" (p. 120). Any expression that does not meet the above requirements is eliminated.

The third step in the process was to cluster the themes of the invariant constituents. "The clustered and labeled constituents are the core themes of the experience" (Moustakas, 1994, p. 121). The fourth step validated the invariant constituents, which included validation whereas the researcher "checks the invariant constituents and their accompanying themes against the complete record of the research participant" (p. 121). The researcher examined the data for themes that are explicitly expressed, compatible but not explicitly expressed or neither compatible or expressed explicitly. If the themes were not compatible or expressed explicitly, they were considered not relevant and are deleted (Moustakas, 1994).

The fifth step included the Individual Textural Description of the experience. It records "verbatim examples from the transcribed interview" to support the textural description of the experience (p. 121). The next step involved the "Individual Structural Description of the experience based on the individual textural description and imaginative variation" (p. 121). The final step was the "construction of each participant a textural-structural description of the meaning and essences of the experience, incorporating the invariant constituents and themes" (Moustakas, 1994, p. 121).

The first step was "listing and preliminary grouping" [and this step led to] "horizonalization" (p. 120). Horizonalization identified every relevant word to the lived experience and places it in a list. Horizonalization helped with listing themes derived from the participant, where Moustakas (1994) stated "horizonalization illustrates the importance of being receptive to every statement of the participant, granting each comment equal value and thus encouraging a rhythmical flow between the researcher and the participant, interaction that inspires comprehensive disclosure of experience" (p. 122).

NVivo 8 software package was used to code the data. Data coding included an analysis of responses to all questions. Categories for the answers were devised to code the data on both the open-ended and closed-ended questions. Specific data were categorized into age ranges to enable meaningful comparison of sub-groups such as the ages within the four generations. The QSR, NVivo: N8 software package was used for data analysis. Data cleaning was completed after the responses were entered in the NVivo software system to check for any inconsistencies or outliers.

Findings

This section contains the findings of the Welcher 2011 study. Five themes emerged from the responses of the 20 nurses. The presentation of findings will include direct quotes from the participants and implications will follow.

Theme 1: Level of Commitment and Proficiency in Technology were the Main Differences in Work Habits between Older and Younger Generation Nurses.

Based on the thematic category, difference in work habits, fifteen unique codes emerged from the data. The thematic category pertained to the perceived differences of nurses regarding the different working habits of nurses belonging in different generations. Level of commitment (10 out of 20 participants, 50%) and proficiency in technology (10 out of 20 participants, 50%) emerged as the most popular code based on the responses of the participants. The use of technology in health care environments increased over the past decade and the younger generation used technology throughout most of their lives. Hence, the younger generation is technologically perceptive, whereas the older generation is more comfortable using a paper record and is not comfortable with technology.

Theme 2: Change was the Main Conflict that Existed Between Older and Younger Generation Nurses

The second thematic category, conflicts between older and younger generation nurses, change emerged as the most cited response from the participants. The thematic category pertained to the perceived conflicts that existed between younger and older generation nurses. Older nurses believed younger nurses were lazy and did not like helping others whereas younger nurses believed older nurses refused to change and wanted things to remain as it were even though the younger nurses could prove through best practices that change was more efficient.

Theme 3: Different Perceptions of Change and Different Levels of Motivation were the Challenges in Working with Older and Younger Generation Nurses

The third thematic category, challenges of working with younger and older generation nurses, 10 unique codes emerged from the data. Different perceptions of change (5 out of 20 participants, 25%) and willingness to work/help/motivation (4 out of 20 participants, 20%) as the most cited responses. The thematic category pertained to the perceived challenges that were experienced by the 20 nurses working with older and younger generation nurses.

Theme 4: Generational Difference had no Perceived Effect on Performance

For the fourth thematic category, effect of generational difference on performance, most of the participants believed that generational differences had no effect on job performance. Only four participants were affected positively by the generation differences in the nursing staff.

Theme 5: More than 40 Hours of Working was Acceptable among Nurses

The fifth thematic category, feelings about working more than 40 hours, six unique codes emerged from the data. Most of the participants (5 out of 20 participants, 25%) were accepting of the working hours.

Implications

Based on the findings that emerged from the data, several implications were apparent. First, generation differences can be broadly classified into older (Veterans and Baby Boomers) and younger (Generation X and Y) generation nurses. The two groups seemed to share similar attitudes and beliefs. These similarities and differences are supported by previous researchers such as Anthony (2006), Swearingen and Liberman (2004), and Weston (2006).

Second, differences in attitudes, beliefs, and practices exist between older and younger generation nurses; however, these differences do not necessarily translate to conflicts. The results of the Welcher 2011 study indicated that conflicts may arise due to generational differences, but with understanding and awareness, conflicts can be avoided. The implication of the results is that generation differences should be addressed appropriately to offset or limit possible conflicts that could arise from the generational differences.

Third, based on the results of the study, different perceptions of change between older and younger generation nurses appears to be a core issue in a generationally diverse nursing staff. The generational differences in the nursing staff seem to manifest primarily on the different perceptions toward change in attitudes, practice, and beliefs. Hospital leaders should take the different coping styles of nurses with regard to changes.

Recommendations

This section contains the recommendations of the researcher. The recommendations are based on the results that emerged from the interview data. The recommendations are geared towards three main stakeholders: (a) hospital leaders, (c) nurses, and (c) future researchers.

Recommendations for Hospital Leaders

The results of the 2011 Welcher study suggested that if there is awareness and understanding of generational differences in the nursing staff, conflicts can be avoided. Hospital leaders should consider incorporating awareness and sensitivity toward generational differences on professional development programs. The incorporation of generational differences cannot only prevent conflict among co-workers; it can also encourage more positive interaction among different nurses who belong to different generations.

While diversity training has been incorporated in health care organizations, the focus of that training has not been on generational differences. Leaders of health care organizations may benefit by implementing awareness training for employees. The training would benefit health care leaders in being aware of issues related to four generations in the workplace. Once issues are identified, strategies can be developed and implemented to decrease conflict that may result from the four generations working together in health care organizations. The employees may benefit by understanding why employees in other generations perform in the manner they perform. Employees may be able to improve team relationships and job performance.

Another recommendation is to conduct assessment methods that could determine if nurses are affected by generation difference in terms of job performance. The results of the 2011 Welcher study indicated that nurses believe that generational difference did not affect their job performance. By focusing on the aspect of conflicts caused by generational differences in the nursing staff, hospital leaders might be able to prevent unnecessary conflicts to occur within the nursing staff.

Recommendations for Nurses

The results indicated that conflicts may arise between the older and younger generation nurses such as conflicts pertaining to perceptions on change and working habits. These potential conflicts do not necessarily translate to actual conflicts if nurses can recognize their differences and work together as part of a team. Older and younger nurses can learn from each other to enhance their knowledge and skills as nursing practitioners.

Recommendations for Future Studies

The findings of the study provide a few research areas that can be explored and examined by future researchers. One area that could be explored by future researchers is how change affects the different generation of nurses. Future researchers can explore what aspect of change is a problem among the different generation of nurses. This future study can be significant in providing a richer understanding of the nature of change that can be a problem for nursing staffs that are generationally diverse.

The participants in the study believed that generational difference did not affect the job performance of nurses. Future researchers could conduct a quantitative study, validating this finding. Future researchers can conduct a comparative analysis regarding the job performance of nurses who believed that their performance are affected by generational difference in the staff and nurses who believed that performance are not affected. Job performance could be measured in terms of evaluation feedback from their supervisors.

No distinction emerged regarding the attitudes of nurses from different generations on working more than 40 hours a week. This finding was not consistent with the hypothesis of previous studies. Future researchers can expand the sample of the study to explore further if a difference exists among the four different generations on attitudes on working more than 40 hours a week.

Summary

The purpose of the Welcher 2011 study was to explore generational conflict related to four generations working together and the values, beliefs and attitudes held by each generation in local hospitals in Georgia. Exploration of this phenomenon revealed five themes:

1. Level of commitment and proficiency in technology were the main differences in work habits between older and younger generation nurses

2. Change was the main conflict that existed between older and younger generation nurses

3. Different perceptions of change and different levels of motivation were the challenges in working with older and younger generation nurses

4. Generational difference had no perceived effect on performance

5. More than 40 hours of working was acceptable among nurses

Based on the emergent themes, several recommendations were made. For the stakeholders, the recommendations were centered on (a) programs that would enhance the understanding and awareness of nurses regarding generational differences; and (b) assessment methods that could examine how generational differences in the nursing staff affect job performance of nurses. For future researchers, recommendations pertained to further exploration of the nature of the differences regarding perceptions on change, quantitative comparative studies on job performance, and further exploration of the perceptions of nurses belonging in different generations on working more than 40 hours a week.

Leaders have a social responsibility to ensure adequate staff is available to perform safe and effective nursing care to consumers of health care. Recognizing the causes of potential conflict and strategizing early to alleviate the conflict may allow leaders an advantage toward conflict resolution. Identifying strategies to alleviate or decrease conflict may decrease staff turnover and improve staffing levels in health care organizations.

REFERENCES

Anthony, M. K. (2006). The multigenerational workforce: Boomers and xers and nets, oh my! *Online Journal of Issues in Nursing, 11*(2), 11–15. doi:10.3912/OJIN.Vol11No02ManOS

Aro, M., Rinne, R., Lahti, K., & Olkinuora, E. (2005). Education or learning on the job? Generational differences of opinions in Finland. *International Journal of Lifelong Education, 24*(6), 459–474. doi:10.1080/02601370500279928

Berger, E. D. (2009). Managing age discrimination: An examination of the techniques used when seeking employment. *The Gerontologist, 49*(3), 317–332. doi:10.1093/geront/gnp031

Bowlby, G. (2007). Defining retirement. *Perspective on Labour and Income, 19*(1), 55–60. Retrieved from http://www.statcan.gc.ca/pub/75–001-x/index-eng.htm

Bowles, C., & Candela, L. (2005). Student nurse update: First job experiences of recent RN

graduates. *Nevada RNformation, 14*(2), 16–19. Retrieved from http://www.nvnurses.org

Calo, T. J. (2008). Talent management in the era of the aging workforce: The critical role of knowledge transfer. *Public Personnel Management, 37*(4), 403–416. Retrieved from http://www.ipma-hr.org/publications

Chen, P., & Choi, Y. (2008). Generational differences in work values: A study of hospitality management. *International Journal of Contemporary Hospitality Management, 20*(6), 595–615. doi:10.1108/09596110810892182

Cooper, E. E. (2003). Pieces of the shortage puzzle: Aging and shift work. *Nursing Economics, 21*(2), 75–79. Retrieved from https://ehis.edscohost.com/eds/pdfviewer

Cooper, D. R., & Schindler, P. S. (2006). *Business research methods* (9th ed.). Singapore: McGraw Hill International.

Creswell, J. W. (2005). *Educational research: Planning, conducting, and evaluating quantitative and qualitative research* (2nd ed.). Upper Saddle River, NJ: Merrill Prentice-Hall.

Denzin, N. K., & Lincoln, Y. S. (1998). *Strategies of qualitative inquiry.* Thousand Oaks, CA: SAGE.

Dols, J., Landrum, P., & Wieck, K. L. (2010). Leading and managing an intergenerational workforce. *Creative Nursing, 16*(2), 68–76. doi:10.1891/1078-4535.16.2.68

Doyle, W. R. (2008). The Baby Boomers as faculty: What will they leave behind? *Change, 40*(6), 56–59. https://ehis.edscohost.com/eds/pdfviewer

Fabian, N. (2007). Rethinking retirement-and a footnote of diversity. *Journal of Environmental Health, 69*(10), 86–87. Retrieved from https://ehis.edscohost.com/eds/pdfviewer

Giancola, F. (2006). The generation gap: More myth than reality. *Human Resource Planning, 29*(4), 32–37. Retrieved from http://www.hrps.org/

Goodman, J. C. (2005). Baby boomer retirement. *Vital Speeches of the Day, 71*(17), 529–531. Retrieved from http://www.vsotd.com/

Greene, J. (2005). What nurses want: Different generations, different expectations. *Hospitals and Health Networks, 78*(3), 34–42. Retrieved from http://www.hhnmag.com/hhnmag/hospitalconnect/search/article.jsp?

Kaufman, K. A. (2009). Annual survey of schools of nursing academic year 2006–2007: Executive summary. Headlines from the NLN. *Nursing Education Perspectives, 30*(2), 136–137. Retrieved from http://www.nlnjournal.org/

Kiyonaga, N. B. (2004). Today is that tomorrow you worried about: Meeting the challenges of a changing workforce. *Public Personnel Management, 33*(4), 357–361. Retrieved from https://ehis.edscohost.com/eds/pdfviewer

Kupperschmidt, B. R. (2006). Addressing multigenerational conflict: Mutual respect and carefronting as strategy. *Online Journal of Issues in Nursing, 11*(2), 14. Retrieved from http://www.nursingworld.org/ojin

Lang, S., Poitier, R., Ferguson, H., Carraher, S. M., & Ford, S. (2009). Baby boomers at 60: Effects on retirement plans, benefits, and the workforce in the Bahamas, Japan, and the sea. *Proceedings of the Academy for Studies in International Business, 9*(1), 11–15. Retrieved from http://news-business.vlex.com/vid/effects-retirement-plan-workforce227783343

Lutz, S. L., & Root, D. (2007). Nurses, consumer satisfaction, and pay for performance. *Health Care Financial Management, 57*–63. Retrieved from https://ehis.edscohost.com/eds/pdfviewer

Manion, J. (2004). Nurture a culture of retention. *Nursing Management, 35*(4), 28–39. Retrieved from http://www.nursingmanagement.com

Moustakas, C. (1994). *Phenomenological research methods.* Thousand Oaks, CA: Sage Publications.

Neuman, W. L. (2003). *Social research methods: Qualitative and quantitative approaches* (5th ed.). Boston, MA: Allyn and Bacon.

Nicholas, A. (2009). Generational perceptions: Workers and consumers. *Journal of Business and Economics Research, 7*(10), 47–52. Retrieved from http://www.journals.cluteonline.com

Rivers, P. A., Tsai, K. L., & Munchus, G. (2005). The financial impacts of the nursing shortage. *Journal of Health Care Finance, 31*(3), 52–64. Retrieved from https://ehis.edscohost.com/eds/pdfviewer

Ro, S. (2006). Leading a multigenerational nursing workforce: Issues, challenges and strategies. *Online Journal of Issues in Nursing, 11*(2), (5P). Retrieved from http://www.nursingworld.org/ojin

Sherman, R. O. (2006). Leading a multigenerational nursing workforce: Issues, challenges, and strategies. *Online Journal of Issues in Nursing, 11*(2), 13–19. Retrieved from http://www.nursingworld.org/ojin

Simon, M. K. (2006). *Dissertation and scholarly research: Recipes for success.* Dubuque, IA: Kendall/Hunt.

Swearingen, S., & Liberman, A. (2004). Nursing generations: An expanded look at the emergence of conflict and its resolution. *The Health Care Manager, 23*(1), 54–64. Retrieved from https://ehis.edscohost.com/eds/pdfviewer

Weston, M. J. (2006). Integrating generational perspectives in nursing. *Online Journal of Nursing, 11*(2), 12–23. Retrieved from http://www.nursingworld .org/ojin

Whitley, R., & Crawford, M. (2005). Qualitative research in psychiatry. *Canadian Journal of Psychiatry, 50*(2), 108. Retrieved from https://ehis.edscohost .com/eds/pdfviewer

Wood, S. (2005). Spanning the generation gap in the workplace. *American Water Works Association Journal, 97*(5), 86–89. Retrieved from http://apps .awwa.org/waterlibrary/scholarabstract.aspx?

About the Author

University of Phoenix, Augusta GA Professor, Dr. Barbara P. Welcher, holds several accredited degrees; a Bachelor of Science Degree in Nursing (BSN) from the Medical University of South Carolina, Charleston South Carolina, a Master of Science in Psychiatric and Mental Health Nursing (MSN) from the Medical University of South Carolina, Charleston, South Carolina, and a Doctorate in Health Care Administration (DHA) from the University of Phoenix School of Advanced Studies.

Dr. Barbara is known to her students as "Dr. B" at the University of Phoenix where she is on faculty. She facilitates classes in the College of Natural Sciences and has been employed by the University since 2007. She is also employed as a Commander with the United States Army Reserves and works at the Charlie Norwood Veterans Administration Hospital as a Telephonic Triage Nurse.

Dr. Barbara is an active member of Sigma Theta Tau International, American Nurses Association, Georgia Nurses Association, and Chi Eta Phi Nursing Sorority. Dr. Barbara is also an active member of Toastmasters International.

To reach Dr. Barbara Welcher for information on any of these topics, please e-mail pettibar@bellsouth.net

The Value of Innovative Leadership Practices on Corporate Social Responsibility (CSR)

Dr. Emad Rahim, Dr. Vishakha Maskey, & Dr. Darrell Norman Burrell

For-profit entities around the world have explored, evaluated, and implemented initiatives relative to social responsibility. These efforts, developed in academia and by various business industry practitioners, have become publically salient following the 2008 financial crisis. The production of goods and services can generate earnings but also have indirect social impacts, whether it is through economic, legal, ethical, or environmental changes. Boli and Harsuiker (2001) suggested that 90% of Fortune 500 firms embraced Corporate Social Responsibility (CSR) as an essential element within their organizational goals, and actively promote their CSR activities in annual reports.

Business organizations that currently do not use social responsibility initiatives or perhaps, do not have an understanding of how social responsibility is beneficial to the company's future prospect. However, this perspective is not common. According to Bowen (1953), CSR had begun as a field of study since Fortune Magazine published a 1946 article in which the editors suggested that CSR "meant that businessmen were responsible for the consequences of their actions in a sphere somewhat wider than that covered by their profit and loss statements" (p. 44). Moreover, establishment of business communities, such as Business for Social Responsibility

(BSR) in 1992 and Ethical Corporations in 2001 are some examples of the CSR phenomenon (Carroll & Shabana, 2010).

Although CSR is a global initiative, the preponderance of organizations within the United States has built extensive plans to implement socially responsible activities into their annual business as a way to reducing behavioral damage (Kolodinsky, Madden, Zisk, & Henkel, 2009). This research paper examines some barriers of adopting CSR as well as the number of benefits for doing so. This research effort also will describe the important issues and current dilemmas that surround CSR, identify a few organizations and discuss their CSR activities as well as provide insight regarding how the organizations can rationalize incorporating social responsibility in their organizational strategy.

Background

CSR Defined

CSR is a method to manage a business by considering the impact of activities on customers, suppliers, employees, shareholders, communities, and other stakeholders as well as the environment. Often, CSR links to business goals, although debate about this statement among academics and corporate managers. Many organizations have acknowledged the importance of CSR and have made considerable contributions to the welfare of the societies in which they operate (Kinard, Kinard, & Smith, 2003). For example, the Chevron Corporation provides community support through education and career training programs in West Contra Costa County California, where unemployment is more than 18%. Twenty-two percent of families in Richmond, California, have incomes below the United States federal poverty level (Kinard, Kinard, & Smith, 2003). To help the communities address these challenges, Chevron contributed $3.7 million in 2010 to nonprofit groups in Richmond and to the county for education, youth leadership programs, economic development, and job training. Procter & Gamble has contributed greatly to the earthquake relief in Turkey as well as to community building projects in Japan, and schools in China, Romania, and Malaysia (Kinard et al., 2003). Solid public images and respectable public perception can go a long way in positively influencing customers and other stakeholders, thereby, contributing to the competitive advantage of corporations who practice CSR by strengthening brand loyalty (Gupta, 2002).

Previous research has defined CSR in both corporate and academic perspectives. Most CSR definitions are categorized by specific interests, for example reducing development and implementation of the conservation (Van Marrewijk, 2003). Dahlsrud (2006) identified five dimensions of CSR through content analysis. These dimensions are social, economic, environmental, stakeholder, and voluntariness. Based on the context of this paper, the definition for CSR will mirror the definition outlined in a 2009 study conducted by Kolodinsky et al. (2009). The definition stated CSR as an organization's ethical duty, beyond its legal requirements and fiduciary obligation to shareholders, sensitivity to consider and effectively manage its effect on its internal and external relationships and environments (Kolodinsky et al., 2009). Mckenzie (2004) discussed triple bottom line of "People, Planet and Profit" [as] "a mode of corporate reporting that encompasses environmental and social as well as economic concerns" (p. 6). Therefore, definition of CSR varies but generally encompasses both stakeholders and shareholders.

Business Case for CSR

Corporate citizenship uses the same themes and concepts as corporate social responsibility. A corporation is regarded as a legal entity that possesses many of the rights, duties, and powers and assumes some of the same obligations as those of the individual citizen (Kinard et al., 2003). Just as there are expectations that individuals will act as a responsible citizens by performing duties that contribute to the common good and welfare of the community at large, these actions are also expected of organizations. Advocates of the corporate citizenship theory employ the same themes and concepts as corporate social responsibility (Carroll, 1999). These advocates believe that maintaining a positive image or good reputation as responsible citizens would greatly enhance the organization's long-term success. Carroll (1998) implied that corporate citizenship is just another term for corporate social responsibility, corporate ethics, or social performance of corporations, which involves businesses responding to stakeholders, which include shareholders, consumers, and the community in which the businesses operate. Carroll stated that corporate citizenship represents the four faces of a citizen's social responsibilities: economic, legal, ethical, and philanthropic, and should fall not only private citizens but on companies as well (Carroll, 1998). The author did not see the term "corporate citizenship" *as* different from "corporate social responsibility" because, in effect, he defined corporate citizenship using the same four elements he used to define corporate social responsibility (Carroll, 1998). Valor (2005) agreed with the notion that the terms "corporate citizenship" and "corporate social responsibility" have the same meaning. Valor expanded the idea by stating that corporate citizenship, corporate social responsibility, and business ethics are all terms used to discuss corporate accountability.

A trend in contemporary literature emphasizes the use of corporate social responsibility as a public relations and marketing strategy. Research studies have found that consumers do care and are paying attention to corporations contributing to the betterment of society (Gupta, 2002; Kinard et al., 2003). Kinard et al. (2003) stated that leaders of businesses must be concerned with societal problems, such as cancer, the environment, child labor, and human rights because consumers around the world care and will make purchasing decisions based on corporate social responsibility. Prominent scholars and authors continue to document the importance of CSR, not only to communities and other stakeholders, but also to the companies that have social responsibility policies and practices.

Previous research reveals that by engaging in CSR activities, private firms can increase earnings growth in the long-run (Carroll & Shabana, 2010). In addition, CSR can enhance a firm's competitive advantage, leading to stakeholders, and stockholders gain. The firms identified as socially responsible and ethical have a greater returns than S&P 500 companies, hence confirming it pays to be ethical (Ethisphere, 2012).

Basic Case Studies

The reference made in this chapter discusses business entities with extensive CSR programs. These examples will examine the relationship that some private organizations have made with society itself. For example, Starbucks Corporation is an organization that has built several CSR programs and has an official CSR statement. The Starbuck's statement is as follows:

> At Starbucks, we strive to be a great enduring company by championing business practices that help produce social, environmental, and economic benefits for the communities in which we operate. Starbucks focuses its efforts on providing a great work environment for our partners (employees); making a positive contribution to our communities; working with coffee farmers to help ensure their long-term success and minimizing our environmental impact. (Starbucks Coffee Company, 2009, p. 5)

Starbucks refers to CSR as a global responsibility, or the *"shared planet"* initiative. The initiative is a major component of the Starbuck's franchise objectives. As part of their global responsibility initiatives, Starbucks emphasizes the following activities: "coffee purchasing practices, growth and expansion, environmental impacts, health and wellness, and workplace practices" (Starbucks, 2009, p. 9).

Another organization known for its extensive CSR program is Ben & Jerry's Homemade Holdings, Inc. By now, most people have seen or experienced the social initiatives Ben & Jerry's have brought to the market. The Ben & Jerry's social mission reads as

> To operate the company in a way that actively recognizes the central role that business plays in society by initiating innovative ways to improve the quality of life locally, nationally and internationally"(Ben & Jerry's, 2008 Highlights). To demonstrate the practice and value of CSR consider that in 2008 Ben & Jerry hosted a Social Mission Summit, held in Burlington, Vermont, home of the organization's headquarters, which included company leaders from around the world. The goal of the "Social Mission Summit" was to present CSR and social initiatives the company has been undertaken.

Goals set for their CSR initiatives included:

1. Use our Company to further the cause of Peace and Justice;

2. Harmonize our global supply chain and ensure its alignment with our values; and

3. Take the lead promoting global sustainable dairy practices. (Ben & Jerry's, 2008, p. 4)

Although Starbucks and Ben & Jerry's are smaller in scale than organizations such as Ford, IBM, or Microsoft, these companies are good examples of what organizations are doing in terms of their social responsibilities. As mentioned before, the efforts displayed by Starbucks and Ben & Jerry's are huge leaps from 50 or 60 years ago when the concept of corporate social responsibility was emerging. A study completed by Esben, Rahbek, and Pederson (2009), *Modeling CSR: How Managers Understand the Responsi-*

bilities of Business Towards Society outlined the current business environment relative to CSR. Pederson (2009) discovered that

> corporate activities have broad impacts on society, but the findings from the analysis indicate that managers still have a relatively narrow perception of societal responsibilities, which can be summarized as taking care of the workers and making products and services that the customers want in an environment-friendly way. (Pederson, 2009, p. 23)

According to Pederson, this perception is narrow because of the traditional line of thought that the organization is running soundly if profit margins remain high and stakeholders are satisfied. Current dilemma with more organizations adopting corporate social responsibility initiatives similar to those Starbucks Coffee and Ben and Jerry's have implemented often a lack a clarity of what is an effective and viable approach (Korkchi, 2009). In addition, business effectiveness is measured in other intangible factors than just financial and individualistic emphases, and business behavior has both economic and non-economic impact (Kolodinsky, et. al., 2009). Also, Ben & Jerry's can realize business effectiveness through the public's perception of an organization as evidenced again. As Ben Cohen, co-founder of Ben & Jerry's indicates that once consumers see examples of prosperous companies integrating social concerns into their business practices, they were emboldened to demand the same of other businesses (Greenfield & Cohen, 1998).

CSR Models

Economic theory originally presented by Nobel Prize winning economist Milton Friedman's shareholder model is still a prominent business model. Friedman's (1970) view proposed a theory of a shareholder model and stakeholder model. According to shareholder model, the sole responsibility of a corporation is to maximize shareholders wealth and satisfaction, which is consistent with the economic theory of self-interest and rational behavior. By contrast, the stakeholder model maximizes profits and has multiple stakeholders including shareholders, such as employees, customers, suppliers, governments, and local communities as well as secondary stakeholders, such as media, special interest groups, and trade associations.

According to Indra Nooyi, the Chief Executive Officer of PepsiCo Inc., profit is defined as revenue minus costs of goods sold, less costs to society (Williams, 2010), which is an intriguing example of the stakeholder model. Based on the examples of corporations and the visions of their leaders, we propose following arguments regarding why organizations are still reluctant to adapting CSR initiatives. In following sections, brief history of CSR

Evolution

The history of corporate social responsibility (CSR) goes back thousands of years and perhaps, to the beginning of private business operations. The word *business* is derived from combining two Latin words, *cum* and *panis,* which translates to "breaking bread together" (Miami University, 2009). According to Henriques (2003), Quakers, such as Barclays and Cadbury as well as socialists, such as Engels and Morris, experimented with socially responsible and values-based forms of business" [and] "Victorian philanthropy could be said to be responsible for considerable portions of the urban landscape of older town centers today" (p. 33). In the 1790s, the earliest recorded boycott of a product surrounded the use of slave-labor harvest sugar. During this time, consumers only purchased sugar harvested by free-laborers that had received a form of wages. This boycott is a great example of how the public and consumers forced an industry to change its behaviors or production with the social aspect as a single driver.

Another recent example of social activism surrounding business practices is protesters demonstration around Apple retail stores around the world because customers were concerned about how Apple's suppliers treat their factory workers in China and other overseas locations (Segall, 2012). Gucci also faced allegations in Shenzhen, China from former employees of operating as high-end sweatshops (Lai, 2011).

Businesses began including the social responsibility objectives directly into their corporate strategic plans. Organizations structured these social responsibilities around core objectives in a way that it fostered the social cause, without becoming a marketing scheme to obtain only social acceptance. Social responsibility initiatives should not revolve around an individual, such as the personal initiatives of a business executive. An appropriate example of a company with initiatives to make society a better place without serving one person's aspirations is the Starbucks Corporation. Starbucks intertwines its environmental stewardship initiatives, such as climate change and understanding and improving their environmental footprint, into its corporate business plans (Starbucks, 2009).

Not putting sufficient resources into its social responsibility projects can hurt organization. Given that organizations exist primarily on the profits of consumers, who directly or indirectly contribute to the organization's profits, without consumers and the society in which they reside, the organization would not exist. Giving back in some fashion to society is not only an ethical responsibility but also a financially as well. "While recognizing that profits are necessary for any business entity to exist, all groups in society should strive to add value and make life better. Businesses rely on the society within which they operate and could not exist or prosper in isolation" (University of Miami, 2009, p. 68). Some of the benefits worth mentioning for organizations to take part in social responsibility include brand recognition, brand marketing, brand insurance, and crisis management. These factors were relevant in 1982, when the

Johnson & Johnson company avoided a potentially brand damaging event surrounding the recall of millions of bottles of Tylenol, which cost the company more than $100 million dollars (University of Miami, 2009). The two potential downsides to maintaining a social responsibility program or initiative, as mentioned in the Johnson & Johnson case, are time and money. However, CSR has evolved over time to the point that public expects organizations to give back to society. Potential consumers often will turn away from the companies not vested with their social responsibilities in favor of those offering the same products that include CSR programs. Therefore, companies must have a clear goal, vision, and metrics to measure the control activities that tie back to strategic plans. These are utilized through advertising, promotional materials, annual reports, or on corporate websites because stakeholders do not want to see activities confused with results or do not want to see that an organization's CSR efforts as insincere (Korkchi, 2009). As a way to gauge perceptions about their actions, businesses will often conduct stakeholder focus groups, customer surveys, and community impact studies (Korkchi, 2008).

Debates have surrounded the initiatives of CSR perhaps since its conception. Businesses that employ CSR initiatives also have to consider the costs of doing so. The whole premise of a business is whether the business is making a profit or not. If the business is not making a profit, the business eventually will cease to exist. The goal of any business is to make a profit and to expand upon that profit to increase its capital gains for long-term stability. Wenzel and Thiewes (1999) investigated whether socially responsible firms financially outperform firms not defined as socially responsible and found no significant difference in Return on Equity (ROE) between both. However, Stock Return (RET) of socially responsible firms was significantly higher than those of the control sample.

If a new CSR initiative is introduced, a business would need to establish a way for the initiative to support itself or at the very least, make enough profit that the business can support the CSR initiative. Some of the factors that hinder CSR initiatives are efficiency and leadership. Some of the arguments to create CSR department, as iterated by Godelnik (2011), are talent management, leadership to build and execute strategies, and a separate department. On the other hand, not having enough public scrutiny and shareholder demands can lead companies not to adopt a CSR strategy (Maharaj, 2011). Surveys of 82 private companies in Canada stated CSR as "nice to have" attribute rather than a priority (Maharaj, 2011).

Those businesses that do not employ CSR initiatives either do not believe in the long-term value of CSR or, quite simply, cannot afford to launch such initiatives. Therefore, the debate for many businesses is the affordability of CSR practices that are provides sustainable competitive advantage. The concept of long-term investment that reduces operational costs needs to be carried out through thorough benefit-cost analysis that includes tangible and non-tangible transactions. Unfortunately for many businesses are concerned towards short-term goals and costs. In a recent debate over CSR, Kevin Moss, the head of Corporate Social Responsibility at BT Americas, stated, "Every manager should be worrying not only about today's profit but about tomorrows and next year's profit too. Using up a resource faster than it is being replenished might deliver short term returns, but will compromise tomorrow's business" (Moss, 2009, p. 54). In the article, Moss (2009) contested a recent article in The Financial Times, written by Stefan Stern who stated that it is "okay for businesses to employ child laborers and pursue environmentally unsustainable activities so long as it is within the law and it is in the interests of being competitive" (Moss, 2009, p. 54).

Moss (2009) insinuated that given the current economic climate, businesses need to do what businesses need to do to survive. This would include pushing the envelope regarding some questionable activities just so businesses can produce a profit and continue to survive. Although the debate is a practical one, many would side with the points made by Kevin Moss, as they are rational, responsible, and especially tolerable. Business leaders normally are resistant to change and are more concerned towards staying afloat as opposed to looking for new and creative ideas to embrace a venture such as CSR.

In contemporary times, there is an expectation that organizations do more with less. Competitions among industries in the current economy are much more intense, forcing organizations to look for alternative ways of doing business, before competitors find these new ways first. Technology certainly has become a large part of how organizations function these days. Some might say that organizations rely heavily on the technological advancements that have become available. For example, in the field of health care, doctor's offices, clinics, and hospitals, large and small, are always looking for the latest technology so they can improve the quality of care, increase the number of patients seen, and decrease costs, such as medical record storage and paper. One of these technologies many health care facilities have implemented is Electronic Medical Records (EMRs). EMRs offer a way for the health care industry to meet CSR goals by decreasing costs to the consumer, increasing the speed in which to see patients, and of course, EMRs also decrease or even eliminate the need for paper, saving trees, and improving the environment. According to Brennan and Johnson (2004), technology within businesses to meet social responsibility goals is crucial and can improve financial performance, environmental practices, and corporate social responsibility (CSR). The article also suggested there are three positive outcomes possible, given conscientious management of an organization's technologies. They are:

Keeping Products Competitive—technology substitution may be undertaken, supplanting an older technology with a new one.

Proving the Basis for New Products and Services—advances in technology—enable corporations to offer new products and services.

Changing Operational Conventions—changing institutional beliefs about what is possible, such as integrating the supply chain, improving customer relationship management, and focusing on enterprise resource planning. (Brennan & Johnson, 2004, p. 12)

Another great example of introducing new technologies in business, not only to improve business but also to exercise corporate social responsibility efforts, comes from Starbucks Corporation. As mentioned earlier, Starbucks places a considerable emphasis upon its social responsibility efforts. What is more impressive than the efforts of Starbucks is the organization tends to include its employees and customers on expeditions to coffee bean farms (suppliers) around the world to introduce new techniques for better farming. Company literature about these expeditions' states:

> Spending time at a coffee cooperative in Costa Rica can be a transformational experience. Starbucks Earthwatch Expeditions offer our partners (employees) and customers the chance to become active members of a scientific research team on coffee farms in Costa Rica's CoopeTarrazú cooperative. Those selected for the expedition conduct research that encourages environmentally sound farming practices at 24 C.A.F.E. Practices–approved farms. (Starbucks Coffee Company, 2009, p. 2)

Ben & Jerry's also often have projects underway to promote a cleaner, healthier environment, as evidenced by their new freezer technology:

> These new freezers use alternative refrigerants that, unlike current freezer gases, do not contribute to global warming or the deterioration of the earth's ozone layer if released to the atmosphere. That's two big leaps forward on the path to more envi-

ronmentally friendly refrigeration! (Ben and Jerry's Homemade, 2010, p. 4)

Most of the literature about corporate social responsibility argues for a strategic approach. Bruch and Walter (2005) contended that even though corporate philanthropy has been widely accepted as a viable business strategy, most companies are not achieving a substantial and lasting societal influence because they lack an effective philanthropy strategy. Academics and practitioners have been advocating the relevance and importance of using philanthropy as a business strategy (Bruch & Walter, 2005), where authors have contended that company leaders should use charitable activities to produce opportunities for their organization as well as those who benefit from their philanthropy (Bruch & Walter, 2005). Companies that adopt a social responsibility strategy maintain that the corporate social responsibility approach contributes to the growth of their companies' own value (Longo, Mura, & Bonoli, 2005).

Future Direction

Social responsibility initiatives demonstrated by almost all organizations dates back many centuries. As more businesses institute environmentally sound practices and products, and show success for doing so, other follower businesses are obligated to do the same. The businesses classified as followers are those who have not employed CSR in their business practices. Identifying barriers to adapt CSR in could be financial or lack of knowledge regarding benefits of CSR.

As stated earlier, one of the biggest factors influencing CSR priorities include the vision of a company's leaders and its organizational culture. It is possible that the strategic vision of an organization's leader is explained using Kohlberg's stages of moral development (Kohlberg, 1981). Most business decisions relating CSR originates from leader's initiatives. Consequently, a business leader at the pre-conventional level of moral development decides on business activities that are profit seeking (self-interest). Business leaders at the conventional level of moral development make decisions that conform to societal expectations and follow their competitor's CSR models (societal expectations). By contrast, organization leaders at post-conventional level of moral development use internalized ethical principles to innovate and adapt new CSR measures (Internalized Principles). Therefore, it is arguable that an organization's decision of whether to adapt a shareholder model or stakeholder model is tied back into the personal moral development of its leaders (Korkchi, 2008).

Kolodinsky et al. (2009) suggested, that several potential reasons the leader's CSR attitudes are not influenced sufficiently to make a change. These include spirituality, ethical ideologies, materialism, relativism, and idealism (Kolodinsky et al., 2009). Kolodinsky et al. stated that, "business effectiveness requires more than just financial and individualistic emphases, and business behavior has both economic and relational impact" (Kolodinsky et al., 2009, p. 19). Perhaps in business schools around the world, corporate social responsibility is not included into the core curriculum as much as it should. Kolodinsky et al. suggested that this is possibly the result of a need for more of a "human-centered educational approach" (p. 19). This requires "the teaching of ethics and social responsibility [which] requires an emphasis and understanding of impact of decisions and behaviors on others" (Kolodinsky et al., 2009, p. 19). According to Christensen et al. (2007), 42% of the top global MBA programs require CSR in the core content of curriculum. Moreover, Boli and Hartsuiker (2001) stated "90% of Fortune 500 firms embraced CSR as an essential element in their organizational goal, and actively promoted their CSR activities in annual reports" (p. 67). Research has confirmed that CSR is good for business; it is good for the environment, consumers, and for its employees. Why not select business managers and leaders who have post-conventional morality to create greater socially responsible organizations that go beyond traditional philanthropy and risk management, by building its core operations toward strategic CSR. In that context, a new business model that has emerged in previous years is B-corporation or Benefit Corporation. These entities were created when the establishment of state-level legislation provided the guidelines for these organizations. These corporations have the highest standards of performance, accountability, and transparency. A B-corporation sets standards for a better way of doing business that focuses on suppliers, buyers, environment, and community (B-Corporation, 2012).

A B-Corporation is a relatively new business concept that provides social benefits to the public observable and accredited by a third party, the B-lab. The B-Lab is a nonprofit group that provides information on B-Corporations and has an extensive website dedicated to the B-Corporation movement. This organization has developed an index used to grade the success of various B-Corporations. The factors that affect the final grade of each B-Corporation entity include governance, workers, community, and environment. This index and grading system do not account for earnings or financial losses but includes only a variety of public benefit factors.

This new trend could be an innovative approach to businesses instigated by the leadership that values CSR in its business models, or a new business strategy that gives them competitive advantage. In any case, this innovative business model by definition is "a new type of corporation which uses the power of business to solve social and environmental problems" (B-Corporation, 2012, p. 27). Therefore, the previous stockholder model is replaced by a shareholder model, where corporations are enforced by a legal structure, which expands corporate accountability, transparency, and performance standards; so they are required to make decisions good for society, not only shareholders. In addition, the performance standards of B-Corporations enable consumers to support businesses that align with their values, investors to drive capital to higher impact investments, and governments and multinational corporations to implement sustainable procurement policies. This new certification process could be the most effective way to achieve triple bottom line of People, Planet, and Profit. With 561 corporations in six states within the U.S., Canada, and Europe, B-corporation could be the answer to CSR. So far with $2.9 billion in revenues and $2 million in savings (B-Corporation, 2012), this innovative model that extends to the external benefits to stakeholder could be the new CSR strategy that may gain popularity. In turn, the success of this business strategy eventually will be adapted by the fence sitters still reluctant to adopting CSR in their business model because of the pressure by the stakeholders, and competitors. As previously described by various case studies and recent trends toward corporate social responsibility, it can be believed that the only future business model that could compete globally would be stakeholder model. With emerging social entrepreneurs and conscious consumers, adopting CSR would be a new paradigm shift, where businesses without some form of CSR practices would have to exit industry.

Consider the amazing social and societal impact of the Occupy Wall Street protests and it is not hard to understand the importance of that the media coverage of this movement has had on encouraging organizations to engage in social responsibility initiatives. This article explored the nuances and significance of developing management practices and organizational cultures that support and encourage corporate social responsibility. To move this issue forward, scholars and organizations should consider the impact of their operations on communities and their ability to improve the lives of others through community outreach.

REFERENCES

Ben & Jerry's Homemade, Inc. (2009). Hydrocarbon: The new cool! The cleaner, greener, freezer. *Activism.* Retrieved from http://www.benjerry.com/activism/environmental/hc-freezer/

B-Corporation. (2012). *2012 corporate annual report.* Retrieved from http://www.bcorporation.net/

Boli, J., & Hartsuiker, D. (2001). Work culture and transnational corporations: Sketch of a project. Proceedings of *International Conference on Effects of and Responses to Globalization, Istanbul.*

Brennan, L., & Johnson, V. (2004, Spring). Technology management for corporate social responsibility. *IEEE Technology and Society Magazine,* 40–48. doi:10.1109/MTAS.2004.1273471

Business for Social Change. (2009). Leveraging business for social change; Ben Cohen. *Social Venture Network.* Retrieved from http: //www.svn.org/index.cfm?pageId=688

Bruch, H., & Walter, F. (2005). The keys to rethinking corporate philanthropy. *MIT Sloan Management Review, 47*(1), 49–55. Retrieved from http://sloanreview.mit.edu/the-magazine/2005-fall/47111/the-keys-to-rethinking-corporate-philanthropy/

Carroll, A. B. (1998). The four faces of corporate citizenship. *Business and Society Review, 100/101,* 1–7. doi:10.1111/0045–3609.00008

Carroll, A. B. (1999). Corporate social responsibility: Evolution of a definitional construct. *Business & Society, 38*(3), 268–295. doi: 10.1177/000765039903800303

Carroll, A. B., & Shabana, K. M. (2010). The business case for corporate social responsibility: A review of concepts, research, and practice. *International Journal of Management Review:* doi:10.111/j.1468–2370.2009.00275.x

Dahlsrud, A. (2006). How corporate social responsibility is defined: An analysis of 37 definitions. *Corporate Social Responsibility and Environmental Management, 15,* 1–13. doi:10.1002/csr.132

Ethisphere. (2011). *World's most ethical companies.* Retrieved from http://ethisphere.com/2011-worlds-most-ethical-companies/

Friedman, M. (1970, September 13). The social responsibility of business is to increase its profits. *The New York Times.* Retrieved from http://select.nytimes.com/gst/abstract.html?res=F10F11FB3E5810718EDDAA0994D1405B808BF1D3

Godelnik, R. (2011). Is it time to ditch the CSR department? *Triplepundit.com*. Retrieved from http: //www.triplepundit.com/2011/12/time-ditch-csr-department/

Greenfield, J., & Cohen, B. (1998). *How to run values led business and make money too*. New York, NY: Simon Shuster Publishing.

Gupta, S. (2002). *Strategic dimensions of corporate image: Corporate ability and corporate social responsibility as sources of competitive advantage via differentiation*. Ann Arbor, MI: ProQuest Information and Learning Company.

Henriques, A. (2003). Ten things you always wanted to know about CSR (but were afraid to ask); Part One: A brief history of corporate social responsibility (CSR). *Ethical Corporation Magazine*. Retrieved from http://www.ethicalcorp .com/content.asp?ContentID=594

Kinard, J., Smith, M. E., & Kinard, B. R. (2003). Business executives' attitudes toward social responsibility: Past and present. *American Business Review*, 87–91. Retrieved from http://www.mendeley.com/research/business-executives-attitudes-toward-social-responsibility-past-present/

Kohlberg, L. (1981). *Essays on moral development, Vol. I: The philosophy of moral development*. San Francisco, CA: Harper & Row.

Korkchi, S. (2008). *Corporate social responsibility: The limits and dangers with corporate codes of conduct*. Heidelberg, Germany: VDM Verlag.

Korkchi, S. (2009). *Corporate Social Responsibility: Why responsibility is a mainstay for 21st century Business*. Heidelberg, Germany: VDM Verlag.

Kolodinsky, R., Madden, T., Zisk, D., & Henkel, E. (2009). Attitudes about corporate social responsibility: Business student predictors. *Journal of Business Ethics*, 91, 167–181. doi:10.1007/s10551–009–0075–3

Lai, A. (2011, October 12). Gucci faces 'sweatshop' claims in China. *Business 360, CNN.com*. Retrieved from http://business.blogs.cnn.com/2011/10/12/ gucci-faces-sweatshop-claims-in-china/

Longo, M., Mura, M., & Bonoli, A. (2005). Corporate social responsibility and corporate performance: The case of Italian SMEs. *Corporate Governance*, 5(4), 28–42. doi:10.1108/14720700510616578

Maharaj, A. (2011). *Why did CSR make its way to the bottom of the list?* Corporate Secretary: Governance, risk and compliance. Retrieved from http://www .corporatesecretary.com/articles/corporate-social-responsibility/11893/why-did-csr-make-its-way-bottom-list/

McKenzie, S. (2004). Social sustainability: Towards some definitions. *Working Paper Series*, University of South .Australia: Hawke Research Institute, Magill.

Moss, K. (2009). The CSR debate. *CSR Perspective*. Retrieved from http://www .csrperspective.com/2009/02/csr-debate.html

Pederson, E. (2009). Modeling CSR: How managers understand the responsibilities of business towards society. *Journal of Business Ethics, 91*, 155–166. doi:10.1007/s10551–009–0078–0

Rettab, B., Brik, A., & Mellahi, K. (2008). A study of management perceptions of the impact of corporate social responsibility on organizational performance in emerging economies: The case of Dubai. *Journal of Business Ethics, 89*, 371–390. doi:10.1007/s10551–008–0005–9

Segall, L. (2012, February 9). Protestors target Apple stores in "ethical I-phone" Campaign. *CNNmoneytech*. Retrieved from http://money.cnn.com/2012/02/08/technology/apple_foxconn_petition/index.htm?cnn=yes&hpt=ibu_c2

Starbucks Coffee Company. (2009). Starbucks earthwatch expeditions. *Ethical Sourcing*. Retrieved from http://www.starbucks.com/sharedplanet/ethicalinternal.aspx?story=earthwatchexpeditions

University of Miami. (2009). *A guide to corporate social responsibility*. Retrieved from http://www6.miami.edu/ethics/pdf_files/csr_guide.pdf

Valor, C. (2005). Corporate social responsibility and corporate citizenship: Towards

corporate accountability. *Business & Society Review, 110*(2), 191–212. doi: 10.1111/j.0045–3609.2005.00011.x

Van Maarrewijk, M. (2003). Concepts and definitions of CSR and corporate sustainability: Between agency and communion. *Journal of Business Ethics 44*, 95–105. Retrieved from http://www.jstor.org/

Wenzel, L. A., & Thiewes, H. F. (1999). Corporate social responsibility: Does it pay? *Journal of Accounting and Finance Research, 7*(4), 48–58. Retrieved from http://www.docslibrary.com/cgi-sys/suspendedpage.cgi

Williams, C. (2010). *MGMT4 20011-2012 edition*. Mason, OH: South-Western Cengage Learning.

About the Authors

Emad Rahim

Dr. Emad Rahim is an award winning author, educator, entrepreneur and civic leader. Dr. Emad holds several accredited degrees; an AACSB Post-Doctoral Diploma in Marketing and Management Research from Tulane University, Doctorate of Management and Master of Science in Project Management from Colorado Technical University, and a Bachelor of Science from SUNY Empire State College. He is also a Certified Manager (CM), Project Manager (PMP), and earned an Executive Leadership Certificate from Cornell University and MIT.

Dr. Rahim is currently the University Dean for the School of Business at Colorado Technical University and the Chief Learning Officer at Global i354 LLC. He served as a Beyster Scholar for the Beyster Institute at UC San Diego, Laureate Visiting Scholar for Laureate International Universities, Professor-in-Residence for the Student Sandbox at Syracuse University, Entrepreneurial Delegate for the Experiential Classroom at Oklahoma State University and a Research Coordinator for the SUNY Research Foundation.

Dr. Rahim has taught at SUNY Morrisville State College, Walden University, Empire State College, Kaplan University, Colorado Technical University, Northcentral University, the Jack Welch Institute, and lectured at Syracuse University, Cornell University, Colgate University, University of Scranton, and Cazenovia College.

Dr. Rahim was the recipient of the Certified Manager of the Year Award, 40 Under Forty Award, Entrepreneurial Teaching Excellence Award, Community Leadership Congressional Award, and was a finalist for the CEC Educator of the Year Award. He is an active member of PMI, ICPM, Intellectbase International Consortium, Innovation Roundtable, and Leadership Greater Syracuse.

To reach Dr. Emad Rahim for information on entrepreneurship, project management, or workforce development, please visit his website: http://www.coloradotech.edu or follow him on Twittter @CTUBusiness

Dr. Vishakha Maskey

Dr. Vishakha Maskey holds several accredited degrees; an AACSB Post-Doctoral Bridge to Business Certificate in Marketing and Management from Tulane University, Ph.D. in Natural Resource Economics from West Virginia University, and a Master of Science in Ecology and Environmental Sciences with focus on Natural Resource Economics and Policy from University of Maine. She also held a Post-Doctoral Fellowship at Regional Research Institute (RRI) at West Virginia University.

Dr. Maskey is an Assistant Professor of Management at Gary E. West College of Business at West Liberty University in West Virginia. Her research interest falls under the premises of Sustainable Enterprise, Historic Preservation, and Corporate Social Responsibility. She has published and presented nationally and internationally. She was the recipient of the Outstanding Doctoral Research Paper Award at West Virginia University, Davis College of Agriculture, Forestry, and Consumer Sciences; the Outstanding Scholarship Award at the College of Business, West Liberty University; the Best Paper Award at Academy of Business Research; and an International Fellowship from American Association for University Women (AAUW).

Dr. Maskey continually serves as a reviewer for many journal articles and textbooks. She has coached finalist student in statewide business plan competition, and mentored several student research projects. Dr. Maskey primarily teaches management, international business, and economics courses.

To reach Dr. Vishakha Maskey, please e-mail: vmaskey@gmail.com

Dr. Darrell Norman Burrell

Dr. Darrell Norman Burrell is an assistant professor of Business Administration in the executive PhD program in Human Capital Management at Bellevue University. He is a former Presidential Management Fellow. Dr. Burrell has been a faculty member at George Mason University. He has also taught in the Doctor of Health Sciences at A.T. Still University. He teaches in the on-line "Green" MBA in Sustainability Development at Marylhurst University. He received a doctoral degree in Health Education in Environmental Public Health from A. T. Still University. He has an EdS (Post Master's Terminal Degree) in Higher Education Administration from The George Washington University. He has graduate degrees (2) in Human Resources Management and Management from National Louis University and a graduate degree in Sales and Marketing Management from Prescott College.

Dr. Burrell can be reached at: dburrell@atsu.edu

Succession Planning in Municipal Governments: Adapting to Change through Knowledge Transfer

Dr. Christi Sanders
& Dr. Michael Millstone

Municipal governments in Texas will face a shortage of qualified employees between 2008 and 2028 (Texas State Auditor's Office, 2006). As the generation known as the Baby Boomers (born 1946–1964) begins to retire, a shortage of workers throughout the United States is expected to cause a deficiency of experienced leaders (Ashworth, 2006; Bakey, 2008; Reester, 2008). Many municipal governments in Texas have a large percentage of employees who will become eligible for retirement within the next 10 years, but have no documented succession plan in place to prepare the next generation of workers to take leadership positions, as older workers retire (The Waters Consulting Group, 2008). The lack of a formal succession plan not only fails to provide for the preparation of future leaders, but also fails to capture the knowledge and experience of those workers who have been leading local governments for many years (The Waters Consulting Group, 2008). This failure to plan could lead to problems in providing services to citizens throughout the state of Texas and the country (The Waters Consulting Group, 2008).

Overview of the Study

The aging workforce and future shortage of workers in the United States has been common knowledge to researchers for more than 15 years (Society for Human Resource Management [SHRM], 2006). The first of the Baby Boomers filed for Social Security in 2007 (Reester, 2008). These older workers will continue to retire over the next 20 years, creating an opportunity for younger workers to move forward in their careers and begin to accept leadership positions (SHRM, 2006). However, most local government entities in the state of Texas have not begun to prepare future leaders to fill the roles of retiring predecessors, thereby creating a gap that could cause problems throughout the state (The Waters Consulting Group, 2008).

The lack of formal succession programs has the potential to cost Texas taxpayers millions of dollars through lost efficiency and experience. The recession that began in 2008 has resulted in widespread municipal budget cuts (Pountain, 2011). Although cheaper to hire younger and less experienced workers, the loss of tacit knowledge by the retiring Baby Boomer generation could lead to mistakes that could cost more than paying the higher wages for more experienced workers (McConnell, 2006).

Succession planning should be a part of an organization's strategic plan to identify, train, and retain qualified employees who can advance into positions of leadership as incumbent employees retire (Texas State Auditor's Office, 2006). However, municipal governments are often entrenched in old methods of staffing that do not sufficiently consider the age, diversity, and skill gaps becoming an issue as the workforce continues to age (Texas State Auditor's Office, 2006). The growing skill gap between older and younger workers indicates that as older workers retire, the skills they take with them will be difficult to replicate if younger workers do not acquire those skills from more seasoned employees (McKinnon, 2008).

The lack of formal succession planning in municipal governments in Texas could be problematic for cities as older workers begin to retire. For example, in the City of Stephenville, Texas, 26% of the workforce is eligible to retire within the next 5 years (M. Kaiser, personal communication, October 16, 2010). With no formal plan in place to identify and train other employees to step into these positions, the City of Stephenville faces a loss of expertise and experience when older workers retire, in addition to the risk of losing qualified employees to other cities. A succession plan can serve the purpose of capturing valuable insight and experience from older workers while preparing younger employees to assume future leadership roles.

To prepare Texas municipalities for the coming retirement of Baby Boomers, education for human resources managers and other city officials concerning succession planning should be included as a part of the strategic plan of each city (Houlihan, 2009). By increasing the understanding of how succession-planning works, more Texas municipal leaders can begin the task of developing their own succession plans (Herrera, 2002). The focus of this current research was to establish the need for succession planning in Texas municipal governments and to provide information to municipal leaders who will create a dialogue within individual municipalities concerning the concept of succession planning (Sanders, 2011).

Conceptual Theory

According to systems theory, systems are composed of many smaller elements that work together to make up the whole (von Bertalanffy, 1950). Research by Senge, Scharmer, Jaworski, and Flowers (2004) resulted in a modified version of this theory, known usually as living systems theory, whereby a business organization can be likened to a living organism in that the organization must change continually and replenish itself to remain viable. These interrelated theories were chosen as the framework for this research study because they provided insight into the complex relationships between municipal government leaders and their approach to succession planning considering the exodus of the Baby Boomer generation from the workforce.

By adopting a living systems theory framework, the effects of the failure to prepare for the loss of expertise was shown in context of both economic and social implications. Because each function of city services is interrelated with other functions, the application of living systems theory would indicate that mass retirement of Baby Boomers could substantially affect an organization. If knowledge is lost because of the retirement of many employees in a short amount of time, the loss of that knowledge may result in lower efficiency, poor decisions resulting from lack of experience, and higher labor costs as organizations compete for skilled employees. The systems that comprise a municipal government also affect individual taxpayers and the community at large, thereby influencing an increasingly larger system as time goes by. The problems that may result from the failure to prepare for Baby Boomer retirement, based on living systems theory might have the potential to affect the entire state of Texas, and perhaps the entire country.

Shaver (2003) cited works by von Bertalanffy (1950) and Senge et al. (2004) concerning organizational power and politics and posited that political environments often have a greater effect on progress toward organizational goals than elements such as finances or other resources. Because both general systems theory and living systems theory hypothesized that all things are an interrelated sum of their parts, a reasonable assumption would be that each part of the whole carries equal weight in the overall scheme of the system. Shaver (2003) disagreed with this philosophy, writing that the political powers of particular players or parts of the system were inherently more powerful than other players or parts of the system, thereby creating a power vacuum that could influence the outcome of organizational plans. Because Texas municipalities are political organizations, the value regarding succession planning by those with the most power will determine the course of action concerning succession planning.

Research Methodology and Design

Qualitative research methods provided opportunities to gain insight into the thoughts and attitudes of study participants, using open-ended interview questions to solicit information from study participants and allow themes to emerge across the sample (Berrios & Luca, 2007). Qualitative research "is a means for exploring and understanding the meanings individuals or groups ascribe to a social or human problem" (Creswell, 2009, p. 4). Because the goal of the research was to determine what values are influencing municipal actions concerning succession planning as well as to ascertain if municipal leaders are aware of the possible effects that mass retirement could have on current operations, the qualitative research design was the best approach.

A phenomenological qualitative research method was selected so that open-ended questions could be used to provide insight into the practices of succession planning in municipalities in Texas (Sanders, 2011). Phenomenological research is an investigative process whereby the researcher develops an understanding of a particular phenomenon through the comparison and contrast of study participants (Creswell, 1994). Moustakas (1994) explained, "The method of reflection that occurs throughout the phenomeno-logical approach provides a logical, systematic, and coherent resource for carrying out the analysis and synthesis needed to arrive at essential descriptions of experience" (p. 47). Because the goal of the research was to understand the experiences of the participants concerning succession planning, a phenomenological research design was appropriate.

Data Collection

The city managers at 10 Texas municipalities were contacted via phone to request permission to interview him or her and members of his or her staff for the study. After receiving general permission from the city manager, invitations to participate were sent to municipal employees, whose job titles indicated a position of leadership in the municipality, specifically seeking municipal leaders such as city managers/city council members, HR professionals, and mid-level managers. The municipal leaders were identified via examination of the individual municipal websites. Five cities and three leaders from each city were selected from the responses received and the individual interviews commenced using a developed protocol as a basis for interview questions, so that all interviewees were asked the initial same questions.

Data Analysis

Following each interview, the audio recording was transcribed into a Microsoft Word document to identify common themes that emerged during the collective interviews. A content analysis technique was used to categorize the data and identify emergent perceptions concerning succession planning in municipal government (Williams, 2007). Because the goal of the research was to determine what value municipal leaders place on succession planning activities, the emergent themes from the data helped to identify specific perceptions and experiences that influence the decisions concerning succession planning across the sample.

The conceptual framework of living systems theory hypothesizes that all organizations are made up of many multiple parts working together to form the whole (Senge et al., 2004). By comparing data from three different leadership positions within each municipality, common perceptions that indicated value placed on succession planning were observed. Because each municipal leader's perceptions and values influence succession planning, the separate values must, according to living systems theory, inherently influence the entire organization. Therefore, the individual perceptions were identified as related to the value placed on succession planning as an organization.

Findings

Initially, each participant identified himself or herself so that a determination could be made regarding his or her status as a municipal leader in the state of Texas. Interviews took place with city managers, HR directors, police chiefs, a fire chief, a director of operations, a finance director, a park and community services director, and a transportation and public works director. The theories by von Bertalanffy (1950) and Senge et al. (2004) indicated that each part of the organization makes up the whole of the organizational body. Therefore, to obtain an accurate measure of how the municipal leaders in different departments or components of each organization perceive succession planning activities, a variety of departmental directors were chosen. These interviews took place at the location of the participant, in person, and were audio recorded.

The cities were purposefully selected for varying size and proximity as well as availability and willingness of the municipal leaders to participate in the study. Table 1 displays the demographic information of each participating municipality, and represents the collected answers for the question asking how many employees each municipality currently has on staff.

TABLE 1. *MUNICIPAL DEMOGRAPHIC INFORMATION*

City Identifier	Population	Number of Full-Time Employees
City 1	120,000	1,502
City 2	31,168	318
City 3	5,000	31
City 4	500,000	6,400
City 5	27,050	350

Participants were asked to identify the percentage of employees currently eligible to retire, but have not. The responses varied. Even within the same organization, the numbers ranged from 10–30%. In the case of City 2, the HR director and the city manager had completely different viewpoints regarding this number. The city manager indicated "about 10 people" (Participant 2) are currently eligible to retire, and the HR director indicated "30% of the workforce" (Participant 3) was currently eligible to retire. This view is a substantially different perception, and one easily documented. The other municipal leaders also answered with indecision with answers ranging from 10% to 40% of the workforce, spread across all municipalities in this study, are currently eligible to retire. Some of the disparity can be explained because answers were given in terms of specific departments, rather than overall municipal demographics, and it is possible that particular departments could maintain a much higher level of retirement-eligible employees that the average for the whole municipality.

The next question asked probed the knowledge of the municipal leaders to specify how many employees would become eligible to retire in the next 5 years and the answers ranged from one or two employees to as much as 40% of the workforce. Two participants indicated that they did not know the answer and would not guess. Most answers given were in the range of 10% to 20% of the workforce.

The same trend continued for the next question, which asked the municipal leaders to identify further the percentage of employees who would become eligible to retire in 10 years. Two of the participants did not know and would not guess. The other answers ranged from 10% to 100% of the workforce, with several answers indicating 40% to 60%. These answers indicate an alignment with the findings of the literature review because the number of retirees is predicted to increase substantially as Baby Boomers begin to retire from the workforce.

The next question asked the municipal leaders to identify if they have an official or unofficial succession plan. Out of the five municipalities, only two had anything resembling an official succession plan. Both of those municipalities have, in the past, had a *Leadership Development Program* (Cities 1 and 4) (see Table 1), but because of the economic downturn that began in 2008, both of these programs were eliminated from the budget, and have not been reinstated.

Several other participants indicated that they have informal departmental programs where a few key positions have been identified as critical and employees are developed to fill those key positions as they become available. During this phase of questioning, a strong theme emerged that substantially affects succession planning in municipal governments in the state of Texas. Police and fire departments in the state of Texas frequently fall under Chapter 143 of the Civil Service Code, by virtue of the size of the municipality, whether or not the municipality has a paid police or fire department, and if that municipality has elected to adopt the civil service code to govern the municipality (Texas Constitution and Statutes, 2009). All of the municipalities, with the exception of City 3, fall into the civil service category. What this means for both police and fire departments is that promotions cannot be made on merit, succession planning, or employee development alone. Prior to any advancement, with the exception of the police or fire chief, and the deputy chiefs immediately under them, an employee must take a civil service examination for that position. For instance, if an opening exists for a police lieutenant, all patrol officers who meet the minimum eligibility requirements must take a civil service examination. The highest score on the test dictates who receives the promotion. This means an officer who performs poorly in the field but tests well, may be promoted over an officer who performs exceptionally in the field, but tests poorly. Therefore, several of the public safety (police and fire) directors interviewed perceives no beneficial reason to spend time or resources developing employees until they become eligible to receive appointment to a deputy chief position. Although these department directors reported some of the highest rates of employees eligible to retire within the next 10 years (20%–30%), they expressed that the department director's ability to develop employees was limited by the Civil Service statutes.

The next four questions concern municipalities that have an official or unofficial succession plan. City 1 is a municipality that had a leadership development program in the past that they have deemed to be successful, although it has not been operational for almost 4 years. The leaders of City 1 were delighted to offer a copy of the manual, the application, and all supporting documentation, and the cooperation of their training coordinator offering assistance and further information about the program. The second subset question asked what the goal of the succession planning program was. Even those participants whose development activities and internal attempts at preparing leaders had the same concept in mind: To capture the knowledge of current leaders and pass to those employees who could lead in the future. The methods to achieve this result are varied, and have varying rates of success, but the goals are the same.

The success rate of the succession planning programs was the focus of the third subset question. As previously mentioned, the two municipalities who had formal development programs in the past are no longer operating those programs. However, municipal leaders at both organizations indicated that graduates of the program are in leadership and upper management positions in the organization. Both cities that have implemented leadership development programs have experienced success with those programs and resulting employee promotions. The departmental directors who have internal departmental programs could not determine if their programs have been successful, as the opportunity to promote has not yet occurred.

The last subset question asked if the municipal leaders were actively trying to capture and retain the knowledge of older workers. Each participant who responded to this question indicated that he or she was, but responded differently from anticipated. Two participants, both from different municipalities, responded in terms of the benefits they offer to employees to reward longevity and keep older workers employed longer. Whereas keeping older workers on the job certainly can benefit a municipality, no mention was made about how the knowledge of the older workers is transferred to younger employees. Two of the participants (both from City 1) indicated that the city manager is stressing succession planning, but since the elimination of the leadership development program, no clear idea of how to accomplish the sharing of knowledge between older and younger workers is apparent.

The next question asked participants to explain what motivated municipal leaders to develop a succession planning program. Both of the responding participants revealed a strong emotional tie to the organization where they work, and a desire to see it remain successful in the future. This type of dedication is also evidenced by the fact that both of these participants already have more than 30 years of service to the municipality, are currently eligible to retire, and are actively involved in training and developing an employee to be ready to take their place when they are ready to retire.

The participants who indicated that their municipality does not have an official or unofficial succession plan were asked why their municipal leaders choose not to develop such a program in the next question. The answers were predictable: Time, money, size of the organization, lack of planning, and that succession planning "has never been done here before (Participant 7)." Because of the poor economic environment that began to affect municipal governments in 2008, which caused municipal leaders to institute a hiring freeze, lay off employees, and eliminate any unnecessary expenditures; training budgets were slashed or eliminated without restraint in all of the organizations selected for this study.

The municipal leaders who indicated that they do not have an official or unofficial succession-planning program were asked to indicate how they plan to deal with vacant positions because of the increasing numbers of retirees. The answers received were sobering. Several of the municipal leaders indicated that they would simply fill the positions, as is the customary and usual practice when a vacancy occurs. However, those same municipal leaders predicted some of the highest levels of turnover over the next 10 years, and do not take into account the expected shortage of 35 million workers expected as Baby Boomers begin to retire (Aiman-Smith, Bergey, Cantwell, & Doran, 2006). The notion that municipal leaders will be able to fill positions as easily in 2020, and they could do so in 2011, could be a statement of the ignorance of some municipal leaders concerning the coming shortage of workers. If municipal leaders are not educated about this potential issue in the next 3–5 years, and a sense of urgency is not developed concerning the possible labor shortage, these specific leaders may find themselves unable to retain their most qualified help as competitive wages increase, and they cannot fill positions with even poorly qualified candidates.

Municipal leaders were asked to predict what effects, if any, they expect to experience from the retirement of Baby Boomer employees. Several of the participants indicated that they anticipate the impact to be none or minimal. Other participants indicated that the loss of institutional knowledge would be problematic. However, one other participant noted that bringing in *new blood* could benefit the municipality because younger workers are more comfortable with technology, more conscious of environmental issues, and have a different perspective. This participant viewed the younger mindsets as assets to the organization and could be a beneficial effect of Baby Boomer retirement.

The most striking example given by a participant for this question was provided by the City Manager from City 2. The participant stated that the policy has been to allow employees to accrue vacation leave, sick leave, and holiday leave without limitation, and that upon retirement, those employees receive a lump sum for those benefits. The City Manager further stated:

> We've got probably about six and a half million dollars in liabilities if everybody walked out the door today. How do you pay for that? So that's the detrimental impact and that's the prevailing question, is how do you satisfy that obligation of debt, and how do you avoid or minimize the future impact of similar debt continuing on with current employees? (Participant 14)

The same participant also stated that because of the laws governing civil service, it would be impossible to do anything to change the way these benefits are allowed to accrue for current employees, but that the municipal leaders were considering a cap on vacation and sick leave accruals for future employees. The City Manager stated that he has seen an employee retire and receive a check for $250,000 in accrued benefits, and the money to pay all these benefits would substantially affect the municipality if the employees all decided to retire at one time.

This is a frightening prospect, and this City Manager was the only participant to put the effect of Baby Boomer retirees in such finite terms. If other municipal leaders have looked at the financial effect of retirement payouts of this nature, they did not indicate such during the interviews. In theory, the funds to pay the employee benefits should have been budgeted and set aside each year, so that those funds would be available when an employee retired. However, the poor economy has affected municipal finances, and whether or not the city will be able to pay out those benefits is questionable. If the municipal leaders indicate that they are going to attempt to change the rules on the accrual limits, employees eligible to retire will do so immediately and demand payment in full of their benefits, before the rule can be changed. If that happens, not only will the municipality lose a tremendous amount of institutional knowledge and experience, but also they will be faced with limited resources and large number of vacancies immediately. If the municipality is not able to pay all the accrued benefits to retirees, they will be faced with lawsuits that will further affect the economics of the municipality.

The final question asked of each participant was if municipal leaders see succession planning as a critical part of strategic planning. Only one participant said that he or she does not. The other participants all indicated that their highest level of city management does see succession planning as critical, but several indicated that city councils were less convinced. Several participants indicated that city councils were not aware of the potential effect of the retirement of Baby Boomers, did not know how many employees were currently eligible to retire, and how many would become eligible to retire in the next 5 or 10 years, or that the municipality currently did not have a long-term strategic plan for the future, or were just starting to develop one. The inclusion of succession planning as part of a strategic plan seems to be an almost foreign concept to the Texas municipal leaders who were interviewed. Although all seem to agree that planning strategically to reduce or limit the impact of mass retirement is a good idea, few leaders are putting those ideas into concrete action.

Summary

Texas municipalities are facing a serious shortage of qualified employees over the next 10 years. Many municipalities are not preparing for the coming retirement of Baby Boomer employees through active succession planning. Further, many municipal leaders are unaware of the potential effect in terms of loss of knowledge, vacant positions, and the financial effect of retirement on municipal governments. This lack of knowledge could lead to reductions in service levels to citizens if the problems are not addressed proactively. City managers must educate upper-level managers as well as city council members about the risks associated with the failure to plan for mass retirement, and together they must develop a strategic plan that will allow Texas municipalities to remain strong and viable. Municipal leaders must create a sense of urgency about succession planning, and must exhibit a culture that creates value for succession planning activities. Without proper planning, the consequences may be that municipal offices throughout the country may be unable to meet the minimum requirements of service to their constituents. Thus, an inherent social responsibility exists to recognize, plan, and implement succession plans for municipal government sustainability.

Conclusion

The implications for positive social change and responsibility for this study indicate that a shift in thinking concerning succession planning in municipal governments in the state of Texas could have significant effect on future operations of municipal governments. If Texas municipal leaders fail to plan for retirement of Baby Boomer employees, the citizens of those communities could expect higher employee costs and lower quality services. Texas is a growing state and citizens want nice park facilities, good libraries, exceptional police and fire protection, clean water, reliable and affordable electricity, and good streets. Each is necessary for a well-developed community. However, each are *services*, meaning provided by *people*. Municipalities use public funds to hire and pay employees who work to produce the services that citizens want and need.

If Texas municipal leaders fail to recognize the effect of large numbers of Baby Boomers in the workforce and plan to avoid the problems that could result from mass retirement, the leaders will be failing to maintain the public trust. The public will not understand or care why the municipal leaders decided that succession planning was not important, citizens would understand and care that the services paid for with their tax dollars have become substandard or nonexistent because their city leaders neglected to consider succession planning a priority.

REFERENCES

Aiman-Smith, L., Bergey, P., Cantwell, A., & Doran, M. (2006). The coming knowledge and capability shortage. *Research Technology Management, 49*(4), 15–23. doi:10.1109/EMR.2011.6019089

Ashworth, M. J. (2006). Preserving knowledge legacies: Workforce aging, turnover, and human resource issues in the U.S. electric power industry. *International Journal of Human Resource Management, 17,* 1659–1688. Retrieved from http://www.tandf.co.uk/journals/routledge/09585192.html

Bakey, P. (2008). Winning the talent competition. *Public CIO, 6*(3), 2–3. Retrieved from http://www.govtech.com/pcio/

Berrios, R., & Lucca, N. (2007). Qualitative methodology in counseling research; recent contributions and challenges for a new century. *Journal of Counseling and Development, 84*(2), 174–187. Retrieved from http://www.counseling.org/publications/journals.aspx

Creswell, J. W. (2009). *Research design: Qualitative, quantitative, and mixed methods approaches.* Thousand Oaks, CA: Sage.

Herrera, F. (2002). Demystifying succession planning. *Employment Relations Today, 29*(2), 25- 31. doi:10.1002/ert.10037

Houlihan, A. (2009). Survive the Baby Boomer exodus. *Official Board Markets, 85*(1), 8–9. Retrieved from http://wpsglobal.files.wordpress.com/2010/09/obm_ipccutenergycosts_1-3-09.pdf

McConnell, B. (2006). 'Lost knowledge' threatens business growth, safety. Retrieved from http://www.shrm.org/Publications/HRNews/Pages/CMS_016538.aspx

McKinnon, C. (2008). Preparing for the Baby Boomer retirement wave. *Pharmaceutical Processing, 23*(7), 38–40. Retrieved from http://connection.ebscohost.com/c/ articles/33937769/preparing-baby-boomer-retirement-wave

Moustakas, C. (1994). *Phenomenological research methods.* Thousand Oaks, CA: Sage.

Pountain, M. (2011). The struggle to cut costs without cutting service. *Journal of Property Management, 76*(2), 10. Retrieved from http:/www.irem.org/sechome.cfm?sec=JPM

Reester, Jr., K. (2008). Dynamic succession planning: Overcoming the Baby Boomer retirement crisis. *Journal of Public Works & Infrastructure, 1*(1), 97–106. Retrieved from http://www.henrystewart.com/jpwi/index.html

Sanders, C. (2011). *A phenomenological exploration of the value of succession planning by municipal government leaders in Texas* (Doctoral study). Available from ProQuest Dissertations and Theses database. (UMI No. 3489744)

Senge, P., Scharmer, C., Jaworski, J., & Flowers, B. (2004). Awakening faith in an alternative future. *Reflections, 5*(7), 1–11. Retrieved from http://www.solonline.org

Shaver, S. (2003). *Organizational power and politics: More than meets the eye in program planning* (Ed.D. dissertation). Available from ProQuest Dissertations and Theses database. (UMI No. 3103630)

Society for Human Resource Management. (2006). *SHRM workplace forecast.* Retrieved from http://www.shrm.org/Research/FutureWorkplaceTrends/ Documents/06–0492_WorkplaceForecastExecSumm_small.pdf

The Waters Consulting Group, Inc. (2008). *The future is now.* Dallas, TX: Author.

Texas Constitution and Statutes. (2009). Local Government Code Chapter 143: Municipal Civil Service for Firefighters and Police Officers. Retrieved November 13, 2011 from http://www.statutes.legis.state.tx.us/Docs/LG/htm/LG.143.htm

Texas State Auditor's Office. (2006). Workforce Planning Guide. February, 2006. Report Number 06–704. Retrieved from http://sao.hr.state.tx.us/Work force/06–704.pdf

von Bertalanffy, L. (1950). An outline of general systems theory. *Emergence: Complexity & Organization, 10*(2), 103–123. Retrieved from http://www.emer-gence.org

Williams, A. (2007). *An examination of Generation Nexters and Baby Boomers value systems in a service organization* (Doctoral dissertation). Available from ProQuest Dissertations and Thesis database. (UMI No. 3388313)

About the Authors

Dr. Christi Sanders

Dr. Christi Sanders, a Texas native, holds a Bachelor of Science Degree in Communication from Tarleton State University; a Master of Science degree in Human Resource Management, also from Tarleton State University; and a Doctor of Business Administration Degree with an emphasis in Leadership from Walden University. Dr. Christi also holds a Senior Professional Human Resources (SPHR) Certification.

Dr. Christi is the Human Resource Director for the City of Granbury, Texas. She also serves as an adjunct faculty for Indiana Wesleyan University and Daymar College, and as a subject matter expert for Central Texas College.

Dr. Christi recently completed her doctoral dissertation: *A Phenomenological Exploration of the Value of Succession Planning by Municipal Government Leaders in Texas.* Other publications include *Leaving a Legacy: Succession Planning in Texas Municipal Governments,* and *The Learning Curve: Finding Ways to Connect with Students in Online Learning Environments.*

Dr. Christi is also an accomplished trainer and public speaker, specializing in employee development, management skills, and interview skills for job seekers and interviewers.

Dr. Christi can be reached at Christi.sanders@ymail.com

Dr. Michael Millstone

Dr. Michael Millstone earned his PhD in Business (Organization and Management) from Capella University, a Master of Arts in Business (Accounting and Finance) from Webster University, a Bachelor of Science (Liberal Arts) from The University of the State of New York, and an Associate of Applied Science degree from the Air University—Community College of the Air Force.

Dr. Michael joined the United States Air Force right out of college and served his entire career in the Space and Satellite Operations career field, specifically in various training roles from OJT instructor, course development, and delivery, to training group leadership and management. His last assignment was the Superintendent of Space Operations for Headquarters, Air Force Space Command. After retirement from the Air Force, he continued in the corporate world joining several excellent hi-tech corporate Learning and Development organizations. He has certifications as a Project Management Specialist (PMI) and a Certified Return on Investment Professional (CRP).

Dr. Michael is a Graduate School Dissertation Chair at a prominent online institution accredited by the Higher Learning Commission (HLC), the North Central Association of Colleges and Schools (NCA), and the Accreditation Council for Business Schools and Programs (ACBSP). Dr. Michael serves as a Dissertation Chair for many aspiring doctoral students from the Schools of Education; Business and Technology Management; and Behavioral and Health Sciences.

He is a Senior International Chess Master, General Secretary, and member of the Executive Board of the International Correspondence Chess Federation (ICCF) and an FAA Commercial pilot with instrument, multi-engine, and instructor endorsements.

To reach Dr. Michael Millstone, please e-mail dr_millstone@yahoo.com

CHAPTER 7

Federal Employees and Instructors: Serving the Public Trust

Dr. Julie M. Ducharme & Dr. Sheila Embry

Corporate Social Responsibility (CSR) has been a controversial topic among corporations and federal entities. Enron's lack of effective CSR in October 2001 caused a ripple effect of destruction for the company and sparked the downward spiral of the Californian economy, partnering companies, and caused deaths at hospitals and homes of the elderly due to rolling blackouts (Bloomberg, 2002). Eleven years later, the United States General Services Administration (GSA) made news for hosting an $800,000 conference for employees in Las Vegas, Nevada; more than triple the cost of prior conferences. The conference included mind readers, clowns, and videos of some GSA staff members making light of the United States financial oversight processes conducted by United States Office of Internal Audit and the United States Congressional Oversight Committees (Davidson, 2012).

The GSA example is important because of the economic status of the United States since the 2008 economic shift, created when its taxpayers were forced to pay more than $700 billion to bail out failing banks, loan institutions, and their insuring corporations (Henriques & Beresen, 2008); a move that created a downgrade in the United States credit rating for the first time in history (Goldfarb, 2011). Since then, federal jobs have been cut (from 2.8 million to 2.1 million) and federal salaries have been frozen for 4 years (Fox, 2012). Federal agencies have been asked to cut out any unnecessary expenses (Yoder, 2012). Still GSA, the agency responsible for federal real estate, determined hosting an extravagant conference for its Western Region employees was an acceptable and necessary expense because the Western Region *always* hosted extravagant conferences. Despite the adverse publicity the GSA Western conference raised, it was reported that another government agency, the National Oceanic and Atmospheric Association (NOAA), created a request for a magician to perform at its Training Conference to illustrate change management (Clark, 2012).

Scandals permeate the school systems too—from K-12 through college, especially in for-profit colleges. One school, which is consistently in the headlines, is the Education Management Corporation (EDMC), which is the target of a multibillion-dollar lawsuit by the U.S. Department of Justice and six states that are accusing this publicly traded company for defrauding the federal government. EDMC went against a federal law that does not allow colleges to give commission to admission recruiters based on the number of students they bring in (Burd, 2011).

> Among other things, EDMC has been accused of pumping up its enrollment numbers by aggressively recruiting unqualified students, loading them up with debt, and failing to help them find gainful employment in the fields in which they trained. The company has also been charged with cooking the books on the job placement rates that it discloses to students and reports to accreditation agencies and state regulators. (Burd, 2011 para. 3)

Corporations and government companies need vigorous CSR to reestablish the public trust. CSR is how a business views the impact the company has on the economy, the society, and the environment. Research shows a lack of public trust and concern among the stakeholders and customers.

If business leaders develop a better understanding of how their organizations can influence society beyond the financial aspects, they will be able to develop policies and decisions that better the business. When leaders embrace CSR, stakeholder interests are viewed differently to determine what possible risks and what opportunities exist in the business as well as the social and environment implications; creating a competitive advantage for the company. A CSR philosophy might help cut waste costs and benefit the environment. CSR could, "contribute to the five drivers of productivity identified by Michael Porter of the Harvard Business School: investment, innovation, skills, enterprise and importance to company's CSR records, and progressive employment practices" (Bloomberg, 2002, para. 4). Public trust can be rebuilt, and companies can become open to how to improve relationships with stakeholders and customers (Bloomberg, 2002).

Statement of the Problem

The preponderance of the 2.1 million federal employees is hardworking, sincere, committed, and conscientious. Many chose the federal government or public school vocations because they believe in the value and spirit of public service (Fox, 2012). With a continual news cycle reporting each found fraudulent occasion in corporations, businesses, governments, and educational systems, the general problem is the lack of trust in organizations, public and private, within the United States.

The specific problem is the lack of public trust in federal agencies and the public school systems. The mixed-methods descriptive study was an investigation of social responsibility with some federal employees and some instructors working in the public school system. The specific population who participated in the current study included federal employees who attended an Executive Program and instructors who worked in a California public school system.

The data collection instruments in the current study were two online surveys composed of open- and close-ended questions used to collect the perceptions of interacting individuals. The focus of data analysis was perspectives of some federal employees and some public school instructors about social responsibility. The general population of the first survey consisted of federal employees who had just completed an Executive Program. A second survey was conducted with instructors teaching in a California public school system. Due to confidentiality laws, the name of the public school system cannot be released.

Purpose of the Study

The purpose of the mixed-methods study was to examine and explore social responsibility and federal employees and instructors. Other researchers successfully used quantitative Likert-type items to measure social responsibility. A qualitative component in the study was appropriate for the exploration of opinions of federal employees and instructors regarding social responsibility listed in the comments field (Creswell, 2009). In the mixed-methods study, the quantitative component consisted of testing the demographic similarities of the participants, and the qualitative component consisted of exploring comments listed by federal employees and instructors. The descriptive design included the measurement of a potential association between federal leaders and social responsibility and instructors and social responsibility. Descriptive designs provide detailed, accurate pictures of particular characteristics within a study and provide focus (Cone & Foster, 2006).

Overview of the Research Method

The study incorporated a mixed-methods descriptive approach with a cross-sectional online survey to identify predictor and criterion variables relationships (Creswell, 2009; Leedy & Ormrod,

2010). The mixed-methods descriptive approach included quantitative and qualitative components (Vogt, 2005). According to Vogt (2005), the boundary between quantitative and qualitative is easily blurred. A quantitative survey was appropriate to provide answers about how experience as federal employees and instructors (predictor variables) influenced social responsibility (criterion variables) (Creswell, 2009). The study included a series of quantitative Likert-type measures and open-ended questions to describe and explore social responsibility and federal employees and instructors (Creswell, 2009).

Overview of the Design Appropriateness

The purpose of the descriptive design and closed questions was to evaluate quantitatively the relationships between the predictor and criterion variables. The open-ended questions were used to examine comments on social responsibility. An online survey was appropriate because of the capability to reach a large population in geographically dispersed locations. The online survey offered the advantages of easy management, anonymity, and remoteness (Leedy & Ormrod, 2010).

Research Questions

Research Question #1

The first research question asked, what relationship, if any, exists between federal employees and social responsibility?

The following is the hypothesis corresponding to the first research question:

$H1_0$—There is no significant correlation between federal employees and social responsibility.

$H1_A$—There is a significant correlation between federal employees and social responsibility.

Research Question #2

The second research question asked, what relationship, if any, exists between instructors and social responsibility.

The following is the hypothesis corresponding to the second research question:

$H2_0$—There is no significant correlation between instructors and social responsibility.

$H2_A$—There is a significant correlation between instructors and social responsibility.

Research Question #3

The third research question allowed for general open-ended comments.

Definition of Social Responsibility

Margaret Gilbert (1996), philosopher, stated "as social beings we form collective relationships with others based on shared, not summative, goals in joint commitments to one another. These commitments are holistic and interdependent" (para. 5). Society leaders provide expectations on how individuals need to be morally responsible to society and our family. These leaders provide expectations for businesses and federal agencies to be socially responsible as they develop socioeconomic relationships. The World Business Council for Sustainable Development (2000) defined,

> Corporate Social Responsibility [as] the continuing commitment by businesses to behave ethically and contribute to economic development while improving the quality of life of the workforce and their families as well as of the local community and society at large. (para. 4)

CSR is difficult to define because each country and culture has different priorities and values, which change the shape of how businesses view CSR. The definition used by Business for Social Responsibility is operating a business in a manner that meets or exceeds the ethical, legal, commercial, and published expectations that society has of business. Goodwin (2001) stated, "businesses should help to anticipate and plan for the future needs and constraints of society and of the natural world within which society—and its subset, business—are imbedded" (p. 262).

The definition used in the United States is focused on a philanthropic model where companies making profits with no hindrance except the paying of taxes, encourages donations of a portion of profits to a charitable cause assuming a financial gain over time. The European business model focuses on the company's core socially responsible by investing in the community. This model has shown to be a successful model of investing in the community and in turn the community investing back into the company (Goodwin, 2001).

Assumptions

The following operational assumptions were identified for the current study:

1. A representative sample from the population of federal employees who attended an Executive Program would be willing to participate in the study.

2. A representative sample for the population of instructors from a California public school system would be willing to participate in the study.

3. Individuals who participated would provide honest and accurate responses. Self-reported data can contain inaccurate perceptions based on faulty memories or a hesitancy to provide answers presenting the organization negatively (Cone & Foster, 2006).

4. The quantitative component of the study design would permit the sampling of a large number of individuals. Unlike qualitative methods, which often include small samples, large samples reduce the risk of self-reported bias from any single respondent (Creswell, 2009).

5. The use of an anonymous online survey might have increased the participants' perception of the confidentiality and anonymity of their participation, in turn increasing the accuracy and honesty of the self-reported answers (Leedy & Ormrod, 2010).

Summary

The scope of the analysis included students within one Executive Program. The analysis included instructors within a California public school system. Delimitations to the study included 4 weeks for online data collection. Figure 1 shows elements organizations should consider within their definition of CSR, where outside stakeholders continue to have an interest in the companies they are vested in. Many are looking at what the outer circle is showing in the model listed below—what the companies do to be socially responsible or are not doing to be socially responsible in the areas of products and services and how it affects the local environment and community.

Does morality and ethics play a role in the creation of the definition for CSR?

Since interactive rational human choice is necessary to the function of the corporation in the marketplace, economic analysis ought to seek and find social legitimacy as a moral intention of corporate decision-making. The notion of interactive choice in the economic market system involves social interdependence among stakeholders—in business and society. (Hausman, 1996, p. 671)

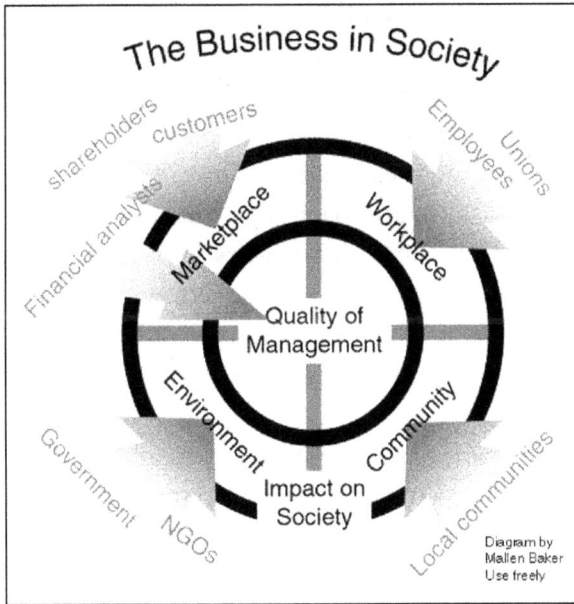

Figure 1.
The Business in Society

"The question whether *morality* constitutes a constraint on the prudent management of motivating interests is a good example, because morality does seem to require us at least sometimes to put the interests of other people ahead of our own" (Kahane 1989, p. 511). For organizational leaders to build back the lack of public trust, they must widen their definition and view on CSR and start to implement actions that show social responsibility. CSR is more than the existing philanthropy model. Organizations have constant responsibility to society and the environment; a responsibility that can be realized by working with the local community to ensure their service or product incorporates quality and reliability.

Methodology

The mixed methodology for the current study was appropriate to examine the relationship between federal employees and social responsibility and instructors and social responsibility. Using qualitative and quantitative methods, the study was an investigation of the correlation between the predictor variables of experience as a federal employees and social responsibility and experience of instructors and social responsibility. A combination of quantitative and qualitative approaches provided two perspectives of social responsibility increasing readers' understanding of the gathered data (Creswell, 2009; Leedy & Ormrod, 2010). In the quantitative component of the study, the use of empirically validated measures allowed quantitative comparisons of the participants' responses.

The quantitative portion of the study consisted of correlating the predictor and criterion variables of social responsibility. The qualitative open-ended questions facilitated the exploration of the trends identified in the quantitative data. The exploratory nature of qualitative questions allowed the participants to explain situations rather than simply respond to specific scenarios in the survey (Cone & Foster, 2006; Leedy & Ormrod, 2010). Triangulation between the methods allowed convergence and comparison of trends in the data not available with either a qualitative or a quantitative approach alone (Creswell, 2009; Leedy & Ormrod, 2010).

Descriptive Design

Descriptive designs are used to measure a situation *as is,* and the research process does not change the situation under study (Leedy & Ormrod, 2010; Schwandt, 2007). Creswell (2009) suggested descriptive designs were effective to identify problems within organizations and to discover potential solutions. Federal employees and instructors provided their perceptions concerning social responsibility. The use of the mixed-methods descriptive design was consistent with other studies of social responsibility.

Population and Sampling Frame

The study topic was social responsibility and federal employees and social responsibility and instructors. The random population consisted of 90 employees in an Executive Program. In addition, this population also included 100 instructors in public education in the California public school system.

The unit of analysis consisted of individuals within an Executive Program and those whom they forwarded the survey. A probability sampling approach provided 190 participants an opportunity to participate in the online survey (Creswell, 2009; Leedy & Ormrod, 2010). A total of 127 participants were targeted for the study based on the Sample Size Calculator with a confidence level of 95% for a population of 90 federal employees and 100 public school instructors (Creative Research System, 2012).

The participants received access to two Uniform Resource Location (URL) links to take the survey electronically. The Web hosting service recorded the participant's Internet Protocol (IP) address that functioned as the participant's electronic signature consenting to the survey. To ensure the confidentiality of all participants, the online survey was constructed on a secure, firewalled Web site. Names or other personally identifiable information were not collected. To ensure the participants completed the survey only once, the Web hosting service locked out the user's IP address after completion of the questionnaire.

Geographic Location

The study was conducted to examine participants of an Executive Program and instructors in a California public education system. Potential participants were in federal offices nationally and six California public schools. The participants included all categories of students within an Executive Program and all instructors in six California public school systems.

Data Collection

Data from the study were collected from a sample of federal employees and instructors through an online survey. Two URLs were made available to the participants. Online questionnaires are expedient and confidential. Availability 24 hours a day and seven days a week helped increase the response rate (Creswell, 2009; Leedy & Ormrod, 2010).

The online questionnaire allowed for (a) the extrapolation of data over a longer period, (b) participation throughout geographically dispersed locations, (c) a large population, and (d) confidential and truthful responses (Cone & Foster, 2006; Creswell, 2009; Leedy & Ormrod, 2010). Researchers chose the online method for data collection when studying an *as is* environment rather than face-to-face interviews, experimental, and causal-comparative techniques (Cone & Foster, 2006; Leedy & Ormrod, 2010). The secure online data collection platform for responses was the most efficient technique for gathering data (Cone & Foster, 2006; Leedy & Ormrod, 2009).

Research Map

The surveys were made available to all participants through two URLs published on fliers. After four weeks, the Web sites were closed and coding of the data began. Coding recorded on a data spreadsheet enabled sorting of responses in multiple categories with a unique, confidential tracking code assigned to each participant.

Instrumentation

Along with the standard questions, the survey included demographic questions. The participants were asked to indicate their geographical and departmental locations, whether they served in the military, what leadership program they attended, and how long they had served in the public sector. Two open-ended questions were included to allow the participants to offer comments and suggestions on what is social responsibility and whether or not federal employees are socially responsible. The survey instrument was piloted to ensure validity and reliability.

Validity

An instrument measuring what is intended to measure is considered valid (Creswell, 2009). Systematic evaluation of content validity ensures the data collection instrument is adequate for the subject of interest (Creswell, 2009). Validity is the determination of how well the results of a study apply to the entire population studied. The sample studied must represent the target population so the results can represent the general population (Creswell, 2009; Leedy & Ormrod, 2010). The target population for the current study was 190 (90 federal employees and 100 instructors). The survey was opened to all participants through two online secure, confidential URLs. Researchers found online data collection through Web sites encouraged increased participation, anonymity, and honesty (Creswell, 2009; Leedy & Ormrod, 2010).

Summary

Data was collected with a cross-sectional survey instrument. Quantitative data analysis was used to examine participants' perceptions of social responsibility. Content analysis was performed on the qualitative open-ended data from federal employees and instructors.

Results

The purpose of the current mixed-methods study was to examine if a relationship exists between social responsibility and federal employees and instructors. A quantitative method was appropriate to study perceptions of federal employees and instructors' on social responsibility with a sample from a large population of geographically dispersed Executive Program participants. A qualitative method was appropriate to explore (Creswell, 2009) relationship between social responsibility and federal employees and instructors. The mixed-methods study included a quantitative test of the relationship between social responsibility and federal employees and social responsibility and instructors.

The descriptive design provided clarification within the study with detailed characteristics identified in the study (Cone & Foster, 2006). Descriptive correlational designs are appropriate to analyze federal employees and instructors' perceptions because the designs generate descriptions as well as systematic tests of relationships between variables (Leedy & Ormrod, 2010). The goal was to test the correlation between the predictor variables of experience of federal employees and instructors and the criterion variable of social responsibility. The population included 90 federal employees in an Executive Program and 100 instructors in the public school system in California.

Data Collection

The survey was administered to examine social responsibility between federal employees and instructors. Open coding simplified the examination of the written data to identify correlations between responses. The mixed methodology study was conducted to assess the correlations between social responsibility and federal employees and social responsibility and instructors.

The survey instrument was used to measure the study variables in a two-dimensional grid showing the relationship between social responsibility and federal employees and the relationship between social responsibility and instructors. The data were collected over four weeks through secure, exclusive URLs. The URL sites hosting the survey recorded each participant's IP address and allowed only one response from each IP address.

Findings

Distribution Methods

The federal employee URL site had 75 participants (83%). The instructor URL site listing had 60 participants (60%). Except for differences in locations of work, and asking whether the person had served in the military, all questions on each URL were identical. Results were considered statistically significant with a probability of .05 or less, indicating at least 95% confidence in conclusions.

Response Rate

Based on the Sample Size Calculator with a confidence level of 95% for a population of 90 federal employees in an Executive Program and 100 instructors in the California public school system, the study required 123 completed surveys to obtain its targeted population (Creative Research System, 2012). After 4 weeks of data collection, 135 individuals participated in the study. With 135 completed surveys, the study exceeded the target population by 12 respondents.

Frequency, Demographics, and Descriptive Statistics

Information on the 135 participants who completed the study was categorized. Designations included locations, departments, years of experience, whether or not the participant served in the military, and what area of education they were in classified, administrative, or faculty. The open manner in which participation was solicited led to 35 recorded responses from participants who did not attend an Executive Program or were California public school instructors. The statistical comparison indicates that participants were:

- 56% federal employees and 45% instructors;

- 37% male and 73% female;

- 40% academics and 60% administrators, supervisors, managers, executives, and general office staff; and

- 14% were in the position less than 1 year, 27% were the in position less than 5 years, 19% in position 6–10 years, and 40% in position 11–19 years.

When asked are most federal employees socially responsible, 67% answered yes and 33% answered no. When asked are most public school instructors socially responsible, 75% answered yes with 25% answering no. Participants' definitions of social responsibility are listed in Table 1.

TABLE 1. SOCIAL RESPONSIBILITY DEFINED BY THEME

In order of frequency chosen	Federal Employees	Public School Instructors
Helping others even when there is no immediate benefit to self	1	2
Ethical behavior	2	1
Financial accountability	3 (tie)	5
Environmental sustainability	3 (tie)	6
Selling safe products	4	7 (tie)
Sound business practices	5	4
Other	6	7 (tie)
Skipped	7	7 (tie)
To act in such a way that the people around you are not adversely affected.	8	3

Qualitative responses indicate selling safe products, sound business practices, environmental sustainability, and financial accountability were top themes for social responsibility among federal employees and public school educators as well have similar responses with selling safe products or sounds business practices that translates into good teaching practices, and financial accountability as well as environmental sustainability as top themes for instructors. In open fields entitled General Comments, other suggestions included themes of

- Social responsibility equaling serving the country

- Having self-respect and integrity

- Helping other people

- Doing the right thing

- Having alternative viewpoints that included:

  ○ were more socially responsible years ago than those hired within the last 10 years,

  ○ are concerned with the eight to five and doing only what is needed as part of the job but show a great concern for the clients they serve, and

  ○ do not work hard enough to deserve the stability of their employment.

- Final comments included social responsibility is the primary reason that the United States is a global leader, and social responsibility is innate in federal employees and instructors' positions.

Summary

The purpose of Research Question 1 (RQ1) was to investigate the correlation between social responsibility and federal employees.

Research Question 1 asked, what relationship, if any, exists between federal employees and social responsibility. The $H1_0$ stated there is no significant correlation between federal employees and social responsibility. The $H1_A$ stated there is a significant correlation between federal employees and social responsibility. Since quantitative responses on federal employees and social responsibility were ordinal, Spearman's Rho was more appropriate than Pearson's Product Moment Correlation (Vogt, 2005). There is a high level of association between social responsibility and federal employees.

The purpose of Research Question 2 (RQ2) was to test the correlation between social responsibility and public-school instructors. Research Question 2 asked, what relationship, if any, exists between instructors and social responsibility. The $H1_0$ stated there is no significant correlation between instructors and social responsibility. The $H1_A$ stated there is a significant correlation between instructors and social responsibility. Since quantitative responses on instructors and social responsibility were ordinal, Spearman's Rho was more appropriate than Pearson's Product Moment Correlation (Vogt, 2005). There is a high level of association between social responsibility and instructors.

Conclusions and Recommendations

The current mixed-methods study was an examination of the relationship between social responsibility and federal employees and social responsibility and instructors. The descriptive design allowed for an analysis of the participants' perceptions by systematically testing relationships between the variables and by using open-ended qualitative questions to gather detailed and accurate pictures of particular characteristics (Cone & Foster, 2006). Limitations of the analysis included students within one Executive Program and those they invited to complete the survey, and instructors within California public school system. Delimitations to the study were a four-week timeframe and the use of the survey for data collection.

Data Collection

Data collected for the study derived from a sample of federal employees and instructors through an online survey using 10 questions: seven demographic questions, and three social responsibility questions. The study was conducted to assess the correlations between social responsibility and federal employees and instructors. The survey was the instrument used to measure the study variables in a two-dimensional grid showing how supervisor leadership and leadership could predict employee performance.

Data were collected on two Internet Uniform Resource Locators (URL) from March 19, 2012, through April 18, 2012. Survey announcements and URLs were listed on fliers distributed in employee break rooms and cafeterias and through private social networks such as *Facebook, Linked In,* and *Twitter.* The data was collected over 4-weeks through secure, exclusive URLs. Each result was reviewed and coded through the URL analytics program.

Data Findings

The URL site listing federal employees had 90 participants (47%) while the URL site listing public school instructors had 100 participants (53%). Based on the Sample Size Calculator with a confidence level of 95% for a population of 90 federal employees and 100 California public school instructors, the study required 123 completed surveys to obtain the targeted population (Creative Research System, 2012). After four weeks of data collection, 135 individuals participated in the study. The study exceeded the target population by 12 respondents. Information on the 135 participants who completed the study was demographically categorized by geographic location, departmental location, leadership program, time in the public sector, and whether or not the participant served in the military. The survey recorded responses from 26% (35 participants) who did not work for the specific categories studied.

Correlational Analysis

Three questions qualitatively addressed RQ1 and 2. The RQ3 was addressed with questions to evaluate federal employees' perception of social responsibility and instructors' perception of social responsibility. The purpose of Research Question 1 (RQ1) was to investigate the correlation between social responsibility and federal employees. The purpose of Research Question 2 (RQ2) was to test the correlation between social responsibility and instructors. A strong positive relationship between the two variables was revealed. Social responsibility was significantly correlated with federal employees and instructors.

Gap Analysis

Fifty-six percent (56%) of the participants who responded were federal employees and 45% of the participants who responded were California public school instructors. Forty percent (40%) of the respondents were in academics while 60% of the respondents listed themselves as administrators, supervisors, managers, executives, and general office staff. Sixty percent (60%) of those who answered the survey were in their positions 10 years or less, while 40% percent were in their positions 11 years or more. Additionally, 73% of the respondents were female while 37% were male.

Summary

Assumptions were made at the beginning of the study. One was that a representative sample from the population of 190 participants would agree to participate. To meet the targeted population, 123 participants were needed. 135 respondents completed the survey. The quantitative component of the study design would allow for the sampling of a large number of individuals. Unlike qualitative methods, which often include small samples, large samples reduce the risk of self-reported bias from any single respondent. Use of an anonymous online survey would increase the participants' perceived confidentiality and anonymity, in turn increasing the accuracy and honesty of the self-reported answers (Leedy & Ormrod, 2010). Another assumption was the individuals who participated would provide honest and accurate responses. Self-reported data can contain inaccurate perceptions based on faulty memories or a hesitancy to provide answers presenting the organization negatively (Cone & Foster, 2006).

A purpose of the mixed-methods study was to discover the perceptions of federal employees and instructors regarding social responsibility. Research Question 1 asked, are federal employees socially responsible. The $H1_O$ stated there is no significant correlation between social responsibility and federal employees. The $H1_A$ stated there is a significant correlation between social responsibility and federal employees. A significant correlation was found between social responsibility and federal employees.

Research Question 2 asked, are instructors socially responsible. The $H1_O$ stated there is no significant correlation between social responsibility and federal employees. The $H1_A$ stated there is a significant correlation between social responsibility and federal employees. A significant correlation was found between social responsibility and California public school instructors.

Research Question 3 asked to define social responsibility and answer the question are federal employees and public-school instructors socially responsible.

- When asked if they believed most federal employees were

socially responsible, 50 out of 75 respondents (67%) answered in the affirmative.

- When asked if they believed most public school instructors were socially responsible, 45 out of 60 respondents (75%) answered in the affirmative.

- When asked to define social responsibility by themes federal employees chose helping others even when there is no immediate benefit to self as their first choice while California public school instructors chose ethical behavior as its first choice. California public school instructors chose helping others even when there is no immediate benefit to self as their second choice while federal employees chose ethical behavior as its second choice.

Based on findings in the current study, respondents believed the majority of federal employees and instructors are socially responsible. Examples were given regarding individual instances of non-social responsibility, yet respondents believed them to be isolated incidents. Written comments from the participants of the current study indicated that even those public workers who appeared to be just *punching an 8 to 5 time clock* still cared deeply about the people their jobs affected.

Researchers have studied Corporate Social Responsibility extensively, but little research was found as it relates to the federal government. The Obama administration promised transparency within the executive branch, making this an opportune time to study the 2.1 million federal employees (Brodsky & Newell, 2009; Herbert, 2009). Longitudinal studies (annual or bi-annual), grounded in theory should track social responsibility over time with special attention paid to the demographic data collection to ensure a clearer understanding of the studies throughout a wider audience base.

Federal workers and instructors must maintain a high standard because they are the guardians of the taxpayer money, the people's trust, and the country's future leaders (Davidson, 2012). Continued studies in this area will add to the body of educational, federal employee, and social responsibility knowledge. Longitudinal studies (annual or bi-annual), grounded in theory, should track social responsibility with special attention paid to the demographic data collection to ensure a clearer understanding of the studies throughout a wider audience base.

REFERENCES

Argyris, C. (2008). *Teaching smart people how to learn.* Cambridge, MA: Harvard Business Classics.

Ben-Har, L., & Shiplett, M. H. (2009, January 28). Management matters. *National Journal Group.* Retrieved from http://www.governmentexecutive.com/story_page.cfm?filepath=/dailyfed/0109/012809

Bloomberg, M. (2002, January 13). The Enron scandal. *Bloomberg Businessweek.* Retrieved from http://www.businessweek.com/magazine/toc/02_04/B3767enron.htm

Brodsky, R., & Newell, E. (2009). Memo to the president-elect. *Government Executive, 41*(1), 25–30. Retrieved from http://cdn.govexec.com

Clark, C. (2012). Magic acts at conferences can add substance, professionals say. *Government Executive.* Retrieved from http://www.govexec.com/oversight/2012/05/magic-acts-conferences-can-add-substance-professionals-say/55591/?oref=top-story

Cone, J. D., & Foster, S. L. (2006). *Dissertations and theses from start to finish: Psychology and related fields.* New York, NY: Springer Publications.

Creative Research System. (2012). *Sample size calculator.* Retrieved from http://www.surveysystem.com/sscalc.htm

Creswell, J. W. (2009). *Research design: Qualitative, quantitative and mixed methods approaches* (2nd ed.). Thousand Oaks, CA: Sage Publications.

Davidson, J. (2012, April 18). *Ripple effects of GSA scandal.* Washington, DC: The Washington Post. Retrieved from http://www.washingtonpost.com/politics/ripple-effects-of-gsa-scandal/2012/04/18/gIQAE1WmRT_story.html

Fox, T. (2012, April 20). Amid government scandals with GSA and the secret service, advice for federal leaders. The Federal Coach. *The Washington Post.* Retrieved from http://www.washingtonpost.com/blogs/ask-the-fedcoach

Ford, W. (2008, September 30). *The 2008 wall street scandal: An American nightmare.* Retrieved from http://www.wilsdomain.com/blog/news/the-2008-wall-street-scandal-an-american-nightmare

Goldfarb, Z. (2011, August 5). S&P downgrades U.S. credit rating for the first time. *The Washington Post.* Retrieved from http://www.washingtonpost.com/business/economy/sandp-considering-first-downgrade-of-us-credit-rating/2011/08/05/gIQAqKeIxI_story.html

Hausman, D., & McPherson, M. (1996). *Economic analysis and moral philosophy.* Cambridge, UK: Cambridge University Press.

Henriques, D., & Beresen A. (2008, December 14). *The 17th floor: Where wealth went to vanish.* The New York Times. Retrieved from http://www.nytimes.com/2008/12/15/business/15madoff.html?pagewanted=all

Herbert, D. (2009, February 2). Agencies struggle to make connections online. *National Journal.* Retrieved from http://www.govexec.com/story_page_pf.cfm?articleid=42201

Leedy, P. D., & Ormrod, J. E. (2005). *Practical research: Planning and design* (7th ed.). Upper Saddle River, NJ: Merrill Prentice Hall.

Schwandt, T. (2007). *The SAGE dictionary of qualitative inquiry.* Thousand Oaks, CA: SAGE Publications.

Vogt, W. P. (2005). *Dictionary of statistic and methodology: A nontechnical guide for the social sciences.* Thousand Oaks, CA: SAGE Publications.

Yoder, E. (2012, March 29). *House backs job cuts: Extends federal freeze. The Washington Post.* Retrieved from http://www.washingtonpost.com/blogs/federal-eye/post/house-backs-federal-job-cuts-extended-pay-freeze/2012/03/29/gIQAdndZjS_blog.html

About the Authors

Dr. Julie Ducharme

Dr. Julie Ducharme holds several accredited degrees; a Bachelor of Arts (BA) from San Diego Christian College, Masters of Business administration (MBA) from National University, Doctorate of Business administration from University of Phoenix.

Dr. Julie has been working with corporations, colleges, and universities in San Diego and outside of San Diego as well. Dr. Julie is a public speaker and has spoken with and at many universities across the U.S. and corporations on leadership, business, and marketing. Dr. Julie is also a published author with a children's book, *Amy the Clumsy Angel,* a master thesis published, and her most recent publication her dissertation on *Women in Senior Leadership Positions in Academia.*

She currently is the owner/creator/CEO of JD Consulting LLC, and the owner/creator/CEO of Julie's Party People. Dr. Julie currently is a Methodologist for the DBA Program at Walden University. She regularly consults businesses and schools in various areas of business, public outreach, curriculum, program design, and many other topics in the business realm.

To reach her, please e-mail: juliemducharme@gmail.com

Dr. Sheila Embry

Dr. Sheila Embry holds a Doctor of Management (DM) in Organizational Leadership from University of Phoenix School of Advanced Studies, a Master of Arts (MA) in Human Resources Development from Webster University, and a Baccalaureate (BA) in Business Administration from McKendree College. She is also a graduate of Spencerian College and a three-time graduate of the Federal Law Enforcement Training Center. Dr. Sheila is a Branch Chief with a large federal agency where prior assignments included Branch Chief, Program Manager, Supervisor, and Officer. Previously she served as Local Projects Coordinator for Congressman Romano L. Mazzoli, and worked with the Hilton Hotels Corporation, and The Irvine Company.

Published works include *A Mixed Method Study: Understanding Employee Performance at the Department of Homeland Security; Leadership and Communication: Key Essentials To Employee Performance, Morale, Turnover, and Productivity; Have We Tipped Yet: Are We Ready To Demand Ethical Behavior From Our Leaders; The Three Ps of Leadership: Pulling, Pushing and Patting;* and articles *A Life on (Temporary) Hold: From ABD to DM in 366 days + 3 years;* and *Leadership and Communication; The To Performance.*

To reach her, please e-mail: drsheilaembry@gmail.com

CHAPTER 8

Ethics in Sports:
The Social Responsibility of Elite Athletes

Dr. Dustin J. Pawlak

To help our children make the right choices, they need good examples. Athletics play such an important role in our society, but, unfortunately, some in professional sports are not setting much of an example. The use of performance-enhancing drugs like steroids in baseball, football, and other sports is dangerous, and it sends the wrong message—that there are shortcuts to accomplishment, and that performance is more important than character. (President George W. Bush, State of the Union Address, 2004, para. 58)

Ethical behavior in sports has declined steadily since the early 1990s; for example, there have been performance-enhancing scandals in the past three Olympics Games, professional football, and baseball as well as in college athletics (Brenner, 2009; Diacin, Parks, & Allison, 2003). The barrage of home runs hit by professional baseball players Sammy Sosa and Mark McGuire in the 1998 and 1999 baseball season can be alluded to by some as an example of the ethical decline (Brown, Basil, & Bocarnea, 2003). Since 2000, questions again have been raised about the social responsibility of professional athletes in relation to their ethical actions and integrity. One particular area of interest is concerning the use of performance-enhancing substances such as steroids and human growth hormones (Kelly & Chang, 2007).

Existing literature depicts numerous illustrations in which professional athletes admit social misjudgments and unethical decision making (Weir, 2008). A primary example is American Olympian, Marion Jones, who in 2004 stated, "my response all along is the fact I've never accepted nor taken nor been offered any performance-enhancing drug from anyone" (Crumpacker, 2004, para. 4). Three years later, Jones rescinded her declaration in front of the United States District Court Judge in 2007, when she remarked "I consumed this substance (the clear) several times before the Sydney Olympics and continued using it after" (Associated Press, 2007, para. 28). Other illustrations include American cyclist Floyd Landis, who was stripped of his Tour de France victory for using performance enhancers, National Hockey League defenseman Sean Hill, and baseball player Jason Giambi, who also admitted using performance-enhancing substances to increase his athletic performance (Berry, 2008; Weir, 2008).

Another example is professional baseball player Jose Canseco. Canseco authored a book titled *Juiced,* a chronicle of Canseco's egregious use of illegal performance-enhancing drugs (Canseco, 2005). In *Juiced,* Canseco admitted to using steroids for nearly the entire duration of his professional baseball career. In addition to accounting his daily regimen of illegal steroid use, Canseco named several prominent professional baseball players he claimed also participated in the use of illegal performance-enhancing drugs.

Diacin et al. (2003) found in their study that male collegiate athletes are strongly influenced by others, those influences include the use of performance-enhancing substances. Yusko, Buckman, White, and Pandina (2008) noted one of the most significant issues confronting college leadership is alcohol and drug use, to include performance-enhancing drugs. In a survey of more than 900 Tennessee high school coaches, nearly 90% believed high school student athletes are experimenting with various forms of performance enhancers, such as steroids and sports supplements

(BlueCross BlueShield [BCBS], 2006). A survey of 902 Iowa student athletes showed results indicating 8% of men and 2% of women reported using some form of performance enhancer (Jenkinson & Harbert, 2008). The most common sources of influence are parents, coaches, athletic trainers, friends, teammates, and professional athletes (Behrendt, 2008; Buckman, Yusko, White, & Pandina, 2009; Donohue, Miller, Crammer, Cross, & Covassin, 2007; Hoffmann, 2008).

Leadership, teamwork, fairness, ethics, honesty, and respect are fundamental values to any athletic competition (Goldstein & Iso-Ahola, 2006). Athletic competition has been known to bring out the best and the worst in individuals; in fact, it is commonly said that sports do not build character; they reveal it (Doty & Lumpkin, 2010). The character one builds through the participation in organized athletics is important, as it lays a foundation for future leadership traits and behaviors.

Over the course of the past several years, the use of performance-enhancing substances has been on the rise (BCBS, 2006; Yusko et al., 2008). From a leadership perspective, competitive sports are a character-building activity that leads to the formation of ethics, empathy, and good judgment. The ethical development of the next generation of leaders relies upon the athletes leadership figures: coaches, teachers, parents, and athletic directors. Bolman and Deal (2003) commented on the importance of leaders' abilities to instill a vision in their followers by stating, "A vision needs to address both the challenges of the present and the hopes and values of followers" (p. 362). Similarly, coaches have a social responsibility to infuse a vision in their players who follow the principles of transformational leadership, including keeping the athletes focused on larger communal goals versus solely centering on individual ambitions (Asgari, Silong, Ahmad, & Samah, 2008).

The current social and behavioral patterns of professional athletes are not teaching future leaders valuable leadership traits such as integrity, empathy, and personal values. The next generation of leaders is being led to believe compromising individual ethics and integrity for the sake of personal advancement is appropriate. Leadership is not about self-advancement, but rather the advancement of others.

Conceptual Development

The objective of this study was to explore the principle that professional athletes are at least in part socially responsible as role models to amateur athletes (Giuliano, Turner, Lundquist, & Knight, 2007; Rapp, 2009). The actions and behaviors of professional athletes leave the potential for collegiate athletes to believe it is acceptable to engage in socially destructive behaviors such as steroid and performance-enhancing substance use (Hoffmann, 2008). Ethical theories represent guiding principles based on an attempt to comprehend coherent and systematic fundamental ideologies (Reilly, 2006). This research accentuated the responsibility of leaders, primarily collegiate coaches, to be cognizant of the views and perspectives future leaders have pertaining to professional athletes. Jones (2004), stated that the backbone of a sensible coaching philosophy commences with the coaches' display of ethical behavior.

The study was designed to investigate the ethical views of collegiate athletes, focusing on individuals participating in collegiate sports programs. This study provided an analysis of the decision-making theory in conjunction with the use of performance-enhancing substances by collegiate athletes based on their beliefs and perceptions generated by observing the actions of professional athletes (Nichols, 2006). According to Nichols (2006), student athletes make a cognitive decision when determining their willingness to make a choice.

Historical Overview

Goldstein and Iso-Ahola (2006), noted the premise of *sport* is to instruct and train sportsmanship as well as the ideals of competition, equality, and teamwork. Contrary to those principles, the use of performance-enhancing supplements by amateur and professional athletes has become a growing concern in the United States (Feinberg, 2009; Garzon, Ewald, Rutledge, & Meadows, 2006). In fact, the use of performance enhancers has become so prevalent in competition the World Anti-Doping Agency (WADA) and the United States Anti-Doping Agency (USADA) have increased their list of banned substance to include nearly all viable performance enhancers (Hampton, 2006; Hanstad & Waddington, 2009; Rapp, 2009). WADAs initiatives are virtuous; however, unethical behaviors by individuals in positions of sports leadership are not revolutionary issues as noted by the steroid and performance-enhancing substance scandals dating back to the ancient Olympic Games (Fernandez & Hosey, 2009; Reddy, Beotra, & Ahi, 2009; Staudohar, 2005).

Melzer, Elbe, and Brand (2010) noted there assumption that athletes are in favor of anti-doping policies even though most sporting events are perpetuated by the win at all cost mentality. The win at all cost mindset has made team and individual contests ultra-competitive for several reasons including the will to be successful, the riches to be gained, and the thrill of victory (Melzer et al., 2010). Lack of regulations and a lack of stringent consequence are also culpable (Leone, Gray, Rossi, & Colandreo, 2008; Mahoney, 2009). Hutton (2006) attributed some of this unethical behavior to the "benefit/cost analysis" (p. 171) favoring cheating, meaning the benefit of cheating to win, outweighs the stigma of being caught.

Athletes, from junior high school to the professional level, men and women, decide to use anabolic steroids or the designer, less detectable, performance enhancers (Ford, 2008; Jenkinson & Harbert, 2008; Mayo Clinic Staff, 2008). Even though this action is illegal, the performance enhancers' ability to reduce fatigue, build muscle, and improve performance is too tempting for some athletes to ignore (Mayo Clinic Staff, 2008). Some athletes, according to Denham (2006), simply view the use of performance-enhancing substances as socially acceptable and use as a part of "modern-day competition" (p. 813).

Steroids were first developed in the 1930s as a tissue-builder used medicinally to assist when individuals were diagnosed with an incapacitating illness. Although the development of steroids was originally pioneered for noble causes, steroids were eventually found to stimulate growth in healthy individuals as well. Soon countries across the globe were injecting their athletes with steroids to enhance their performance in Olympic completion and in the World Games (Horn, Gregory, & Guskiewicz, 2009). As the International Olympic Committee (IOC) and the International Amateur Athletic Federation (IAAF) recognized the potential enormity of this behavior during the 1960s and 1970s, the organizations began placing specific substances on a banned list (Diacin et al., 2003). Additionally, public health concerns in relation to the epidemic use of performance enhancers in professional baseball worked its way into the mainstream because of the impact it was having on amateur athletes (Lowenfish, 2009).

Although the initial surge of steroids was primarily concentrated within weight lifting, it was only a short time before the course of natural progression moved to football, track, and baseball. Performance-enhancing substance use moved rapidly from the Olympic and World Games on to professional and collegiate athletics (Diacin et al., 2003). Now, performance enhancers include everything from designer steroids, caffeine, and creatine, to ephedrine and erythropoietin (EPO) (Fernandez & Hosey, 2009; Jenkinson & Harbert, 2008).

Socially Accepted Beliefs and Influences

Improving athletic prowess, a pleasing appearance, weight loss, weight gain, there are numerous underlying principles behind a student athlete's decision to start using performance-enhancing substances (Denham, 2006; Elliot et al., 2006; Ford, 2008; Garzon et al., 2006; Tahtamouni et al., 2008). Unfortunately, students at all levels begin to use these substances without the proper knowledge or preparation (Jenkinson & Harbert, 2008). Early studies in the area of ethical decision making of collegiate athletes generally concluded that teammates, peers, and coaches are the primary role models and sounding boards responsible for the ethical decisions of collegiate athletes (Behrendt, 2008; Diacin et al., 2003; Stewart & Smith, 2008).

The success of student athletes rests greatly in the magnitude of their individual accomplishments and in the results generated by their team's success (Fletcher, Benshoff, & Richburg, 2003). Student athletes, when entering college, assume the responsibility not only to perform well academically but also to take on the added pressures of performing well in their athletic disciplines. Scofield and Unruh (2006) delineated not only the thrills of victory but also the agony of defeat for student athletes and with defeat come the fear of being cut from the team, performing poorly, or being injured. Additionally, in order to be socially accepted by the fans and alumni, the coaches and school officials may place unrealistic expectations on winning and team success as opposed to the well-being of the student athlete (Kim & Parlow, 2009; Lowenfish, 2009).

A study conducted by the NCAA in 2001 indicated that nearly 40% of student athletes used some form of athletic performance enhancer during the previous 12-month period (Buckman et al., 2009; Green, Uryasz, Petr, & Bray, 2001). The study cited the two primary viewpoints were that the performance-enhancing substances would improve their athletic performance or they would improve their physical appearance (Elliot et al., 2006; Garzon et al., 2006). Dodge and Jaccard (2007) defined *behavioral beliefs* as "perceptions of an association between the behavior and some consequence or outcome" (p. 45). The outcome for many student athletes is to increase strength, speed, endurance, energy, performance, weight gain, or appearance (Dodge & Jaccard, 2007; Elliot et al., 2006; Garzon et al., 2006; Hoffmann, 2008; Peters et al., 2003; Tahtamouni et al., 2008). In their belief that performance-enhancing substances improve athletic performance, student athletes are remiss to acknowledge the use of performance-enhancing substances does come with consequences.

Common beliefs among student athletes are that performance-enhancing substances are harmless as long as they are used in moderation (Peters et al., 2003). For example, the following are some of the responses from the research pool of Peters et al.'s (2003) study, "If it helps you win then it's okay;" "Use it to get to the next level;" "I need a boost before the game;" "Because I perform better with it;" and "People are not concerned with what's going on as long as they look good" (p. 128). People are concerned, unfortunately, not always those that should be such as the parents, coaches, athletic trainers, and friends (Behrendt, 2008).

Social Influences

Both male and female student athletes claim their parents as a major influence for their use of performance-enhancing substances, followed closely by advice from their coaches. Parents and coaches are simply the first line of motivation behind an athlete's desire to use performance-enhancing substances. On a larger scale, influence of fame, money, and advancing to the professional ranks is leading this movement (Donohue et al., 2007; Hoffmann, 2008).

From a social standpoint, collegian student athletes are driven to succeed, driven to excel, and driven to win (Behrendt, 2008;

Jolly, 2008). This drive and inspiration originate from many external influences. One of the primary sources of student athlete influence is through the media, the Internet, the news, ESPN, *Sports Illustrated, The Sporting News,* and any other outlet that glorifies (or condemns) the professional athletes involvement with performance-enhancing substances (Primm, Preuhs, Regoli, & Hewitt, 2010).

Athletes as Role Models

The development of a strong sense of self-identity is an integral component of the early adolescent stages of a child's life (Buford May, 2009). Adolescence is also the time to build ones moral and social character and integrity for adult years. A key component to achieving this is through the selection of idols and role models (Denham, 2006). A role model can be someone the athlete comes in contact with directly, or through a variety of circumstances, which potentially can influence the individuals consumption decisions (Bush, Martin, & Bush, 2004; Shuart, 2007).

Professional athletes' skills and abilities seem to transcend from the playing field and incite the belief that the athletes are positive influences simply because of their success in sports. Pulley (2001) referenced a quote from a man who is a father and a Little League Baseball Coach who signified the magnitude of professional athletes as role models. The father noted,

> When I take my kid out and hit him ground balls at shortstop, he wants to be Derek Jeter. He doesn't want to be me. So any professional athlete who tells you he's not a role model is full of baloney. (p. 131)

Performance-Enhancing Substances

The NCAA first banned performance-enhancing substances in 1973 and began to conduct random drug testing of their athletes in

1986 (Diacin et al., 2003). Student athletes have taken several varying stances on the practice of drug testing, ranging from testing being unconstitutional to fully endorsing the practice (Young, 2010). Motives for using performance-enhancing substances also vary; some athletes are interested in steroids for the competitive advantage they provide, whereas others are interested simply because they enhance their physical appearance (Elliot et al., 2006; Jenkinson & Harbert, 2008; Petróczi, 2007; Tahtamouni et al., 2008).

Another common assertion by athletes is that they only participate in the use of steroids and other performance-enhancing substances to help them recover from their sports-related injuries. Young people often buy into the misconception they are invincible, and the negative effects of performance-enhancing substance use is not realized for years, student athletes fall prey to tunnel vision. Winning and succeeding become a mindset and the athlete begins to believe second place is failure (Lowenfish, 2009).

An intense measure of emphasis is placed on the importance of winning from the board of directors, alumni, fans, and student body. These outside influences add to the pressures on the student athlete to perform suitably. Aghazadeh and Kyei (2009) recognized the intrinsic value placed on winning to rationalize why universities behave the way they do.

Ethics

Understanding the definition of ethics in sports is an effortless pathway toward understanding athletes' desires to use performance enhancers. Reilly (2006) held that ethics "are nothing but reverence of life" (p. 163). Part of the reverence includes understanding and maintaining principles, standards, and morals while participating in organized sports. Principles include possessing a selfless attitude toward the game, being motivated to excel, and having awareness in relation to physical and mental limitations and boundaries (Waldron & Kowalski, 2009).

Involvement in organized athletics is an excellent character builder (Goldstein & Iso-Ahola, 2006). Whether athletes participate in team or individual sports, the athletes are provided the opportunity to develop concepts of fair play, teamwork, discipline, focus, and ethics. Lomax (2008) believed, "Americans are drowning in a turbulent ocean of cheating" (p. 15). Waldron and Kowalski (2009) referred to this cognitive process as being absorbed in behaviors of *deviant overconformity*, referring to the athletes' actions that ultimately place them in a position of either physical or psychological danger.

Nichols (2006) noted, "one of the most important human skills is our ability to use judgment and make choices" (p. 40). The ethical background for such decision-making can be derived from upbringing, relatives, peers, friends, and many other settings. The outcome of this growth process, our *will power*, affects our ethical and unethical decision-making in the future.

Leadership

Scharmer (2009) described leaders as artists; they can produce new concepts and convey them to the public. Collegiate athletes are competitive and aspire to do well to make an impression on their peers, friends, and their coaches (Leone et al., 2008). Bach (2006) noted the primary objective of organized sports is for the athlete to undergo a positive, worthwhile experience. This can only occur if the athletes are being taught social responsibility and ethical decision making throughout their sporting experience. Dalla Costa, author of *The Ethical Imperative*, provides a very succinct definition of ethics, "Ethics is others" (Cashman, 2008, p. 85).

In sports, ethics are the impasses that leaders face daily, their social responsibilities, financial decisions, administrative decisions, scheduling decisions, most of which involve other people. Leaders at the collegiate level, the coaches and trainers specifically, are estimated to spend 150 to 200 hours with the athletes during the sports season (Elliot et al., 2006). The coaches' guidance as well as others in positions of authority can impact the social and behavioral decision making of the athletes within their span of control. Hutton (2006) suggested unethical decision making is a product of either the student's character flaws or the inability of persons in leadership positions to impose established standards or codes of conduct. "Ethical schools and ethical leadership require ethical leaders" (Reilly, 2006, p. 163).

Cheating and unethical decision-making are significant problems; therefore, leaders should guide the leaders of tomorrow down paths paved with socially acceptable ideas and practices. Cheating at the collegiate level is a growing phenomenon, one that creates an ethical dilemma for coaches, teachers, and administrators (Elias, 2009; Feinberg, 2009). Several governing bodies and programs are available that attempt to dissuade or at a minimum, regulate the actions and behavior of the athletic participants.

Change Agents

The World Anti-Doping Agency (WADA), United States Anti-Doping Agency (USADA), Athletes Training and Learning to Avoid Steroids (ATLAS), and Athletes Targeting Healthy Exercise and Nutrition Alternatives (ATHENA) are some of the programs taking positive steps toward teaching ethics to our future leaders (Hampton, 2006). WADA introduced new guidelines allowing them to catch cheaters by monitoring irregular shifts in an athlete's normal physiological make up (Coghlan, 2009; Foddy, 2006). Understanding and classifying athletes' drug consumption is vital due to the addictive nature of performance enhancers. The threat has become so significant that Congress classifies anabolic steroids as a schedule III controlled substance (Jenkinson & Harbert, 2008).

Schedule III controlled substances are less addictive than schedule I or II drugs, such as heroin, marijuana, cocaine, and lysergic acid diethylamide (LSD). However; Schedule III drugs are still addictive (DEA, 2010) and can cause premature death (Jenkinson & Harbert, 2008). The Mitchell Report (Mitchell, 2007) listed several specific mental and physical side effects of steroid and performance-enhancing drug use in both men and women including liver damage, menstrual irregularities, and death.

The ATLAS program and ATHENA are two programs designed to allow athletes the opportunity to avoid the pressures of unethical decision-making (Kuehn, 2009). The ATLAS program is directed toward male adolescents and educating them in nutritional and safe training techniques. ATLAS concentrates its energy on actively dissuading the use of steroids and introduces students to healthful options of increasing mass and brawn (Elliot et al., 2006; Socher, 2008). Additionally, the ATLAS programs focal point is to keep these male athletes away from all forms of anabolic steroids and any other performance-enhancing supplement (Elliot et al., 2006). The ATHENA program is geared toward female athletes with studies showing that given healthy alternatives, female athletes will participate in healthier activities and repudiate the use of performance enhancers (Garzon et al., 2006).

Methodology

The qualitative method was an appropriate method for determining value of research and fostering the ability to appreciate the phenomena studied (Creswell, 2005; Grant, 2008). It was appropriate specifically to focus of the interpretation of the perceptions and beliefs of collegiate athletes. Qualitative research is an inquiry-based methodology in which a phenomenon is explored through questioning and depicts and scrutinizes up-and-coming themes (Neuman, 2003).

Moustakas (1994) described the phenomenological methodology as a way to assemble data about the "lived experiences of the people involved, or who were involved, with an issue" (p. 8). Giorgi (2008) stated, in line with phenomenological principles, scientific investigation is valid when the knowledge sought is arrived through communication with multiple individuals, making it possible and allowing better comprehension of the true implication and spirit of the experience. Moustakas additionally stated, "Phenomenology is the first method of knowledge because it begins with things themselves . . . attempts to eliminate everything that represents a prejudgment, setting aside presuppositions, and reaching a transcendental state of freshness and openness" (p. 41).

Research Questions

Research questions narrow the purpose statement into precise questions the research is designed to explore (Creswell, 2005). In qualitative research studies, research questions examine the central phenomenon or concept being explored. Proper research questions, according to Neuman (2003), are exploratory, descriptive, or explanatory.

The purpose of a phenomenological qualitative study is much more open-ended than that of a quantitative study; it allows the best answers to be provided from the participants themselves (Creswell, 2005). Creswell noted the importance of selecting a research problem that benefits the individuals being studied. The research questions selected for the study were the following:

RQ1. What are the perceptions and lived experiences of student athletes regarding the unethical behaviors of some professional athletes?

RQ2. What are the beliefs and lived experiences of student athletes regarding the unethical behaviors of some professional athletes?

The central questions were addressed through the following semi-structured questions during the in-depth interview:

1. What is your perception of professional athletes' ethical decision-making?

2. In relation to the use of performance-enhancing substances, how has the decisions of professional athletes influenced your choices toward the temptation to experiment with those substances?

3. From an ethical standpoint, what are your perceptions of professional athletes in relation to their admissions or denials of performance-enhancing substance use?

4. Understanding that beliefs are your viewpoints and your values, what are your *beliefs* about professional athletes' decisions to use illegal performance-enhancing substances?

5. Understanding that perceptions are your opinion, what are your *perceptions* about professional athletes' decisions to use illegal performance-enhancing substances?

6. As a student athlete, what do you feel constitutes ethical decision-making, in relation to athletic competition?

7. How do you feel the competitive nature of collegiate and professional athletics impacts the ethical decision-making of athletes?

8. How are your behaviors influenced by your perception (opinion) of professional athletes' use of performance-enhancing substances?

9. Does the media attention given to professional athletes who have tested positive or admitted to using performance-enhancing substances sway your opinion of a professional athlete's ethical decision-making either positively or negatively? If yes, then please provide me an example.

10. Do you believe it is ever justified for professional athletes to use illegal performance-enhancing substances? If yes, then please provide me an example.

The expected outcomes of the study included the researcher gaining a deeper understanding of amateur athletes' perceptions and beliefs about professional athlete's decisions to use illegal performance-enhancing substances. The phenomenological strategy was used to identify patterns and themes that developed during the interview process, which assisted in categorizing consistent responses and terms. The research site, the time of observation, and the people and events involved were identified once the interviews took place.

Data Analysis

Moustakas (1994), argued the true emphasis of a phenomenon exists in the perception, and it is regarded as a principal source of knowledge, one that should not be questioned. Neuman (2003) viewed data analysis as the collection of information from observed details of social life. The study incorporated both philosophies while working toward examining the patterns, codes, and themes derived from the participant responses.

Research Questions 1 and 2 were designed to formulate a picture of the student athletes' experiences and opinions on the topic of sports performance-related ethics. To examine Research Questions 1 and 2, 14 participants took part in one-on-one interviews. A total of 28 emergent themes were identified, clustered, and organized into five central themes. The five central themes include: (1) Beliefs, (2) Experiences, (3) Justification, (4) Influences, and (5) Decision-making.

Theme 1: Beliefs

The beliefs theme emerged from data patterns pertaining to the participants' descriptions of their beliefs about the professional athletes who chose to use performance-enhancing substances. The central theme became apparent through participant responses and the materialization of the emergent themes: (16) Athletes are selfish, lazy cheaters and (17) Using should be their choice.

Pressures, at all levels of athletic competition, bring with them the temptation for athletes to enhance their execution with performance-enhancing substances (Jenkinson & Harbert, 2008). The participants in the study acknowledged that use of performance-enhancing substances is clearly cheating; however, in some instances it should be the athlete's choice to use. Participant 1 noted "I think that they're taking advantage of a loophole" that if athletes were "a little less lazy" they would be able to get the same results through legitimate workouts.

Theme 2: Experiences

The experiences theme emerged from data patterns pertaining to the participants' descriptions of their beliefs about collegiate student-athletes lived experiences. The central theme became apparent through participant responses and the materialization of the emergent themes: (5) Professional athletes' actions and decisions don't influence me; (6) Consequences give steroids negative appeal; (7) Never had any desire to use; (8) Athletes should be honest and upfront (9) Honesty encourages forgiveness; (12) I disagree with use; (13) Athletes should be allowed to use; (14) Use natural talent/ not steroids; (18) Work/play hard; (20) Respect yourself and others; and (23) Seeing negative consequences discourages me from using.

Collegiate athletes realize there is a pressure to maintain or sustain a competitive advantage against the athletes they are competing with and against (Rapp, 2009). The pressures affect both male and female athletes. Many participants reported strong feelings regarding their experiences seeing the consequences of those who decided to use performance-enhancing substances. Participant 3 stated, "I mean I don't take performance-enhancing drugs nor would I just based on, one, my moral conduct and my ethics growing up, but also seeing all the consequences of it."

Theme 3: Justification

The justification theme emerged from data patterns pertaining to the participants' assessment of the justification process athletes go through when they decided to use or avert the temptation to use performance-enhancing substances. The central theme became apparent through participant responses and the materialization of the emergent themes: (10) I understand why they lie; (11) Using gives athletes an advantage; (15) Using steroids is unnecessary; (26) Use is never justified; and (27) Use is justified for injury recovery.

Although the development of steroids was originally established for righteous causes, once steroids were found to stimulate growth in healthy individuals, the temptation to experiment became too much to overcome for people in the world of highly-competitive athletics. The concept of using performance-enhancing substances in the healing process was noted but was not predominantly well-received by the study participants. Participant 5 said, "I understand why they do, but it—I don't think it's justified at all. I know that a lot of people are using them to get ahead" and Participant 6 agreed saying those who use "get an extra advantage."

Theme 4: Influences

The influences theme emerged from data patterns pertaining to the participants' assessment of what were the influences affecting the athlete's decision to use performance-enhancing substances. The central theme became apparent through participant responses and the materialization of the emergent themes: (3) Unethical decisions are covered by the media; (21) Obtaining competitive/monetary advantage explains using; (22) Competition drives use; (24) Media makes me think negatively of professional athletes; (25) Media has no effect on my opinion of professional athletes; and (28) Fans want to see the best of the best.

Denham (2006) presented a proposal based on the theory of

mass communication, introduced originally by McCombs and Reynolds in 2002. Denham identified the tendency of the media to guide or entice our thought process toward supporting prevailing social norms, principles, and beliefs. The media accomplishes this not by telling people what to think, but by guiding their thought process toward what to think about. More so than the media outlets, Hutton (2006) believed individuals are motivated by egocentricity and individuals make decisions based on the positive outcomes and avoid rationalizing the negative effects.

Studies have indicated most individuals do not have a predisposed tendency to use performance-enhancing substances; they were influenced by trusted sources (Murray, 2008). The most common sources of influence are parents, coaches, friends, teammates, and professional athletes (Bach, 2006; Buckman et al., 2009; Donohue et al., 2007; Hoffmann, 2008; Leone et al., 2008). Study participants frequently reported the largest source of influence, both positively and negatively, is the media. Half of the study participants commented that the media makes them think negatively of professional athletes. Participant 13 replied that the media portrays the athletes who use steroids in a negative light "I would never wanna, wanna have my life scrutinized like that for—especially for making a bad decision."

Theme 5: Decision-making

The decision-making theme emerged from data patterns pertaining to the participants' perceptions of professional athletes' ethical decision-making process. The central theme became apparent through participant responses and the materialization of the emergent themes: (1) Majority makes ethical decisions; (2) Poor decisions are made because of money; (4) Majority make unethical/poor decisions; and (19) Follow the rules.

Decision-making is a cognitive process. Nichols (2006), argued there is no such thing as good or bad decision makers, "only different decision-making styles" (p. 45). Study participants most frequently considered athletes' decision-making process to be respectable. Ten (71%) participants commented that professional athletes' decisions do not influence their own decision-making process; Participant 11 stated, "it's never affected me at all. I've actually never even thought about doing it. Never had a reason to, really."

Findings

The results of the study revealed that although college students are cognizant of the unethical behaviors and decisions of some professional athletes in relation to performance-enhancing substance use, the athletes' perceptions and beliefs are not influenced. When the research participants responded to the open-ended interview questions concerning how the unethical behaviors of some professional athletes influenced the *perceptions* of student athletes, the results indicated that the professional athletes' decisions have little, if any, impact on the perceptions of college athletes. When the research participants responded to the open-ended interview questions concerning how the unethical behaviors of some professional athletes influenced the *beliefs* of student athletes the results indicated that the professional athletes' decisions have little if any impact on the beliefs of college athletes.

Conclusion

The study was an exploration of the fundamental social responsibility and decision-making process of student athletes. Ethics, ethical behavior, role models, and recreational activities are important issues for individuals in leadership positions. The ethical development of the next generation of leaders relies upon the athlete's leadership figures: coaches, teachers, and parents. Coaches must infuse a vision in their players which follows the principles of social responsibility and ethical leadership, including keeping the athletes focused on larger communal goals versus solely centering on individual ambitions (Asgari et al., 2008).

It is the social responsibly of leaders to teach and instill honesty in their followers. The results of 25 years of research by Kouzes and Posner (2007), noted that *honesty* consistently emerged as the number one leadership characteristic crucial to fostering leader-subordinate relationships. Rao (2006), stated leaders are not necessarily motivated by ego as much as the ideals that foster a healthy working environment. The current social and behavioral patterns of professional athletes are not teaching future leaders valuable leadership traits such as integrity, empathy, and personal values. On the contrary, the next generation of leaders is being led to believe compromising individual ethics and integrity for the sake of personal advancement is appropriate. In my opinion, leadership is not about self-advancement, but rather the advancement of others.

REFERENCES

Aghazadeh, S., & Kyei, K. (2009). A qualitative assessment of factors affecting college sports' team unity. *College Student Journal, 43*(2), 294–302. Retrieved from http://www.projectinnovation.biz/csj.html

Asgari, A., Silong, A., Ahmad, A., & Samah, B. (2008). The relationship between transformational leadership behaviors, organizational justice, leader-member exchange, perceived organizational support, trust in management and organizational citizenship behaviors. *European Journal of Scientific Research, 23*(2), 227–242. Retrieved from http://www.europeanjournalofscientificresearch.com/

Associated Press. (2007, October 5). *Jones pleads guilty, admits lying about steroids.* Retrieved from http://nbcsports.msnbc.com/id/21138883/ns/sports-other_sports/

Bach, G. (2006). The parents association for youth sports: A proactive method of spectator behavior management. *The Journal of Physical Education, Recreation, & Dance, 77*(2), 16–19. Retrieved from http://www.questia.com/PM.qst?a= o&d=5017424445

Behrendt, B. (2008). Strategies to curb risk behaviors in adolescent athletes. *Strength and Conditioning Journal, 30*(3), 17–20. doi:10.1519/SSC.0b013e 3181770c65

Berry, D. (2008, August 7). The science of doping. *Nature,* 692–693. doi: 10.1038/454692a

BlueCross BlueShield. (2006, October 3). *Tennessee coaches believe some high school athletes are using performance-enhancing drugs.* Retrieved from http://www.bcbs.com/news/plans/tennessee-coaches-believe.html

Bolman, L., & Deal, T. (2003). *Reframing organizations: Artistry, choice, and leadership.* San Francisco, CA: Jossey-Bass.

Brenner, S. (2009). Internet law in the courts. *Journal of Internet Law, 13*(4), 18–19. doi:10.1080/10941660903310177

Brown, W., Basil, M., & Bocarnea, M. (2003). The influence of famous athletes on health beliefs and practices: Mark McGwire, child abuse prevention, and androstenedione. *Journal of Health Communications, 8*(1), 41–57. doi:10.1080/ 10810730305733

Buckman, J., Yusko, D., White, H., & Pandina, R. (2009). Risk profile of male college athletes who use performance-enhancing substances. *Journal of Studies on Alcohol & Drugs, 70*(6), 919–923. Retrieved from http://www.jsad.com/

Bush, A., Martin, C., & Bush, V. (2004). Sports celebrity influence on the behavioral intentions of Generation Y. *Journal of Advertising Research, 44*(1), 108–118. Retrieved from http://www.journalofadvertisingresearch.com/

Canseco, J. (2005). *Juiced.* New York, NY: HarperCollins.

Cashman, K. (2008). *Leadership from the inside out: Becoming a leader for life* (2nd ed.). San Francisco, CA: Berrett-Koehler.

Coghlan, A. (2009). Passport to catch sports cheats. *New Scientist Archive, 204*(2738), 10. doi:10.1016/S0262-4079(09)63228-0

Creswell, J. (2005). *Educational research: Planning, conducting, and evaluating quantitative and qualitative research.* Upper Saddle River, NJ: Pearson.

Crumpacker, J. (2004, May 14). Marion Jones isn't running from steroid controversy. *San Francisco Chronicle,* p. D2.

DEA. (2010). *DEA, controlled substance act.* Retrieved from http://www.justice .gov/dea/pubs/csa.html

Denham, B. E. (2006). Effects of mass communication on attitudes toward anabolic steroids: An analysis of high school seniors. *The Journal of Drug Issues, 36*(4), 809–829. Retrieved from http://www.questia.com/PM.qst?a=o&d= 5035151111

Denham, B. E. (2011). Alcohol and marijuana use among American high school seniors: Empirical associations with competitive sports participation. *Sociology of Sport Journal, 28*(3), 362–379. doi:10.1177/002204260603600403

Diacin, M., Parks, J., & Allison, P. (2003). Voices of male athletes on drug use, drug testing and the existing order in intercollegiate athletics. *Journal of Sports Behavior, 26*(1), 1–8. Retrieved from http://www.questia.com/library/jp-journal-of-sport-behavior.jsp

Dodge, T., & Jaccard, J. (2007). Negative beliefs as a moderator of the intention-behavior relationship: Decisions to use performance-enhancing substances. *Journal of Applied Social Psychology, 37*(1), 43–49. doi:10.1111/j.0021–9029 .2007.00145.x

Donohue, B., Miller, A., Crammer, L., Cross, C., & Covassin, T. (2007). A standardized method of assessing sports specific problems in the relationships of athletes with their coaches, teammates, family, and peers. *Journal of Sports Behavior, 30*(4), 375. Retrieved from http://www.questia.com/library/jp-journal-of-sport-behavior.jsp

Doty, J., & Lumpkin, A. (2010). Do sports build or reveal character?—An exploratory study at one service academy. *Physical Educator, 67*(1), 18–32. doi:10.2202/1940–1639.1009

Elias, R. (2009). The impact of anti-intellectualism attitudes and academic self-efficacy on business students' perceptions of cheating. *Journal of Business Ethics, 86*(2), 199–209. doi:10.1007/s10551–008–9843–8

Elliot, D., Moe, E., Goldberg, L., DeFrancesco, C., Durham, M., & Hix-Small, H. (2006). Definition and outcome of a curriculum to prevent disorder eating and body-shaping drug use. *Journal of School Health, 76*(2), 67–77. doi: 10.1111/j.1746–1561.2006.00070.x

Feinberg, J. (2009). College students' perceptions of athletes who cheat: The role of performance and history. *Journal of Sport Behavior, 32*(4), 460–475. Retrieved from http://www.questia.com/library/jp-journal-of-sport-behavior.jsp

Fernandez, M., & Hosey, R. (2009). Performance-enhancing drugs snare nonathletes, too. *The Journal of Family Practice, 58*(1), 16–23. Retrieved from http://www.jfponline.com/

Fletcher, T., Benshoff, J., & Richburg, M. (2003). A systems approach to understanding and counseling college students-athletes. *Journal of College Counseling, 6*(1), 35. doi:10.1002/j.2161–1882.2003.tb00225.x

Foddy, B. (2006). The ethics of genetic testing in sport. *International SportMed Journal, 7*(3), 216–224. Retrieved from http://www.ismj.com/

Ford, J. (2008). Nonmedical prescription drug use among college students: A comparison between athletes and nonathletes. *Journal of American College Health, 57*(2), 211–219. doi:10.3200/JACH.57.2.211-220

Garzon, L., Ewald, R., Rutledge, C., & Meadows, T. (2006). The school nurse's role in prevention of student use of performance-enhancing supplements. *Journal of School Health, 76*(5), 159. doi:10.1111/j.1746-1561.2006.00088.x

Giorgi, A. (2008). Concerning a serious misunderstanding of the essence of the phenomenological method in psychology. *Journal of Phenomenological Psychology, 39*(1), 33–49. doi:10.1163/156916208X311610

Giuliano, T., Turner, K., Lundquist, J., & Knight, J. (2007). Gender and the selection of public athletic role models. *Journal of Sport Behavior, 30*(2), 161–198. Retrieved from http://www.questia.com/PM.qst?a=o&d=5021238898

Goldstein, J., & Iso-Ahola, S. (2006). Promoting sportsmanship in youth sports; perspectives from sports psychology; sports psychology provides crucial insight for improving behavior in sports. *The Journal of Physical Education, Recreation & Dance, 77*(7), 18. Retrieved from http://www.questia.com/PM.qst?a=o&d=5017425041

Grant, R. (2008). A phenomenological case study of a lecturer's understanding of himself as an assessor. *The Indo-Pacific Journal of Phenomenology, 8*(1), 1–9. Retrieved from http://www.ipjp.org/

Green, G., Uryasz, F., Petr, T., & Bray, C. (2001). NCAA study of substance and abuse habits of college student-athletes. *Clinical Journal of Sports Medicine, 11*(1), 51–56. doi:10.1097/00042752-200101000-00009

Hampton, T. (2006). Researchers address use of performance-enhancing drugs in nonelite athletes. *JAMA: Journal of the American Medical Association, 295*(6), 607–608. doi:10.1001/jama.295.6.607

Hanstad, D., & Waddington, I. (2009). Sport, health and drugs: A critical re-examination of some key issues and problems. *Perspectives in Public Health, 129*(4), 174–182. doi:10.1177/1466424008094806

Hoffmann, R. (2008). For a few atoms more. *American Scientist, 96*(2), 104–106. doi:10.1511/2008.70.3630

Horn, S., Gregory, P., & Guskiewicz, K. (2009). Self-reported anabolic-androgenic steroids use and musculoskeletal injuries. *American Journal of Physical Medicine & Rehabilitation, 88*, 192–200. doi:10.1097/PHM.0b013e318198b622

Hutton, P. (2006). Understanding student cheating and what educators can do about it. *College Teaching, 54*(1), 171–172. doi:10.3200/CTCH.54.1.171-176

Jenkinson, D., & Harbert, A. (2008). Supplements and sports. *American Family Physician, 78*(9), 1040–1046. Retrieved from http://www.aafp.org/online/en/home/publications/journals/afp.html

Jolly, J. (2008). Raising the question # 9 is the student-athlete population unique? And why should we care?. *Communication Education, 57,* 145–151. doi:10 .1080/03634520701613676

Jones, D. (2004). Domain 1: Philosophy and ethics national standards for sport coaches. *Strategies, 17*(4), 23–24. Retrieved from http://search.proquest.com .ezproxy.apollolibrary.com/docview/214561679?accountid=35812

Kelly, P., & Chang, P. (2007). A typology of university ethical lapses: Types, levels of seriousness, and originating locations. *Journal of Higher Education, 78*(4), 402. doi:10.1353/jhe.2007.0024

Kim, J. Y., & Parlow, M. (2009). Off-court misbehavior: Sports leagues and private punishment. *The Journal of Criminal Law & Criminology, 99*(3), 573–597. Retrieved from http://www.law.northwestern.edu/jclc/

Kouzes, J., & Posner, B. (2007). *The leadership challenge* (4th ed.). San Francisco, CA: Jossey-Bass.

Kuehn, B. (2009). Teen steroid, supplement use targeted. *JAMA: Journal of the American Medical Association, 302*(21), 2301–2303. doi:10.1001/jama.2009 .1711

Leone, J., Gray, K., Rossi, J., & Colandreo, R. (2008). Using the transtheoretical model to explain androgenic-anabolic steroid use in adolescents and young adults: Part one. *Strength and Condition Journal, 30*(6), 47–54. doi:10.1519/ SSC.0b013e31818e3124

Lomax, S. (2008). Whatever happened to America's ethical values?. *Business & Economic Review, 55*(1), 15–18. Retrieved from http://www.moore.sc.edu/fac-ultyandresearch/researchcenters/divisionofresearch/businesseconomicreview.aspx

Lowenfish, L. (2009). Whatever happened to the marvelous importance of the unimportant? A plea for putting today's baseball and all-sports mania in proper perspective. *Nine, 17,* 1–12. doi:10.1353/nin.0.0043

Mahoney, K. (2009). Learning from the mistakes of others: Changing major league baseball's substance abuse arbitration procedure. *Ohio State Journal on Dispute Resolution, 24*(3), 613–640. Retrieved from http://moritzlaw.osu.edu/ students/groups/osjdr/

Mayo Clinic Staff. (2008). *Performance-enhancing drugs: Are they a risk to your health.* Rochester, MN. Retrieved from http://www.mayoclinic.com/print/perfor-mance-enhancing-drugs/HQ01105/METHOD=print

Melzer, M., Elbe, A., & Brand, R. (2010). Moral and ethical decision-making: A chance for doping prevention in sports?. *Nordic Journal of Applied Ethics / Etikk i praksis, 4*(1), 69–85. Retrieved from http://www.tapirforlag.no/node/1563

Mitchell, G. (2007). *Report to the commissioner of baseball of an independent investigation into the illegal use of steroids and other performance enhancing sub-*

stances by players in major league baseball. Retrieved from http://files
.mlb.com/mitchrpt.pdf

Moustakas, C. (1994). *Phenomenological research methods.* Thousand Oaks,
CA: Sage.

Murray, T. (2008). Doping in sport: Challenges for medicine, science and ethics.
Journal of Internal Medicine, 264, 95–98. doi:10.1111/j.1365-2796.2008
.01994.x

Neuman, W. (2003). *Social research methods: Qualitative and quantitative
approaches* (5th ed.). Boston, MA: Pearson.

Nichols, J. (2006). Balancing intuition and reason: Turning in to indecision. *The
Journal of Rehabilitation, 72*(4), 40–52. Retrieved from http://www.rehab
.research.va.gov/jour/jourindx.html

Peters, R., Adams, L., Barnes, J., Hines, L., Jones, D., Krebs, K., & Kelder, S.
(2004). Beliefs and social norms about ephedra onset and perceived addiction
among college male and female athletes. *Journal of Drug Education, 33*(4), 415.
doi:10.2190/NXJ6-U60J-XTY0–09MP

Petróczi, A. (2007). Attitudes and doping: A structural equation analysis of the
relationship between athletes' attitudes, sport orientation and doping behaviour.
Substance Abuse Treatment, Prevention & Policy, 2, 34–48. doi:10.1186/
1747–597X-2–34

Primm, E., Preuhs, R., Regoli, R., & Hewitt, J. (2010). The more things change
the more they stay the same: Race on the cover of Sports Illustrated. *National
Social Science Journal, 35*(1), 118–127. Retrieved from http://www.nssa.us/jour-
nals.htm

Pulley, B. (2001, March 19). *Top of the lineup—Derek Jeter is must-see TV.*
Retrieved from http://www.forbes.com/forbes/2001/0319/130.html

Rao, S. (2006). Tomorrow's leaders. In F. Hesselbein & M. Goldsmith (Eds.), *The
leader of the future 2: Visions, strategies, and practices for the new era* (pp.
173–182). San Francisco, CA: Jossey-Bass.

Rapp, G. (2009). Blue sky steroids. *Journal of Criminal Law and Criminology,
99*(3), 599. Retrieved from http://www.law.northwestern.edu/jclc/

Reddy, I., Beotra, A., & Ahi, S. (2009). A simple and rapid ESI-LC-MS/MS
method for simultaneous screening of doping agents in urine samples. *Indian
Journal of Pharmacology, 41*(2), 80–86. doi:10.4103/0253–7613.51347

Reilly, E. (2006). The future entering: Reflections on and challenges to ethical
leadership. *Educational Leadership and Administration, 18,* 163–167.

Scharmer, C. O. (2009). *Theory U: Leading from the future as it emerges.* San
Francisco, CA: Berrett-Koehler.

Scofield, D., & Unruh, S. (2006). Dietary supplement use among adolescent athletes in Central Nebraska and their sources of information. *Journal of Strength & Conditioning Research (Allen Press Publishing Services), 20*(2), 452–455. doi:10.1519/00124278-200605000–00037

Shuart, J. (2007). Heroes in sport: Assessing celebrity endorser effectiveness. *International Journal of Sports Marketing & Sponsorship, 8*(2), 126–140. Retrieved from http://www.imrpublications.com/journal-landing.aspx?volno=L&no=L

Socher, A. (2008). No game for old men. *Current,* (501), 17–19.

State of the Union Address. (2004). *Briefing room.* Washington, DC. Retrieved from http://www.whitehouse.gov/news/releases/2004/01/20040120–7.html

Staudohar, P. (2005). Performance-enhancing drugs in baseball. *Labor Law Journal, 56*(2), 139. Retrieved from http://hr.cch.com/products/ProductID-632.asp

Stewart, B., & Smith, A. (2008). Drug use in sport: Implications for public policy. *Journal of Sport & Social Issues, 32*(3), 278–298. doi:10.1177/0193723508319716

Tahtamouni, L., Mustafa, N., Alfaouri, A., Hassan, I., Abdalla, M., & Yasin, S. (2008). Prevalence and risk factors for anabolic-androgenic steroid abuse among Jordanian collegiate students and athletes. *European Journal of Public Health, 18,* 661–665. doi:10.1093/eurpub/ckn062

Waldron, J., & Kowalski, C. (2009). Crossing the line: Rites of passage, team aspects, and ambiguity of hazing. *Research Quarterly for Exercise and Sport, 80*(2), 291–302. doi:10.5641/027013609X13087704028633

Weir, K. (2008). Big dopes: Athletes who take performance-enhancing drugs risk their reputations and their health. *Current Science, 93*(9), 6. Retrieved from http://cs-test.ias.ac.in/cs/php/cissue.php

Young, S. (2010). PIAC (pee in a cup)—The new standardized test for student-athletes. *Brigham Young University Education & Law Journal,* (1), 163–190. Retrieved from http://elj.byu.edu/

Yusko, D., Buckman, J., White, H., & Pandina, R. (2008). Alcohol, tobacco, illicit drugs, and performance enhancers: A comparison of use by college student athletes and nonathletes. *Journal of American College Health, 57*(3), 281–290. doi:10.3200/JACH.57.3.281–290

About the Author

Michigan author Dr. Dustin J. Pawlak holds several accredited degrees; a Bachelor of Science (BS) in Occupational Education from Wayland Baptist University; a Master of Arts (MA) in Human Resources Development from Webster University; a Master of Arts (MA) in Management also from Webster University; and a Doctorate of Management (DM) in Organizational Leadership from the University of Phoenix School of Advanced Studies.

Dr. Dustin has over 20 years of civilian and military experience working in leadership, administration, military and international protocol, and educational instruction. He is currently employed by the Department of Defense as the Director of Human Resources at an Air Force Installation in North Carolina. Additionally, Dr. Dustin serves as a commissioned officer in the United States Air Force Reserve.

Dr. Dustin has numerous military and civilian awards including 10 service medals for outstanding military achievement and two Senior Civilian of the Year awards.

He is an active member of the Military Officers Association of America and the Air Force Sergeants Association.

Additional works include his dissertation: *A phenomenological study: The influence of professional athletes' unethical behavior on amateur athletes.*

To reach Dr. Dustin Pawlak, please e-mail: drdjpawlak@gmail.com

CHAPTER 9

Stakeholders, Redesign the Theory to Reposition the Reality

Dr. Magdy Hussein
& Dr. Gamal M. Elmarsafi

The term responsibility is troubling business owners, executives, and board members of what, and how they meet their responsibility. However, the most imperative question in this subject matter is to whom corporations are socially responsible? Theorists have added more confusion to the stakeholder theory by adding many segments to the stakeholders whom they are already well protected by laws, regulations, and open market balancing rules. Greenwood (2007) has been noted that employees are the most crucial group in the list of stakeholders and thus they must hold the biggest power in term of stakeholders' engagement. In this study, an alternative model of the theory suggests one simple equation to live by and that is stakeholder solely means employees and shareholders mean business owners. The workforce in the U.S. has suffered unprotected employment conditions and the consequences of the short-term strategies of downsizing and outsourcing. Making only good numbers in Wall Street has cost many families their jobs, homes, health insurance, and in some cases their lives.

The at-will employment doctrine defines an employment relationship between employer and employee in which either party can break the relationship with no liability ("At Will Employment," 2012). This simple format was affected by theorists to include new influential forces, which share employees in their unique and direct position with business shareholders. Social responsibility toward employees has become much more complicated with the unclear and continuous change of stakeholder definitions.

Freeman (1988) led many theorists defining the stakeholder concept as the right of stakeholders to make claim on the firm. Other theorists line up solidly behind Freeman's stakeholder perspective (Jensen, 2001; Pigé, 2002), but never fixed the gab in the theory. The theory included every single entity that has anything to do with a company from the input-output model. That means investors and suppliers have joined employees in the input, while customers present the output in this format. One wonders what the difference between stockholders and investors is except in the number of owned stocks and sequentially the voting power. Other than these two differences, they both own the business from two different positions. Apparently, Freeman neglected to identify the nature of the stakeholders' claim.

In his article *Jobs, Downsizing and Stakeholders,* David Nitkin (1996), CEO of EthicScan Canada asks whether profits paid to shareholders by large corporations are "generated at the expense of other stakeholders: namely unemployed and dislocated, discouraged but willing, workers?" (p. 11). He argued the bottom line in this debate should not be profits but the "survival of families, communities, the country, and the planet" (p. 11). Nitkin opposes the absolute power of shareholders that may hurt stakeholders' well-being, as do other corporate executives. However, a decade has passed since Nitkin's published article, and the present economy is compelled to ask whether we are any closer to realizing the tenets of stakeholder theory.

On the contrary, Friedman (1970) was so clear positing that the only responsibility of business is to increase shareholder profits. Beauchamp and Bowie (2004) aligned their thoughts with Friedman stating "nearly all business ethicists concur with the general public that one of the purposes of a publicly held firm is to make a profit and thus making a profit is an obligation of the firm" (p. 47).

The Theory

In the last decades of the 20th century, the word stakeholder evolved from the science of sociology into the field of business management. The concept of the shareholder and profit maximization has been challenged by the concept of stakeholders where shareholders represent one participant among many others. However, stakeholder theory is controversial theory due to its broad definition of stakeholders. According to Pige' (2002) "One main difficulty of the stakeholder theory is that there is not a unified concept of stakeholders" (p. 1).

Generally, Freeman (2010) has defined stakeholder as any individual or group who can affect, or is affected by, the achievement of a corporation's purpose, including employees, customers, suppliers, stockholders, banks, environmentalists, and government. According to stakeholder theory, a company's responsibilities are to *all* of its stakeholders. This means that a business has to fulfill the needs and wants of many different people, ranging from the local population and customers, to their own employees. The assumption was that many firms would switch to the stakeholder concept because it improves the image of the firms and special interest groups are less likely to target them. Theoretically, to ensure that a company's practices are not detrimental or damaging to any of its stakeholders, all of a company's stakeholders should be taken into consideration when corporate policy is created and decisions are made.

The significance of applying stakeholder theory in managing a company is the involvement of many participants in the policy-making process that may be in conflict with shareholder interests. This raises multiple questions about the actual degree of involvement and the level of engagement by stakeholders in influencing the corporate direction. If such an argument is applicable, one asks what types of mechanisms need to be present to represent all stakeholder perspectives?

Until quite recently, theorists had not answered that question. Jensen (2001) pinpointed the problem in stakeholder theory that the advocates of this theory failed to specify how to make the necessary tradeoffs among these competing interests. As is, the theory leaves managers stranded with an impractical theory that makes it impossible for them to make proper decisions.

Unless stakeholder theory focuses on employees as one single participant that has a direct effect on a company's performance and has the greatest impact on quality, stakeholders theory will be difficult to provide the proper frame work. It is also important to realize that employees have the greatest interest of the organization's social responsibility. Stakeholder theory might be widened to encompass the fact that unless quality is internalized at the personal level, it will never become rooted in the culture of an organization. Thus, quality must begin at employees level specially today, as one is witnessing organizations asking employees to take more responsibility for acting as the point of contact between the organization and the customer.

Other stakeholder groups have their own influential position to increase their profits, protect their assets, or defend their interest through the nature of commercial relationship, laws, regulations and effective media propaganda. Customers, for instance, have the purchase power to influence corporate behavior, or through the legal approach by consumer protection agencies in case of any misleading or business misconduct. Suppliers, as business subsidiaries, have the choice from the beginning to do business under profitable agreeable terms. The open market advanced the role of the suppliers and placed them in a good negotiating position. Other stakeholders, such as environmentalists, the government, and financial institutions, play a fair game with the corporation through many platforms.

In an effort to redefine companies' obligation toward their stakeholders, Freeman and Reed (1983) modified the theory to classify stakeholders into vital and non-vital stakeholders. The modified theory recognizes employees as a vital group, among stakeholder groups, because of their important role in an organization's success and the finest layer possible of protection against layoffs, downsizing, and outsourcing. Narrowing the definition of stakeholders helped in prioritizing which stakeholders deserve corporate attention and helps to clarify how a corporation can be held accountable and socially responsible without conflict with shareholders' interests. By considering employees and managers as the premier stakeholders, the theory is more applicable and acceptable for larger number of beneficiaries when including employees' families. However, the ongoing downsizing and outsourcing give an indication that the theory is unsuccessful to sway corporations from making strategic decisions without involving all groups of stakeholders. It is evident that the current stakeholder theory failed to live up to its promise.

The Reality

Interestingly, while the compromised stakeholder theory furnishes a common ground where stockholders and employees can meet halfway, a significant gap between employers and employees' views continues to widen in regards to employment conditions. Issues such as salaries and benefits commonly occupy employees' concerns at the time of hiring. Nowadays, these issues are subject to negotiation at anytime due to corporate strategies of downsizing. Similarly, the new trend of outsourcing raises a red flag that may indicate a tie between the outsourcing strategy and the jump in CEOs' salaries, another type of stakeholders.

Seager and Finch (2009) commented on the Guardian's report that a high pay commission would investigate how huge executive rewards affect economic stability and long-term corporate performance, and would consider the social effects of gross inequality. The report questioned if the CEOs, who outsource thousands of service jobs to countries like India, have been rewarded with higher pay. The report suggested that top executives at the 50 largest outsourcers of service jobs made an average of 10 million in 2003, 46% more than they as a group received the previous year and 28% more than the average large-company CEO. These 50 CEOs seem to be benefiting personally from a trend that has already cost hundreds of thousands of U.S. jobs and is projected to cost millions more over the next decade.

It is fair to recognize that the rise in top U.S. executives' salaries matches raises in other countries but not with the same scale to make a global phenomenon. In England, Finch (2004) suggested that top directors' pay leapt 16% on 2003, further widening the gap between the boardroom and employees. In China, the Development Research Center (DRC) reported that executives in Chinese enterprises have received increasing pay in 2004 enlarging the gap with ordinary employees after an economic reform underwent for some 20 years in China. In 1,061 Chinese enterprises, or 61.2% of the total surveyed, general managers were paid three to 15 times higher than employees were, according to the report. While many see the ratio of 15 to 1 in China or 30 to 1 in Europe, of CEO and employee's salary is alarming, many do not feel the drastic ration 300 to 1 in U.S. means anything.

On the side of healthcare coverage, corporations keep shifting more of the burden of managing and funding employee benefits to their employees. This trend is noteworthy given that workers' satisfaction with their benefits can greatly affect their attitudes toward their employer. The imbalance of corporate power, as the stakeholders theory suggested, is the reason that gives board of directors the solo right to make strategic decisions that hurt many employees along with their families.

In reality, there is one solution to the break the absolute control of executives over corporate behavior. This solution suggests that shareholders restrict the conditions of increasing top executives' salaries as well as approving strategic decisions such as downsizing and outsourcing. The solution will stay hypothetical since CEOs and top executive represent the most powerful stockholders in the board of directors.

In Case of the Public Sector

Applying stakeholders' theory in the public sector may take an unusual turn and sets importance of stakeholders in different order. For example, in the private sector, the model of b2c (business-to-consumer) is never the same like g2c (government-to-consumer). In case of the g2c scenarios consumer is not equivalent to citizen Scholl (2001). In addition, one has to differentiate between the purposes of the two sectors to better understand how the stakeholders' theory is applicable. In the public sector, the organization was designed to serve the interest of the public not to increase the wealth of the shareholders as Friedman (2001) has stated. Theoretically speaking, the public sector's shareholders are, in this case, the public themselves. Since citizens have no direct governing role in the public sector, managers, and executives still in charge of the organization and present the shareholders' interest.

Donaldson and Preston (1995) stressed the fact that the stakeholders' theory is broad enough to apply its principles of governing on both sectors, and this is exactly what this paper is arguing. Employees of public sector have somewhat different protections by law than do employees of private sector organizations this becomes the baseline. For example, because the constitution in the U.S. gives rights of protection against invasion of privacy to citizens in general, those rights apply to employees of government. In government, there has to be a clear reason for such information to be shared other than between the employee and his/her supervisor, whereas in the private sector, such information was quite openly shared.

Diversity also was more strongly enforced on the government side; there is low tolerance of any sort of discrimination. On the other side an employee of public sector faces, different set of challenges tend to be inadequate. Fairness and consistency in application of policies such as hiring, raises, promotions, and leave are all management solo perception; there is guideline of policy execution. Deficiency of quality and quantity training to public sector employees lead to vague career path development. Some public organizations go beyond the bureaucratic culture and have a desire to be the employer of choice. They want to move beyond compliance to transformation. They attract and retain top employees because the culture is affirming. They treat employees as stakeholders, on par with customers.

Corporate Governance and Social Responsibility

A comprehensive look to the stakeholders' theory answers the question of why the theory is crippled and un-applicable. The theory is situated within the social responsibilities concept that comprises components of economic, legal, political, ethical, and societal issues involving the interaction of business, government, and society. Stakeholder theory addresses three areas of organizational governance including structure, management style, and the decision-making process. The confounding gap between governing an organization and fulfilling its social responsibilities creates an untenable situation.

On the shareholders' side, Jensen (2001) argued that a corporate vision, strategy, and tactical plan that unite participants in the organization's struggle for competitive dominance must complement the choice of value maximization as the corporate scorecard. Jensen's view displays the traditional and common theory of shareholders that focuses on one purpose of the organization of maximizing the wealth of shareholders. Furthermore, Sundaram and Inkpen (2004) exhibited a commitment to shareholder ideology concluding that the goal of maximizing shareholder value is the only appropriate goal for managers in the modern corporation. In a clear statement, the two authors of disclosed the principal controversy with their opponents is governing the corporation, its goals and the expected consequences.

Further under girding shareholder theory is agency theory, which according to Jensen (2004), is simply a mathematical way to model the relationship between two parties (the principal and the agent), one of whom wants to hire the other to act on behalf of the first. The attraction of agency theory is that it provides convenient means to account for the fact that agents might have goals and incentives that are different from those of the principals. Hence, agency theory is really contract theory, legalistically. Contract theory is a general approach to modeling business relationships. Conveniently, agency theory provides a way for theorists to argue whether a corporation should be understood as a special creation of the state with duties to operate for the public good. The theory should be understood as a contractual mechanism through which an aggregation of shareholders puddle their resources to undertake a business venture, presumably for their own benefit rather than the benefit of the larger society.

On the side of stakeholders, theorists have reexamined many of their views of corporate social responsibilities to consider, to some degree, the main purpose of establishing a corporation. In an attempt to revise their stakeholder position, Freeman, Wicks, and Parmar (2004) conceded that shareholders are important constituent and the corporate purpose of achieving profits should become the result rather than the driver in the process of value creation.

Whether the organization governors are the shareholders, stakeholders, or both, the question remains of how to accommodate corporation's purpose of increasing the wealth of shareholders without defeating the social commitment to stakeholders. Recently, legal theorists proposed a new theoretical approach that may serve as a plausible, tenable, foundation for stakeholder theory.

A New Foundation

Asher, Mahoney, and Mahoney (2005) proposed that the economic theory of property rights could be used to develop strategic management purposes that recognize the importance of stakeholders, as well as stockholders, in value creation and distribution. They further proposed that property rights theory is consistent with resource-based theories, which have been the basis of strategic management theory for several decades. This framework provides solutions for both the issue of wealth creation and of wealth distribution. In their model, Asher and colleagues define property rights broadly as being the sanctioned relationships among decision makers in the use of resources. Included in this arrangement are the social conventions with which parties act as well as the premise for legally enforceable claims. In other words, property and resources would be viewed as bundles of rights rather than as physical entities.

A property rights "theory of the firm" (i.e. who holds what rights, in what circumstances, and who is liable) serves to close the gap in theories of the firm that has previously preempted non-shareholder stakeholders from participation. Ostensibly, for management theorists the next issue to decide is the approach for determining allocation of rights over assets. Specifically, theorists must now develop structural relationships within and across the firm that enable creation, capture, and distribution of mutually owned wealth. Pige' (2002) suggested that an organization structure must meet the interest of stakeholders without disregarding the purpose of the corporation. Accordingly, Pige' recommended the separation between the executive body represented by the CEO and the shareholders' body represented by the board Chair in an attempt to limit executives' influence on the board of directors. Separating the two identities will create an opportunity for stakeholders to present the corporate information in a way that affects the board's decisions. Many American corporations separated the two positions in a step to provide greater accountability of management to the shareholders, and provide independent oversight of management, including the CEO, by the Board of Directors.

In Germany, corporate law applies a two-tier board structure that consists of the management board and the supervisory board. The management board is in charge of managing the company while the supervisory board is the guardian of shareholders' interest, similar to the board of directors in the U.S. The important difference between the American board of directors and the German supervisory board structure is that the German board consists of between twenty to 50% of workers' elected representatives. Such structure maintains the interest of shareholders without disturbing the well-being of the workers. Tüngler (2000) made a comparison between the American board of directors and the German supervisory board in an effort to emphasize that the stakeholder theory is applicable if the company's law changes.

In conclusion, it is clear that economic ideology of various times plays a significant part in shaping corporate law, and affects shareholders/stakeholders relationship. It is reasonable to rethink the old paradigm of corporate governance that omits or undermines the well-being of employees as the most critical stakeholder. Business leaders must base strategic and tactical decisions on the common interest of both shareholders and stakeholders. Otherwise, continuing to make outdated and unjust decisions will continue to harm the legitimate rights of decent work conditions and fair financial recognition of hardworking people.

REFERENCES

Anderson, S., Cavanagh, J., Hartman, C., & Klinger, S. (2004, August 31), Executive Excess 2004, Campaign contributions, outsourcing, unexpensed stock options and rising CEO pay. *Institute for Policy Studies.* Retrieved from http://www.ips-dc.org/reports/executive_excess_2004

Asher, C. C., Mahoney. J. M., & Mahoney, J. T. (2005).Towards a property rights foundation for a stakeholder theory of the firm, *Journal of Management and Governance.* Retrieved from: http://www.business.illinois.edu/working_papers/papers/04–0116.pdf

At-will employment. (2012). Retrieved from http://en.wikipedia.org/wiki/At-will_employment

Beauchamp, T., & Bowie, N. (2004). *Ethical theory and business.* Upper Saddle River, NJ. Prentice-Hall. Retrieved from: http://digilib.bc.edu/reserves/mh300/selt/mh30010.pdf

Charreaux, G. (1997). Vers une théorie du gouvernement des enterprises. In G. Charreaux (Ed.), *Le gouvernement des enterprises. Corporate governance, théories et faits, Économica* (pp. 421–469).

Donaldson, T., & Preston, L. E. (1995). The stakeholder theory of the corporation: Concepts, evidence, and implications. *Academy of Management Review, 20*(1), 63–91. Retrieved from http://zonecours.hec.ca/documents/A2010–1-2410481.stakeholdertheoryofthecorporation,concepts,....pdf

Evan, W., & Freeman, E. (1993). A stakeholders theory of the modern corporation: Kantian capitalism. In Beauchamp, T. L. & N. E. Bowie (Ed.), *Ethical theory and business* (pp. 97–106). Englewood Cliffs, NJ: Prentice-Hall.

Freeman, E. (2010). *Strategic management: A stakeholder approach.* Cambridge, UK: Cambridge University Press.

Freeman, E., & Reed, D. (1983). *Stockholders and stakeholders: A new perspective on corporate governance.* In C. Huizinga, Ed., *Corporate Governance: A definitive Exploration of the Issues.* Los Angeles, CA: UCLA Extension Press.

Freeman, E., Wicks, A., & Parmar, B. (2004). Stakeholder theory and the corporate objective revisited. *Organization Science 15*(3), 364–369. Retrieved from http://orgsci.journal.informs.org/content/15/3/364.abstract

Friedman, M. (1970, September 13). *The social responsibility of business is to increase its profits.* New York, NY: *Times Magazine.* Retrieved from http://www-rohan.sdsu.edu/faculty/dunnweb/rprnts.friedman.dunn.pdf

Greenwood, M. (2007). Stakeholder engagement: beyond the myth of corporate responsibility. *Journal of Business Ethics, 74,* 315–327. Retrieved from http://www.jstor.org/discover/10.2307/25075473?uid=2129&uid=2&uid=70& uid=4&sid=56231785273

Jensen, C. (2001). *Value maximization, stakeholder theory, and the corporate objective function.* European Financial Management, 7(3), 297–317, Retrieved from: http://www.efmaefm.org/Bharat/Jensen_EFM2001.pdf

Nitkin, D. (1996). Jobs, downsizing, and stakeholders. *Ethics in Economics* 2(3), 11. Retrieved from http://www.economicsandethics.org/

Pigé, B. (2002). *Stakeholder theory and corporate governance: the nature of the board information.* Journal of Contemporary Management, 7, 1–17. Retrieved from http://www.efst.hr/management/Vol7No1–2002/1-pige.doc

Scholl, H. (2001), *Applying stakeholder theory to e-government: benefits and limits.* University at Albany/State University of New York, Center for Technology in Government. Retrieved from http://www.ischool.washington.edu

Seager, A., & Finch, J. (2009, September 15). Salary gap widens between workers and their directors. *The Guardian,* 20. Retrieved from: http://www.guardian.co.uk/business/2009/sep/16/guardian-executive-pay-survey-ratios

Sundaram, A., & Inkpen, A. (2004, September 21). The corporate objective revisited. *Organization Science, 15*(3), 350–363. Retrieved from http://www.jstor.org/discover/10.2307/30034738?uid=2129&uid=2&uid=70&uid=4&sid=55946874563

Tüngler, G. (2000). The Anglo-American board of directors and the German supervisory board: marionettes in a puppet theatre of corporate governance or efficient controlling devices? *Bond Law Review,* 12, 230. Retrieved from: http://epublications.bond.edu.au/blr/

About the Authors

Dr. Magdy M. Hussein

A Silicon Valley resident; Dr. Magdy M. Hussein earned his Bachelor of Science in Electrical Engineering (B.S.E.E.) from Helwan University in Cairo-Egypt, a Master of Business Administration (MBA) in Global Management from University of Phoenix, and a Doctorate of Philosophy (PhD) in Organization and Management from Capella University.

Dr. Hussein joined Northwestern Polytechnic University School of Business as a Professor of Management and serving as a doctoral program advisor.

Dr. Hussein's primary research areas of interest include Business Ethics and Corporate Social Responsibility. He believes that ethics is strategic and critical from the absolute core business perspective. Without ethics, the end will always be similar to Enron.

Prior to teaching in higher education, Dr. Hussein worked in the industry for 25 years in areas of Broadcasting System Engineering, Computer Network Design, Medical Equipment, and Multicultural Management Consulting.

To reach Dr. Magdy M. Hussein, please e-mail: mhussein@yahoo.com

Dr. Gamal M. Elmarsafi

Dr. Gamal M. Elmarsafi holds several accredited degrees; Bachelor of Science (BS) and Master of Science (MS) in Engineering and Construction field from New Jersey Institute of Technology, and a Doctor of Philosophy degree in Organization and Management from Capella University School of Business and Technology.

He received Certification in Construction Engineering Technology from National Institute for Certification in Engineering Technologies and is a member of The National Society of Professional Engineers and member of Westlaw Round Table Group's expert network, to serve as expert witness professional. Negotiated construction dispute problems affecting stakeholders and resolved approximately $750 million of disputed claims.

Dr. Gamal managed team of professionals and oversaw numerous government infrastructure contracts for the New York City Department of Environmental Protection and Port Authority of New York and New Jersey. The work involved the coordination of large infrastructure contracts from feasibility studies through construction completion totaling approximately $2 Billion.

Dr. Gamal is a Business and Engineering Consultant, received awards from FEMA for his contribution in the recovery efforts caused by mass flooding in Mendocino County State of California. He also received awards and recognitions from the Governor of Louisiana State and from FEMA for his role in the long-term recovery and strategy plan in New Orleans City and Plaquemine Parish following the damage caused by Hurricane Katrina.

Prior to teaching business and technology at Devry University-Keller Graduate School of business Dr. Gamal published "Interorganizational Collaboration: Transformation Strategies to Reduce Construction Disputes" and conducted seminars in legal aspects of architecture, engineering and the construction process including ethics, organization management and leadership. He uses effective delivery methods that carry academic theory and subject matter to the learner's industry experiences. Stimulate discussion and enrich learning material to pre-existing knowledge base. His primary research areas of interest include Organization Behavior, Managing Quality, and Advanced Program Management.

To reach Dr. Gamal Elmarsafi, please e-mail: gelmarsafi@hotmail.com

CHAPTER 10

Socially Responsible Approaches to Using Technology in the 21st Century

Dr. Claudia Santin
& Dr. Suzanne LeBeau

S ocial responsibility is a principle that has concerned the business world for many years. Corporations want to be considered socially responsible and want stakeholders to view them as having a positive impact on society and the world, while they are financially prosperous. A quick search on the Internet for the term *social responsibility* yields pages and pages of corporate and business sites providing information about organizations touting that they have the answer regarding how to make a company more socially responsible.

No less a concern is the social responsibility, as it relates to technology use within academic institutions. We cannot educate students without the use of technology. A valid concern is if students, professors, administrators, and academic institutions are relating to technology in socially responsible ways. Understanding the reasons socially responsible technology usage is important is part of the equation. Knowing and following the approaches that professors and academic institutions should take in the area of social responsibility and technology usage, and the responsibilities of students to act in a socially responsible manner is key to ensuring ethical behavior and academic integrity.

The Importance of Social Responsibility in Technology

Social responsibility is that which encompasses our obligations to society. This responsibility includes behaving ethically and remaining sensitive toward cultural, social, and economic issues. It also involves our approaches to the environment. Kidder (1995) remarked that the two major issues that would define the following decade would be technology and ethics. In an ever-changing technological world, few activities take place without the use of technology. Technology, computers, and online resources are so ubiquitous that we tend to take them for granted.

Academic professionals as well as academic institutions must realize that the use of these technologies carry a social responsibility. Educators owe it to their students to use technology to facilitate the teaching and learning process ensuring that they have the necessary skills to prepare them to be leaders in their respective fields. This applies to the graduate forum as much as it does the K-12 forum. Nowhere more than in online education does this hold true. Data from the *2011 Survey of Online Learning* reveals that the number of students taking at least one online course has surpassed six million. Nearly one-third of all students in higher education are taking at least one online course (Allen & Seamen, 2011).

If educators can use technology so that students can integrate learning into their everyday activity, this helps moves the learning model from the 20th to the 21st century, where walls or classrooms do not bind learning, and career choices are no longer static or prescribed. If educators can do this while encouraging ethical and good digital citizenship, as well as social responsibility true empowerment takes place. As far back as 1995, Glennan and Melmed (1995) wrote, "Technology without reform is likely to have little value: widespread reform without technology is probably impossible" (p. 18). The reforms considered when Glennan and Melmed wrote this statement have morphed, as much as technology has; to include reforms in the way we approach not only the use of technology in our classroom but also how we educate our students on the proper use of technology. Over 8 years ago, the American Association of University Professors (AAUP) prepared a report on Academic Freedom and Electronic Communications (2004). Noted on the AAUP website, "While basic principles of academic freedom transcend even the most fundamental changes in media, recent developments require a re-examination of the application and implications of such principles in a radically new environment" (para. 1). Eight years after this quote, the rapidly changing conditions regarding the Internet and use of technology, the imperative to re-examine and continue examining if faculty is prepared to not only use but also to model the social, legal, and ethical use of digital resources.

For the past 8 years, online enrollments have grown substantially faster than higher education enrollments (Allen & Seamen, 2011). The increasing growth of online education in higher education is ongoing owing to several factors. These factors are the popularity of the Internet, the increased in human capability of using web-based tools, the increased number of individuals with Internet skills, and the decrease in those individuals not able to access the Internet (Schott, Chernish, Dooley, & Lindner, 2003). Entire academic programs can be obtained online. In the early years of online course delivery, it was enough that faculty existed who were willing to teach online.

With the growth of online course and program delivery and increasing technological skills of the students taking online courses, it now has become necessary for faculty to become skilled in using different technologies to enhance online course delivery. According to Allen and Seamen (2011), there is no specific formula or single approach taken by institutions of higher education as it pertains to training their faculty, adjunct, or full-time instructors teaching online. The survey also reported that most of the training programs are comprised of internally developed and offered courses, in some cases informal mentoring, and to a lesser degree, a formal mentoring program. The content of these training courses, likewise, differs widely. Learning how to use emerging technologies is generally not the focal point of the training, but rather how to use and/or manage the learning platform.

Socially Responsible Approaches to Technology Application in the 21st Century

Modeling has long been the approach that educators at all levels use to help students understand a concept. When educators model what they teach and demonstrate the expected behaviors, they put themselves in a position of serving as an example of the desired behavior. Modeling the social responsibilities of using technology is no different. When modeling occurs at the institutional level, the message is reinforced and more powerful, supporting the faculties' efforts. As an example, we point to Walden University's mission statement: "Walden University provides a diverse community of career professionals with the opportunity to transform themselves as scholar-practitioners so that they can effect positive social change." (Mission, n.d.) In the Walden University Ed.D. program, the entire program with the exception of a required residency is offered online. Technology is the delivery modality. Faculty are expected to employ technology to communicate with students, retain students, and facilitate student learning. Likewise, the expectation is that graduate students must adopt the scholar practitioner approach and assume responsibility for their actions, including how they use technology.

Different types of technology can be used to support and enhance learning. Everything from social media to instant messaging (IM) has been used in classrooms, and new uses of technologies are emerging quickly. Although we know that technology is only the tool that individuals use to complete assignments and projects, there must be a shared understanding of the task and/or project that is the goal. Students and faculty must understand the process they will follow and the expectations of all involved, including individual roles and responsibilities.

Social Media

The social networking sites are varied in approaches and are numerous: Facebook, MySpace, and LinkedIn, to name a few. The general purpose of these sites is to help individuals to communicate with family, friends, and colleagues, to share ideas, and to exchange information. In addition, the use of these sites are as varied as those using them, as it has been shown that social networking tools are used by people of all ages and all walks of life. According to the *PEW Internet and American Life Project* (2010), those using social networking sites have doubled since 2008 and the population of social network site users has gotten older, with over half of all adult users now over the age of 35. According to PEW (2012), the average age of adult-social network site users has shifted from age 33 in 2008 to age 38 in 2010.

Social media has changed how educators engage online with each other and their students. As faculty work with students who use social networking sites, they need to know their responsibility in using these sites for personal use or for communicating with students. We know that the majority of higher education faculty is using social networking sites. A recent survey of more than 900 higher education professionals revealed that nearly 85% have a Facebook account and approximately 67% have a LinkedIn account. Those taking the survey also disclosed that over 32% have *friended* undergraduate students, while 55% said they waited to *friend* students only after the students graduated (Faculty Focus, 2011).

Whether their classes are taught online or face-to-face, faculty must encourage students to communicate with them. It is one of our obligations as educators. Of course, there are many ways in which faculty can communicate with students. While some educators are hesitant to use social networking; for those who do, it is certainly a tool that helps educators to get to know their students and to have a forum other than the classroom for teaching and modeling social responsibility. When students see how we use such social networking sites, we are giving them a powerful message and a lesson in responsibility.

Care must be taken; however, when faculty establishes social networking accounts and befriends students on these sites. The nature of these sites allows users to share personal interests and personal information, educational background, biographical information, and even contact details. All social networking sites have privacy settings that allow users to limit access to some of this information. A best practice for all educators choosing to *friend* students on Facebook or other social networking sites would be to restrict access to some personal profile data.

More institutions are using social networking sites to help promote their institution and their programs. Who can admonish them, as this is where students are found. Social networking sites like Facebook do more than merely advertise and market their school and programs; they provide a social context for the school, which then creates a connection among the people who *like* them. Socially responsible higher education institutions should not use Facebook or other social networking sites to post course content or academic policies or the like; most institutions have excellent gateways and tools to deliver such information. However, what higher education institutions can do is post enough information on these social networking sites to send those who are interested back to the university site. Social networking sites must be used in such a way not to pose a threat of replacing the institution's portal of learning, but used so that it complements the portal.

Students must also consider their social and personal responsibilities when utilizing social media and social networking sites. Current and long-term effects of what students post on social networking sites must be considered in relation to themselves and to the university in which they are enrolled. What is posted on a Facebook wall, remains, in essence, on the Internet forever. Employers and college admissions' offices now check social networking sites almost as regularly as they check the information on applications and resumes. Students must consider their identity that they are portraying on the Internet and that of their school, as this may have serious consequences in their future. Students must realize that with the freedom to post anything, comes the responsibility to consider the future. For instance, a student might post derogatory remarks about their institution or a professor on Facebook. Depending on the interpretation of the institution's Code of Conduct, this could result in punitive action against the student by the institution. Students must reflect on the legal and socially responsible approaches to using social media and take into account the obligations to conduct themselves as students in good standing of the university. Guidance, modeling, lessons, and policies are needed to lead students to use social media for enjoyment but to do so in socially responsible ways. Social networking requires responsibility.

Internet Sharing Sites

A plethora of Internet sharing sites, other than those classified as social networking sites, has surfaced in the last few years. Such sites include: blogs, wikis, photo sharing, music sharing, file sharing, and video sharing sites. These Internet sharing sites are vehicles that empower individuals, faculty, and students alike as well as higher education institutions, giving them a voice and a tool to share views, ideas, and materials in a variety of formats. Ensuring that what is posted on the Internet and shared with others is worthy of an audience is a social responsibility of all. Internet users must be socially responsible when using such sites that share information.

Internet users access websites for current events, news, to interact with others, and to search for information. Such users are bombarded with information, sometimes too much information. When students come to higher education institutions for formal learning, there should be little adjustment for them, as these students are already familiar with finding, processing and then sharing information online. The challenge, and hence, the responsibility, lies in ensuring that what they are absorbing and in turn, processing and sharing, is reliable information. Faculty members are responsible for guiding students to the valid information and to help students to understand their personal responsibility in posting information on the Internet that is acceptable, honest, and true.

Internet sharing sites have become a type of a learning community and all those contributing to this community must be aware of the need to practice ethical and responsible behavior regarding the shared information. This means that all participants must recognize and uphold the principles of intellectual freedom and respect the intellectual property of others. With the ever-increasing Internet sharing sites, the challenge is to strike that balance between protecting the rights of those who publish information on the Internet (no matter how formal or casual the balance may be) and respect and encourage all users to access information freely when they want and need such information.

Lenhart, Purcell, Smith, and Zickuhr (2010) suggested that there have been dramatic increases in content creation and sharing on the Internet by adults that are 18 and older. The researchers reported that since 2006, the online sharing of content by teens has not changed significantly, with 39% of all teens sharing content on the Internet like videos, photos, artwork, and blogs. However, approximately 30% of all adults share content on the Internet, up from 21% in 2007. The amount of information that is posted on the Internet grows exponentially each day. Therefore, there is no wonder why many individuals are confused regarding what is permissible to copy and what is restricted by copyright. As faculty, we must model and create that climate of social responsibility and ethical behavior with respect to content and information on the Internet. The responsibilities of faculty and higher education institutions are countless. In all too many instances, the correct manner of documenting information from the Internet is not made clear to students or faculty. Institutional formatting guidelines for documenting information retrieved from the Internet require routine updating. Modeling citation formats for podcasts and wikis and blogs and other Internet-based sources of content information should be the norm. If we want students to act ethically and responsibly concerning information found on the Internet, we must provide them with models.

Blogging is one area in which social responsibility must be encouraged. One must be a blogger to understand how blogging works. Blogging is a different style of writing than academic writing. A blogger is one who posts thoughts, comments, ideas on a topic often involving emotion and passion. Bloggers rarely take the time they need to think things through carefully. Asking students to keep a blog has now become a strategy used by many faculty and institutions. Educators need to guide students through the process of being socially responsible bloggers and provide students with some guidelines when posting to a blog. Bloggers need to check their facts and credit their sources. Above all, as educators, we need to guide students in being honest and in avoiding harsh comments that will harm others. In academic writing, blogs must be cited if one is referencing material from them, although they are not considered scholarly sources.

As faculty in a higher education institution, it is also our responsibility to respect the rights and the information privacy of our students. Some students may not want their name associated with a blogging assignment or not want to post thoughts, opinions, or assignments on the Internet. In this case, we need to respect their rights and allow students to be anonymous on the Internet. At the same time, we must demand that students, who do blog as part of an academic requirement for a course, maintain a level of scholarly writing and integrity. Educators are called to help develop the next generation of bloggers.

Digital Communication

In 2012, most of us would think that many forms of digital communication are known and understood. After all, email, texting, Voice over Internet Protocols (VoIP) and IM are commonplace. For instance, Skype helps families, friends and co-workers stay connected. Digital communication could enhance faculty-student communication. All faculty need to understand not only the power of using these technologies as it pertains to enhancing and assisting student learning, but also how to instill into students the legal, and social responsibilities surrounding the uses of these digital communication tools.

Email and discussion boards are integrated into most learning management systems as a staple of an online course room. to enhance, augment, or supplement the asynchronous environment faculty often turn to VoIPs, such as Skype or FaceTime. Skype's chat and voice calling features allow for synchronous communication that email and the discussion boards do not. Skype, FaceTime, and other VoIP can help break down the traditional barriers of the classroom walls overcoming the distance that often restricts learners. Cheng-Chang (2005) noted that the use of Skype encourages the student to take an "active and responsible learning role" (p. 2).

VoIP can assist students and faculty to remain connected in a community of practice that might otherwise be impossible.

Two digital communication tools rapidly gaining popularity are text messaging and IM. Irvine (2006) reviewed how young professionals gravitate toward instant gratification communication tools. In the article, Irvine declared that email, IM, and text messaging out date previous technological advances. As the growth in IM usage continues, it will compete with other forms of communications, such as the telephone and email, to become the primary method of communication for business, education, and everyday life.

In a 2006 presentation, Wagner (2006) noted that analysts agreed that college students were using text messaging regularly. Wagner observed that text messaging is the second most frequently used computer-based tool, next to email. IM is third. Faculty must be ready to adapt instructional pedagogy compatible with the mobile lifestyle they live. DuVall, Powel, Hodge, and Ellis (2007) emphasized that if text messaging was appropriately used within an online course for specific objectives, it could offer enhanced social presence and communication among class participants. Some faculty members are using cell phones and text messaging to help students stay organized and to send them reminders about due dates for assignments, upcoming quizzes, webinars and other types of events. While not every faculty does this or may want to do this, faculty can educate their students to set up their own reminders to be sent to cell phones using an online reminder service.

Because of the ease with which digital content may be posted in an online course, or within an email, or a course using Web 2.0/social media technologies, students should be reminded that they must comply with copyright laws, and university-specific policies. Faculty should ensure they are aware of university policy regarding using 21st century technologies, and they should be aware that it is inappropriate to use such technologies to discuss with a student a matter that does not pertain to course-related activities. Electronic communications with students should be sent simultaneously to multiple recipients, not only to one student, except where the communication is specific to them and inappropriate for persons other than the individual student to receive (for example, emailing a message about a student's course performance). In other words, faculty should take care that they do not engage in what may be perceived as inappropriate communication with a student, whether by phone, texting, IM, Skype, social media, or any other method.

Students learning online are expected to understand, through the guidelines posted in the course room, how to use email to ask questions and communicate with their faculty and peers, and the expectations for the content of discussion postings. However, it is prudent that faculty emphasize the institution's code of conduct and acceptable rules of engagement. The same should be done with using text messaging, IM, VoIPs, and any other technology. Faculty need to emphasize that appropriate behavior is expected when using any type of course related communication. T his behavior would include using appropriate academic or scholarly language, maintaining professional tone, obeying copyright rules, reporting any abusive behaviors, and remembering that whatever the forum or degree program level, the student, and the faculty member represent the institution.

Conclusion

Within the advancing application and usage of technology, academic users of the Internet, and the institutions that employ them as faculty or serve them as students, all have a social responsibility. Institutional polices should address best practices and acceptable use regarding social responsibility in technology usage, faculty must know and understand these policies, and model appropriate conduct for the students they serve. Whether using Internet sharing sites, social media, or digital communication tools, those that participate and share in these technologies, and use various technology tools for teaching and learning, all contribute to a larger learning community. The active participants in this learning community have a social responsibility to respect the intellectual property of others and to recognize the principles of intellectual freedom and most important, to practice responsible and ethical behavior regarding communicating, distributing and consuming Internet-based information and using 21st century technologies.

REFERENCES

Allen, I. E., & Seamen, J. (2011). *Going the distance: Online education in the United States.* Needham, MA: The Sloan Consortium.

American Association of University Professors. (n.d.). Academic freedom and electronic communications. Retrieved from http://www.aaup.org/AAUP/pubsres/policydocs/contents/electcomm-stmt.htm

Cheng-Chang, P. (2005). Instructional use of Skype in an online graduate program. Paper presented at the TCC 2005 Worldwide Online Conference, University of Hawai'i, Honolulu, Hawaii. Retrieved from http://tcc.kcc.hawaii.edu/previous/TCC%202005/pan01.pdf

DuVall, B., Powell, M. R., Hodge, E., & Ellis, M. (2007). Text messaging to improve social presence in online learning. *Educause, 30*(3), 24–28. Retrieved from http://www.educause.edu/.../TextMessagingtoImproveSocialPr/161829

Faculty Focus. (2011). *Social media usage trends among higher education faculty.* Retrieved from http://www.facultyfocus.com/free-reports/social-media-usage-trends-among-higher-education-faculty/

Glennan, T. K., & Melmed, A. (1995). *Fostering the use of educational technology: Elements of a national strategy.* Washington, DC: RAND.

Irvine, M. (2006). *Email losing ground to IM, text messaging.* Retrieved from http://www.msnbc.msn.com/id/13921601/

Kidder, R. M. (1995). The ethics of teaching and the teaching of ethics. In Boschmann, E. (Ed.), *The electronic classroom: A handbook for education in the electronic environment.* Medford, NJ: Learned Information.

Lenhart, A., Purcell, K., Smith, A., & Zickuhr, K. (2010). *Social media and young adults.* Retrieved from http://www.pewinternet.org/Reports/2010/Social-Media-and-Young-Adults.aspx

Pew I/internet and American life project. (2012). Retrieved from http://www.pewinternet.org/

Schott, M., Chernish, W., Dooley, K. E., & Linder, J. R. (2003, Summer). Innovations in distance learning program development and delivery. *Online Journal of Distance Learning Administrators, 6(2).* Retrieved from http://www.westga.edu/~distance/ojdla/

Wagner, E. (2006, March). *Mobility and mobile learning: The next phase of anytime, anywhere learning.* Presentation delivered at Educause Learning Initiative (ELI) Spring Focus Session. College Park, MD: University of Maryland.

Walden University. (n.d.). *University mission statement.* Retrieved from http://www.waldenu.edu/About-Us.htm

About the Authors

Suzanne LeBeau

Dr. Suzanne LeBeau has over 35 years of experience as an educator, working with students of varying levels, from elementary and middle school to graduate and doctoral levels. Dr. Sue holds a Doctor of Education degree in Organizational Leadership from Nova Southeastern University, a Master of Arts degree in Instructional Technology from Georgian Court University, and a Master of Education and a Bachelors degree in Elementary Education from Rivier College.

Dr. Sue has been involved with the integration of technology in all areas of education for well over twenty years and has taught university level courses online for over ten years. She presently teaches online graduate courses in Education, Information Technology, and Business; she serves as a dissertation chair, major assessor, lead faculty, and program coordinator for various university programs.

Dr. Sue has published chapters in three books and numerous articles in peer-reviewed journals. She has been a professional development provider and educational workshop presenter for well over 20 years. Dr. Sue has traveled around the world, having visited all seven continents (including Antarctica); in her spare time, she dabbles in digital photography and all things technology and she loves to read. She presently lives in Arizona with her two Havanese puppies, Chloe and Casey.

Dr. Sue LeBeau may be contacted at sue.lebeau@yahoo.com

Claudia Santin

Dr. Claudia Santin is an educational consultant, who has worked in higher education for over 30 years. Dr. "C" holds an EdD in Higher Education Leadership from Nova Southeastern University, and a MA and BA from College of NJ. She has her Graduate Certificate in Marketing Management from Nova Southeastern University. As an early adopter of online education, Dr. C has been teaching in the online format for over 15 years. In addition to taking numerous training and for credit courses in the use of media in online learning, she also has achieved a Certification in Online Instruction.

Dr. "C" currently serves as a professor of leadership, a dissertation chair, a senior researcher, a lead faculty, subject matter expert, and doctoral writing mentor. She has served as a university president, provost, vice-president of academic affairs, a dean of leadership studies and a dean of education. Within the last 3 years, Dr. C has published two books and numerous articles in peer-reviewed journals. She also serves as Vice-President and Executive Director of The eLearning Institute. Dr. "C" lives in Arizona, is the proud mother of a son, who has a PhD in Business and her daughter, an attorney, as well as two granddaughters and three Chihuahuas.

Dr. Santin can be contacted at dr_santin@yahoo.com

Social Irresponsibility Provides Opportunity for the Win-Win-Win of Sustainable Leadership

Dr. Elmer B. Hall & Dr. Edward F. Knab

A simple definition for *sustainability* is living and acting in ways that can go on indefinitely, ways that do not result in externalities or cause a burden on future generations (IPPC, 2007). A key component to sustainability is the magic of compounding when used well and wisely (Freidman, 2009). Many non-sustainable actions use the power of compounding destructively and can be compared to a video of a train wreck with a factual past and present but a Hollywood version of the future in which the train goes off the cliff ahead. Simply stopping the acceleration is the reasonable place to start when addressing the looming disaster (Senge, Smith, Kruschwitz, Laur, & Schley, 2008). Sadly, aspects of land, energy, and water use are slow-motion train wrecks waiting to happen. Government entitlement commitments and rising Federal debt are train wrecks that can be drawn for the future with the simplest of forecasting. The ending of the film with its projected carnage may not be completely accurate, but the children of the future will get to see how it actually plays out. If there are things that should reasonable be done differently today, it would be irresponsible not to do so.

Social irresponsibility occurs in governments, businesses, and by individuals who come from short-term thinking and less-than-responsible planning (Bearden, Money, & Nevins, 2006). A serious and concerted effort from *sustainable leaders* will be required to address the many non-sustainable issues and start to use the magic of compounding positively toward solving these issues. Existing leadership styles need to be adjusted to accommodate sustainability.

The Issues and the Problems

The financial definition of *sustainable growth* is how much can the company grow without raising outside capital; that is, how quickly can the company grow simply by investing profits to fund growth (Ehrhardt & Brigham, 2011). The DOTcom era brought the *irrational exuberance* of financial sustainability down to earth when the stock market bubble burst in 2000 revealing the laws of gravity still work (Greenspan, 2007).

Achieving Sustainability, Now or Later

The global lifestyle, governments, businesses, and consumers, are built on non-sustainable practices. Here are just a few non-sustainability areas in which the power of compounding is at work.

Healthcare Irresponsibility. U.S. Healthcare costs have been growing at about 10% per year (although it has dropped temporarily to 4% in 2012); and healthcare represents more than 17% of the U.S. GDP (Altarum Institute, 2012; Terry, 2010). If inflation is a modest 2% and GDP growth is 2.5% on average for the next few decades, then real GDP growth is about 0.5%. So how many years, with this out-of-control healthcare spending, does it take before the costs of healthcare exceed the U.S. GDP? About 25 years! Within 15 years, healthcare costs would rise to 50% of the U.S. GDP. *Answer:* The out-of-control costs of healthcare are non-sustainable, healthcare costs must be contained.

Lifestyle Irresponsibility. Tobacco use has contributed significantly to deaths and to healthcare costs (CDC, n.d.; Danaei, Ding,

Mozaffarian, Taylor, Rehm, Rehm, Murray, & Ezzatil, 2009). Overindulgence in alcohol and (illegal) drugs results in (traffic) accidents and health complications. Obesity is becoming a huge and ever-increasing epidemic in the U.S. and in the developing countries as the world moves to eating more, eating more meat, and eating more processed foods. To make up for over-indulgence, people exercise less. Gaining weight is what happens when a person consumes 8,000 calories per day, but burns only 2,000. In all, the root causes or contributing causes of most of the mortalities in the US are caused by life style. *Answer:* Change to healthy life styles is needed including not smoking, exercise, and healthy diet.

Entitlement Program Irresponsibility. Social Security and Medicare are known broken systems (Greenspan, 2007; Hall, 2010a; Walker, 2010). One of the problems is that the government spends the money that comes in from current workers immediately and does not bank any of it for those future expenses promised by entitlement programs. In accounting terms, this is cash-based accounting versus the Generally Acceptable Accounting Practices (GAAP) method required of publically traded companies. Painful reality is revealed by visiting the U.S. Debt Clock (2012) to see that the U.S. debt is not about $16T as of May 2012, but more like $119T in GAAP terms when counting unfunded liabilities. *Answer:* Adopt one of the bi-partisan programs to fix entitlements (Walker, 2010). Small changes to the entitlement programs today will make a huge difference to those programs; delaying action simply magnifies the problem and accelerates when they become insolvent.

Government Debt Irresponsibility. The U.S. has twin deficits, the federal deficit, and the ongoing trade deficit each year (BEA, 2012; Greenspan, 2007; Hall, 2010b; Walker, 2010). Neither of these is sustainable, obviously; they continue to grow over time with no surpluses anticipated for decades to offset them. The long-term result of either is inflation within the country and devaluation of the currency. Perpetual overspending and excessive importing cannot go on forever, as demonstrated by the sovereign debt crises in the Southern European Union nations. *Answer:* Years with economic growth should have a mandated improvement in the deficit.

Government Interest Rate Time Bomb. About 10% of the total tax revenues of the federal government go toward paying the interest on the massive U.S. bond debt (BEA, 2012). Although interest rates have been artificially low because of massive monetary policy measures, interest rates can be expected to rise rapidly after 2014. As interest rates rise from artificially low rates, or the U.S. debt rating drops, the costs of servicing the U.S. debt become greater and greater. When interest rates go from below 2% in 2012 to 4%, 6%, 8%, 10%, the percentage of all U.S. Federal tax revenues spent simply to service the debt (not to pay it down) goes from 10% to 50%. Of the bankrupt countries in Southern Europe, Spain has gone up to 6%-7% interest rate (yield to maturity), and Greece to 30%-50%? As the credit ratings for a country's bonds drops into *junk risk ratings,* the country's sovereign debt becomes unserviceable (Investopedia, n.d.). *Answer:* Reduce the federal debt during the years of economic growth, and keep federal debt low. The ways to address a deficit are: growth, raise taxes, and/or cut expenditures. Growth is usually hugely preferred because the expanding economy automatically produces more income and tax revenue while reducing many government expenses related to poor and unemployed.

Consumer Irresponsibility. Consumerism goes through phases, but does not go away (Leonard, 2010a, 2010b). The fads and fashions come and go, but the advertising engines of business are relentless. The demand for ivory, brought elephants to the brink of extinction. The created demand for bottled water has created significant costs to the consumer and massive spillover costs to the environment. (What is the explanation again, why consumers spend $10 per gallon for something that comes nearly free from the tap?) The consumer lives in a linear system where raw materials are mined, manufactured, shipped to the consumer, and then are partially consumed. What is not consumed is occasionally recycled, but generally goes to the landfill. *Answer:* Consumers need to make wiser choices and become more informed consumers. Consumers need to evaluate the corporate social responsibility (CSR) of the companies they do business with as well as the externality costs of products before purchases.

Energy Irresponsibility. Exhaustible energy resources, such as coal, oil, and uranium are not sustainable, i.e., they are non-renewable (Hall, 2010a). Burning wood for energy is renewable, provide the forest is replanted. One way to solve the problem eventually is to let economics resolve the issue with scarcity and higher prices as supplies are exhausted. The economies of the world have to be converted to renewable energy sources eventually, and some researchers believe that *peak oil* and *peak coal* may have already occurred if not for the Great Recession of 2008 (Cernansky, 2010; Roger, n.d.). New finds and non-conventional mining in shell and tar sands may delay peak oil for another decade or two (EIA, 2012a, 2012b). A bigger problem, however, is the externalities of fossil fuels, especially coal. Coal is dangerous to mine (about 10,000 people die each year in mines), and produces ugly chemicals as a byproduct. A dirty little secret of coal is coal ash (Kromm, 2010). Yearly, thousands of people die and millions are sick from coal energy (Lockwood, Welker-Hood, Rauch, & Gottlieb, 2009). *Answer:* Develop long, intermediate, and short-term plans for switching to 100% renewable energy. Governments need to change the costs and incentives; the real costs of coal and oil are more expensive than the direct prices paid at the pump or meter, even before considering the greenhouse gas (GHG) emissions.

Ecological Irresponsibility. The very earth system that maintains life on planet Earth is being broken systematically, but relentlessly

(Botkin & Keller, 2011; Wright & Boorse, 2011). The bottom of the food chain is under duress (plankton and coral reefs) and the top of the food chain is facing extinction (whales, sharks, and tigers). Oceans are overfished; waters are overused and polluted (Chartres & Varma, 2011; Marks, 2009). *Answer:* Moving toward sustainable farming, fishing, and living.

Environmental Irresponsibility of Fossil Fuels II. Fossil fuels—coal, oil, and natural gas—took millions of years to create (Ayres & Ayres, 2010; EIA, 2012a, 2012b; EPA 2009, 2012; Hall, 2010a, 2010b; IPPC, 2007; UNFCC, n.d.; Wright & Boorse, 2011). Humans have been trying to burn most of the fossil fuels over a couple centuries, with one aggressive century already past. Besides heat, there is one primary byproduct of burning fossil fuels: carbon dioxide (CO_2) emission, a greenhouse gas. These tons of coal and 90 million barrels of oil per day are from carbon that has not been in the earth's systems for more than 50 million year when the fossil fuels were formed (Babcock, 2009; EIA, 2012a, 2012b; Wright & Boorse, 2011). The result is the buildup of CO_2 and other greenhouse gases in the atmosphere, climbing to a record 30.6 Gigatonnes (Gt) of CO_2 emissions in 2011 (EIA, 2012a). This is at a time when more plants (and more photosynthesis) are not an option, impervious surfaces and deforestation are reducing the planet's ability to process CO_2 (IPCC, 2007). Oh, and, something that few people realize, carbon dioxide is persistent in the atmosphere with warming factors measured in 100 years (EPA, 2009). So essentially all the carbon ever produced from running fuel vehicles is still persistent in the atmosphere today. Even if everyone stopped every car and closed every fossil-fuel power plant this moment, there would still be the impact from that extra greenhouse gas buildup from the century past. In short, the cost of cheap coal today may be astronomically expensive for future generations; no one really knows, but no one can reasonably say that coal is *cheap* or *clean* (Hall, 2010a). *Answer:*

Start immediately with conservation and energy efficiency measures while transitioning to sustainable energy.

Single-Problem Irresponsibility. An interrelationship exists among earth systems (World Economic Forum, 2011). Addressing only one part of the problem is an ineffective, even irresponsible, way to deal with problems. For example, vast amounts of water are required to make conventional electricity, and if available water runs out, it takes energy to clean and transport water. It takes massive amounts of water and energy to make paper and clothes. It takes a large amount of water and energy (and oil) to make plastics. It takes huge amounts of water to make food, especially grain-fed beef (Mekonnen, & Hoekstra, 2012; Tukker, Cohen, Hubacek, & Mont, 2010). This complex interrelationship is the *water-energy-food nexus* (World Economic Forum, 2011). *Answer:* Solutions must address entire systems, not isolated parts. This will require sustainable leaders with a long-term, integrated, holistic approach.

Individuals—including people with organizations and governments—need to get going on sustainability (Senge et al., 2008). The magic of compounding continues to work in negative ways, not positive. *Wedges* are possible aggressive actions that *might be taken* to start reducing human impacts and reversing damage already done (IPCC, 2007; Walker, 2010). This has to be done sooner, not later, when the problem may be exponentially worse (Friedman, 2009; IPCC, 2007).

All of the above issues are highly complex and can only be resolved through the development of a consensus regarding the solutions and a resolve to apply solutions that will compound benefits over time (Senge et al., 2008). Most of these issues that are of consequence of post-industrialization are at a level of complexity never before experienced by humankind, they were decades in the making. A new type of leadership, sustainable leadership, is needed to address the problems of the future. The following section outlines the general management and a sustainable leadership framework.

Organizational Design and Leadership Models

Significant research has been done on organizational design and leadership. Organizationally, entities that are more sustainable would have to be much more open (vs. closed) as discussed by Scott (2007). A multitude of issues related to the best ways to create an organization to be most effective include organizational structure, specialization, complexity of the environment, boundaries, span of control, centralization, and geographic area (Jones, 2010; McAuley, Duberley, & Johnson, 2007; Robbins & Judge, 2011; Scott, 2007). All of these issues become more complex when universal sustainability is considered that includes the full spectrum of social and environmental factors. The best structure is strongly shaped by the environment in which the management and leadership of the organization must function.

Historically, leadership has focused on characteristics of leaders, task structure, initiating influencing factors (Yukl, 2010). The leadership styles that work best depend primarily on the task environment as well as the characteristics and strengths of the specific leader (Robbins & Judge, 2011; Yukl, 2010). "The behavioral [approach has narrowed] leadership into task-oriented (initiating structure) and people-oriented (consideration) styles" (Robbins & Judge, 2011, p. 439). Charismatic and transformational leadership have met with the best empirical support as effective leadership types (Robbins & Judge, 2011; Yukl, 2010).

Ethical, servant, spiritual, and authentic leadership are not necessarily exclusive of the leadership styles including transformational leadership (Yukl, 2010). Ethical and trusted leaders can have very strong and loyal followers. "A servant leader must attend to the needs of the followers and help them become healthier, wiser and more willing to accept their responsibilities" (Yukl, 2010, p. 349). Ethical leaders would be, and should be, more active at looking for the external impacts of organizations: impacts to society and the environment. Corporate social responsibility (CSR) is a key part of overall ethics of a leader.

Corporate Social Responsibility (CSR)

Corporate social responsibility builds on the concept of trust and ethical behavior of the organization's management (Maon, Lindgreen, & Swaen, 2008). What are all of the impacts, positive and negative, internal and external, of the activities of the organization? "Many studies have identified positive relationship between social responsibility and financial performance" (Thorne, Farrell, & Ferrell, 2010, p. 30). Hartman (2011) outlined the issues of social responsibility in general and for CSR for organizations. The four major models of CSR are economic, philanthropic, social web, and integrative (Hartman, 2011).

An integrative model for CSR planning and reporting looks at the interest of both internal and external stakeholders (Hartman, 2011). Several frameworks for CSR management and reporting have been developed including the Global Reporting Initiative (GRI). Here are examples:

- International Standards Organization (ISO, 2012) has developed standards used for management and reporting purposes globally. The families of ISO standards are:
  - ISO 9000—*Quality management* (quality management approach used in all ISO analysis, statistics, and reporting)
  - ISO 14000—*Environmental management*
  - ISO 26000—*Social responsibility*
  - ISO 31000—*Risk management*
  - ISO 50001—*Energy management*

- Global Reporting Initiative (GRI) is a reporting environment developed in collaborative with the Organisation for Economic Co-operation and Development (OECD), United Nations Environmental Programme (UNEP), United Nations Global Compact (UNGC) and ISO (GRI, 2012; Savitz, & Weber, 2006). This initiative provides support and encouragement for companies to complete CSR activities and report on them directly through the GRI web site. More than 1,800 corporations now provide GRI reports (GRI, 2012).

- CERES (2012) not only helps and encourages CSR reporting, including working with GRI, but CERES provides SR analysis on sustainability progress and other services, such as the Investor Network on Climate Risk (INCR).

- Probably the most useful tool for organizations is the Triple-Bottom Line (TBL) approach to sustainability planning and reporting. John Elkington (Laur, 2007; Savitz, & Weber, 2006), the inventor of the term and the concept of *Triple-Bottom Line,* was also a pioneer in the GRI and CERES movements; he likes that the GRI reporting has taken more of a TBL approach. For a smaller organization, TBL reporting does not have to be that complicated.

- *Campus Ecology* is a reporting process for colleges and universities that includes not only physical plant operations, but also education in sustainability as well. (AASHE, 2008; Hall, 2010b; Hall, Taylor, Zapalski, & Hall, 2009; Martin Akel & Associates, 2006; SEI, 2008; NWF, 2012).

- Several frameworks have already been created for CSR, which can be utilized for developing an integrated planning process that takes all aspects of the business/organization and its environment into account.

Integrated Sustainable Planning

The economic environment, physical environment, and social environment are depicted by *the triple-bottom line* of sustainability (see left side of Figure 1). Savitz and Weber (2006) and other authors discussed using the TBL for socially responsible strategic planning. To create a sustainable world means that the interrelationship of the external environment to people and economic growth must be carefully considered in all business decisions. The interdependence inferred in this sustainability model shows the areas of overlap at the center of the circle is the area of sustainability—those things that can go on indefinitely without spillover costs or negative externalities. For long-term sustainability, these circles must come together as shown in the right side of Figure 1.

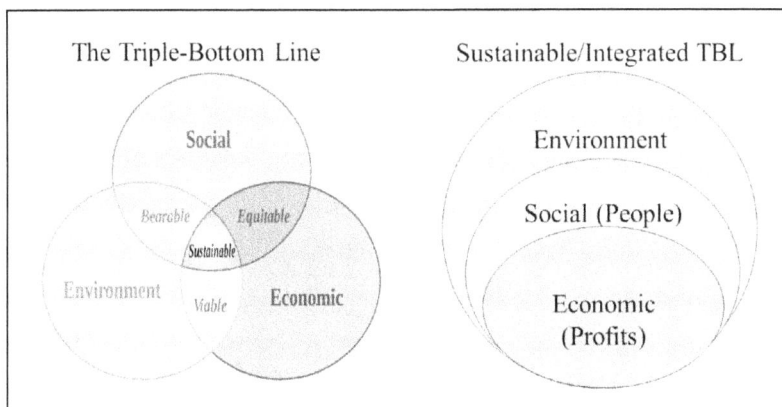

Figure 1. Sustainability: The triple-bottom line and integrated triple-bottom line.

Hall and Hinkelman (2007) developed strategic planning processes for long-term competitive advantage for companies and for economic development (Hall, 2008). What is needed is an integrated planning process for companies that take into consideration the overall community of an economic development plan with the environmental interests of the people who live in the communities (Casey, 2011; Porter, 2008). The *integration sustainable planning* process that includes a holistic approach and the triple-bottom line is shown in Figure 2. Note that the short-term planning should focus on moving and prioritizing the organization toward the overlap areas that are more *sustainable* and consequently better for business, society and the environment. However, the long-term goal would be for a complete overlap. Businesses should not be doing things that are good for them but not for society or for the environment. Long-term harmony of the economy and of society within the environment is the sustainable goal. Anything else is, well, not sustainable.

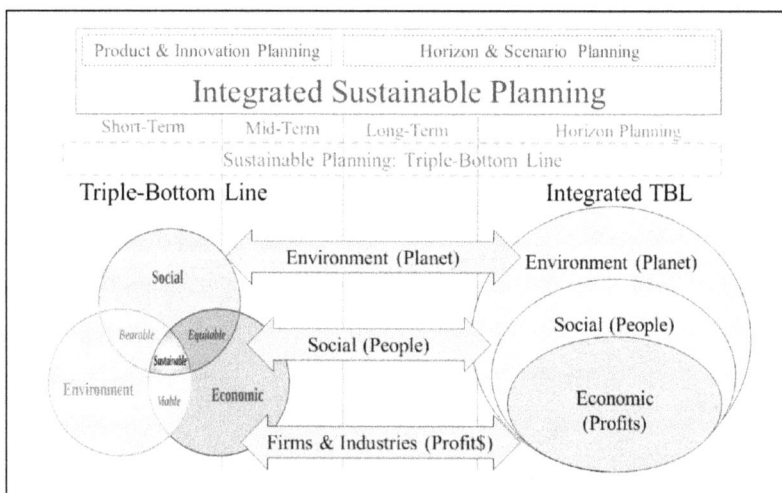

Figure 2. Integrated sustainable planning: From TBL to Integrated TBL planning.

So far, non-sustainable practices have been identified. These are big problems, but certainly not all such issues. Then frameworks for organizations to addressing sustainability in integrated planning have been outline. What type of leadership, then, is required to implement sustainability?

Building a Model for Sustainable Leadership

Even successful leaders find their worlds overwhelming. To also address sustainability, these leaders must have an extraordinary ability to expand their understanding of the issues, identify solutions, and generate the public supported for change. The long-held assumptions that have led the compromise of the health of organizations, communities, and planet earth need to be evaluated. Social irresponsibility is in many ways a consequence of post-industrialization and globalization as the impact of growth neglected to consider the long-term impact on the environment and social organizational structures.

Of the existing leadership styles, there are really two that seem most appropriate for sustainable leadership: servant and transformational. The concepts of transformational and servant leadership form a foundation for a more sustainable type of leadership inclusive of the environment, economic conditions, and social institutions.

Transformational leadership is a methodology that enhances the morale and performance of followers through a variety of organizational systems (Burns, 1978; Hollander, 1986). These include: developing a clear and distinct mission for the organization (Bennis, 1984), and connecting it to the members' (followers') sense of identity (Barnard, 1938), to be a role model for followers that inspires them to achieve the mission of the organization (Bass & Avolio, 1988); and, promoting a sense of ownership in members that aligns members with tasks that optimize performance (Bass, 1985). Four primary elements of transformational leadership provide a foundation for the transition to a new sustainable leadership model (Yukl, 2010). The four key elements include:

1. Individualized Consideration—the degree to which the leader tends to each follower's needs in the form of coaching or mentorship.

2. Intellectual Stimulation—the manner in which the leader challenges assumptions, takes risks, and solicits ideas from the organization.

3. Inspirational Motivation—the manner in which the leader articulates the vision that appeals to and inspires the organizational members.

4. Idealized Influence—the manner in which the leader is a role model instilling high levels of ethical behavior based on trust and respect.

These foundational elements are essential to the development of an effective sustainable leadership model.

The concept of servant leadership is also foundational to the development of a sustainable leadership model. This concept was developed by Robert K Greenleaf (1977) and is built on the idea that servant-leaders achieve results for their organizations by giving priority to the needs of colleagues and to those they serve (Robbins & Judge, 2011; Yukl, 2010). Servant leaders are seen as humble stewards of their organization's resources: human, financial, and physical.

The traditional concept of servant leaders must be enhanced somewhat to include a more robust environmental responsibility, which is a natural extension of the organization's physical resources. The transition of servant leaders to a sustainable leadership includes stewardship of the organization's resources that include human (social), financial (economic) and physical (environmental). In this manner, servant leadership matches as a foundational element of integrated sustainable planning (see Figure 2).

Sustainability leaders are individuals compelled to make a difference by deepening awareness of themselves in relation to the world around them. In doing so, they adopt new methods of seeing, thinking, and interacting that result in innovative, sustainable solutions, solutions that can be applied over the long-term. Sustainable leadership must be an extension of servant and transformational leadership.

Collins (2001, 2005, 2007, 2012) coauthored with Hansen (2011) and Porras (1994) management books *Built to Last, Good to Great*, and *Great by Choice*. *Good to Great* identified the ultimate leadership type associated with long-term great companies. The key to a great company is *Level 5 Leaders*, leaders who are humble yet relentless. Only small extensions are necessary to extend Level 5 Leadership to accommodate sustainability. The decision to be *great*, requires only the addition of sustainability: Do you want to be *sustainably* great? The core competency (hedgehog) and Big Harry Audacious Goal (BHAG) must be sustainable competencies and goals. Moreover, the Level 5 Leadership must be leadership that is committed not only to the company's goals, but also to the community and environment as well, i.e., *sustainable* Level 5 Leadership. The framework that Collins proposed, including the 12 questions to ask, can easily adopt an Integrated Sustainable Triple-Bottom Line planning framework (see Figure 2).

Unfortunately, only a few leaders are, or will be, Level 5, maybe 1%. Not every leader can be great (Caulkins, 2008; Neindorf & Beck, 2008). With sustainability, all leaders need to participate, and participate aggressively to address the looming non-sustainable factors. A sustainable servant leader would do *good*. A sustainable transformational leader would perform triple-bottom line *well*. A *sustainable leader* would achieve the best of both. A sustainable Level 5 Leader would be, well, *great!*

Conclusions

To be more sustainable is not an option, it is an imperative. Because of the magic—or the tragedy—of compounding, sooner is much better than later. There are two problems with later. First, the power and the magic of compounding will be working destructively, not constructively, making any problems far more difficult to resolve and reverse. (To begin slowing down the train, the engine driver must pull back on the throttle.) The second is that the true costs are not being evaluated, so there is no risk assessment regarding how big the problem might be in the future and how much it could cost future generations (CERES, 2012). Looming non-sustainable issues exist in government, in consumerism, in energy and resource use, and in business. Corporate social responsibility planning and reporting seems like a great place to start, including the triple-bottom line. An integrated planning approach is proposed that uses the triple-bottom line that is harmonized for a sustainable future. Corporations need to adjust to CSR as *the way of doing business,* not *a way of doing business.*

Leadership styles need to be adjusted for the long-term, triple-bottom-line necessary to move from less responsible ways of living to more responsible. Servant leaders need to be extended to stakeholders and environmental concerns. Transformation leaders need to use longer-term and broader goals.

Collins and his team may have identified the best approach to implement great organizations that have Level 5 Leadership. With minor adjustments and forward planning Level 5 leadership could become *sustainable leadership* as well. Bill Gates (2010), who is well qualified for the status of a Level 5 Leader at Microsoft and the Gates Foundation, gave one target number at a TED conference. Organizations need to aim for, and attain, zero carbon emissions before 2050. Gates and The Gates Foundation are spending huge amounts of time, money, and energy addressing innovative solutions to the looming global warming and CO_2 emissions problems. Microsoft is aiming to reach that carbon-neutral milestone in 2013 (Guenther, 2012)!

Future leaders need to focus on areas where the environment, society, and the economy win: the triple win of the triple-bottom line of sustainability. Individuals within organizations should aim to become good and ultimately *sustainably great*. The move from socially irresponsibility to sustainability will be led by *sustainable leaders*.

REFERENCES

Altarum Institute. (2012, May 10). Insights from monthly national health expenditure estimates through March 2012. *Health Sector Economic Indicators*. Retrieved from: http://www.altarum.org/files/imce/CSHS-Spending-Brief_May%202012_050912.pdf

Association for the Advancement of Sustainability in Higher Education [AASHE]. (2008, June). *AASHE Digest 2007*. Retrieved from http://www.aashe.org

Ayres, R. U., & Ayres, E. H. (2010). *Crossing the energy divide: Moving from fossil fuel dependence to a clean-energy future*. Upper Saddle River, NJ: Pearson Education.

Babcock, L. E. (2009). *Visualizing earth history*. Hoboken, NY: John Wiley & Sons.

Barnard, C. I. (1938). *The functions of the executive*. Cambridge, MA: Harvard University Press.

Bass, B. M. (1985). *Leadership and performance beyond expectations*. New York, NY: Free Press.

Bass, B. M., & Avolio, B. J. (1988). *Prototypical, leniency and general response set in a rated and ranked transformational and transactional leadership descriptions*. (Report Series 88–2, Binghamton State University of New York, NY: Center for Leadership Studies.

Bearden, W. O., Money, R., & Nevins, J. L. (2006). A measure of long-term orientation: Development and validation. *Journal of the Academy of Marketing Science, 34*(3), 456–467. Retrieved from http://jam.sagepub.com/

Bennis, W. G. (1984). The 4 competencies of leadership. *Training & Development Journal, 38*(8), 14–19. Retrieved from http://www.accessmylibrary.com/archive/411170-training-development-journal.html

Botkin, D. B., & Keller, E. A. (2011). *Environmental sciences: Earth as a living planet* (8th ed.). Hoboken, NY: John Wiley & Sons.

Bureau of Economic Analysis [BEA]. (2010). *Interactive data*. Retrieved from http://www.bea.gov/itable/

Burns, J. M. (1978), *Leadership*. New York, NY: Harper & Row.

Butcher, J., Bezzina, M., & Moran, W. (2011). Transformational partnerships: A new agenda for higher education. *Innovative Higher Education, 36*(1), 29–40. doi:10.1007/s10755–010–9155–7

Casey, T. (2011, November 29). Bloomberg News adds its two cents to sustainability debate. *Triple Pundit*. Retrieved from: http://www.triplepundit.com/2011/11/bloomberg-news-adds-cents-sustainability-debate/

Caulkins, D. (2008). Re-theorizing Jim Collins's culture of discipline in Good to Great. *Innovation: The European Journal of Social Sciences, 21*(3), 217–232. doi:10.1080/13511610802404880

Center for Disease Control and Prevention [CDC]. (n.d.). *Over weight and obesity*. Retrieved from: http://www.cdc.gov/obesity/

CERES. (2012). *Investor network*. Retrieved from: http://www.ceres.org/investor-network

Cernansky, R. (2010, September 6). Will coal supplies peak in 2011? That's the prediction made by a recent study of reserves and historic coal production. *PlanetGreen.com*. Retrieved from http://planetgreen.discovery.com/work-connect/will-coal-supplies-peak-in-2011.html

Chartres, C., & Varma, S. (2011). *Out of water: From abundance to scarcity and how to solve the world's water problems*. Upper Saddle River, NJ: Pearson Education.

Collins J., & Porras, J. (1994). *Built to last*. New York, NY: Harper Business.

Collins, J. (2001). *Good to great*. New York, NY: HarperCollins.

Collins, J. (2005). Level 5 Leadership: The triumph of humility and fierce resolve. (cover story). *Harvard Business Review, 83*(7/8), 136–146. Retrieved from https://hbdm.hbsp.harvard.edu/hbr/

Collins, J. (2012). Effective management. *Leadership Excellence, 29*(4), 3. Retrieved from http://www.leaderexcel.com/

Collins, J., & Hansen, M.T. (2011). Great by choice: Uncertainty, chaos, and luck—Why some thrive despite them all. New York, NY: HarperBusiness.

Danaei, G., Ding, E. L., Mozaffarian, D., Taylor, B., Rehm, J., Rehm, J., Murray, C. J. L., & Ezzatil, M. (2009). The preventable causes of death in the United States: Comparative risk assessment of dietary, lifestyle, and metabolic risk factors. *PLoS Med 6*(4): e1000058. doi:10.1371/journal.pmed.1000058

Ehrhardt, E. F., & Brigham, M. C. (2011). *Corporate finance: A focused approach*, (4th ed.). Mason, OH: Thomas South-Western.

Energy Information Administration [EIA]. (2012a). *International statistics.* Retrieved from: http://www.eia.gov/cfapps/ipdbproject/

Energy Information Administration [EIA]. (2012b). *Annual energy outlook 2012: Early release.* Retrieved from: http://www.eia.gov

Environmental Protection Agency [EPA]. (2009, December 7). *Endangerment and cause or contribute findings for greenhouse gases under Section 202(a) of the Clean Air Act.* Climate Change Division, Office of Atmospheric Programs. Washington, D.C.: Author.

Environmental Protection Agency [EPA]. (2012). *Climate change.* Retrieved from: http://www.epa.gov/climatechange/index.html

Friedman, T. (2009). *Hot, flat, and crowded: Why we need a green revolution—and how it can renew America.* New York, NY: Farrar, Straus, and Giroux.

Gates, B. (2010, February). Bill Gates on energy: Innovating to zero!. *TED2010 Conference.* Retrieved from: http://www.ted.com/talks/bill_gates.html

Global Reporting Initiative [GRI]. (2012). *Reporting.* Retrieved from: https://www.globalreporting.org/reporting/Pages/default.aspx

Greenleaf, R. K. (1977). *Servant leadership: A journey into the nature of legitimate power and greatness.* Mahwah, NJ: Paulist Press.

Greenspan, A. (2007). *The age of turbulence: Adventures in a new world.* New York, NY: Penguin Group.

Guenther, M. (2012, May 24). *Microsoft is going carbon neutral.* Retrieved from: http://www.globalcarbonsystems.com/News/2012–05–24/Microsoft-is-going-carbon-neutral.cfm

Hall, E. (2009). Strategic planning in times of extreme uncertainty. In C. A. Lentz (Ed.), *The Refractive Thinker: Vol. 1. An anthology of higher learning* (pp. 41–58). Las Vegas, NV: The Lentz Leadership Institute.

Hall, E. (2010a). Innovation out of turbulence: Scenario and survival plans that utilizes groups and the wisdom of crowds. In C. A. Lentz (Ed.), *The Refractive Thinker: Vol. 5. Strategy in innovation* (5th ed., pp. 1–30). Las Vegas, NV: The Lentz Leadership Institute.

Hall, E. (2010b). Lessons of recessions: Sustainability education and jobs may be the answer. *Journal of Sustainability and Green Management.* Retrieved from: http://www.aabri.com/OC2010Manuscripts/OC10079.pdf

Hall, E. B. (2007). *Strategic economic development & marketing plan for Highlands County.* Morrisville, NC: LuLu Press.

Hall, E. B., & Hinkelman, R. M. (2007). *Perpetual Innovation™: A guide to strategic planning, patent commercialization and enduring competitive advantage.* Morrisville, NC: LuLu Press.

Hall, E., Taylor, S., Zapalski, C., & Hall, T. (2009). Sustainability in education: Green in the facilities, but not in the classrooms. *Proceedings of the Society for Advancement of Management,* USA.

Hartman, L. (2011). *Business ethics: Decision-making for personal integrity and social responsibility,* (2nd ed.). New York, NY: McGraw-Hill.

Hofstede, G. (2012). *About the U.S.A.?* Retrieved from: http://geert-hofstede.com/united-states.html

Hollander, E. P. (1978). *Leadership dynamics: A practical guide to effective relationships.* New York, NY: Free Press.

Hollander, E. P. (1986). On the central role of the leadership process. *International Review of Applied Psychology,*35, 39–52. Retrieved from http://www.wiley.com/WileyCDA/WileyTitle/productCd-APPS.html

Intergovernmental Panel on Climate Change [IPCC]. (2007). *Climate change 2007: Synthesis report,* (4th ed.). New York, NY: Cambridge University Press.

International Standards Organization [ISO]. (2012). *Management and leadership standards.* Retrieved from: http://www.iso.org/iso/iso_catalogue/management_and_leadership_standards.htm

Investopedia. (n.d.). *Debt securities—Bond ratings.* Retrieved from: http://www.investopedia.com/exam-guide/series-7/debt-securities/bond-ratings.asp#axzz1xKq8BFPu

Jones, G. R. (2010). *Organizational theory, design, and change* (6th ed.). Upper Saddle River, NJ: Prentice Hall.

Kromm, C. (2010, June 4). Coal's dirty secret (a week-long series). *Institute of Southern Studies.* Retrieved from: http://www.southernstudies.org/2010/06/coals-dirty-secret-1.html

Laur, J. (2007). *Twenty years later: An interview with John Elkington.* Retrieved from: http://www.johnelkington.com/downloads/twentyyearsafter.pdf

Leonard, A. (2010, March 22). *The story of bottled water: How "manufactured demand" pushes what we don't need and destroys what we need most.* Retrieved from http://www.storyofstuff.org/movies-all/story-of-bottled-water/

Leonard, A. (2010b). *The story of stuff: How our obsession with stuff is trashing the planet, our communities, and our health—and a vision for change.* New York, NY: Free Press.

Lockwood, A. H., Welker-Hood, K., Rauch, M., & Gottleib, B. (2009, November). Coal's assault on human health. *Physicians for Social Responsibility.* Retrieved from: http://www.psr.org/coalreport

Maon, F., Lindgreen, A., & Swaen, V. (2008). Thinking of the organization as a system: The role of managerial perceptions in developing a corporate social responsibility strategic agenda. *Systems Research & Behavioral Science.* 25(3), 413. Retrieved from http://onlinelibrary.wiley.com/journal/10.1002/%28ISSN% 291099-1743a;jsessionid=6F0BA279FC8688C21E73ED072084D21E.d01t04

Marks, S. (2009). *Aqua shock: The water crisis in America.* New York, NY: Bloomberg Press.

Martin Akel & Associates. (2006, Spring). Institutions of higher education: A study of facilities and environmental considerations. *Educational & Institutional Cooperative Purchasing and University Business.* Retrieved from: http://www.universitybusiness.com/uploaded/pdfs/HiEdGreenFacilitiesStudyECNN.pdf

McAuley, J., Duberley, J., & Johnson, P. (2007). *Organization theory: Challenges and perspectives.* Upper Saddle River, NJ: Prentice Hall.

Mekonnen, M. M., & Hoekstra, A. Y. (2012, January 24). A global assessment of the water footprint of farm animal products. *Ecosystems.* 15, 401–415. doi: 10.1007/s10021-011-9517-8

Minkov, M., & Hofstede, G. (2012). Hofstede's fifth dimension: New evidence from the World Values Survey. *Journal of Cross-Cultural Psychology, 43*(1), 3. doi:10.1177/0022022110388567

Mintzberg, H., Lampel, J., Quinn, J. B., & Ghoshal, S. (2003). *The strategy process: Concepts, contexts, cases* (4th ed.). Upper Saddle River, NJ: Prentice Hall.

National Wildlife Federation. (2008). *Campus environment 2008: A national report card on sustainability in higher education.* Retrieved from: http://www .nwf.org

Niendorf, B., & Beck, K. (2008). Good to great, or just good? *Academy of Management Perspectives, 22*(4), 13. doi:10.5465/AMP.2008.35590350

Porter, M. (2008, November 10). Why America needs an economic strategy. *Business Week,* 38–42. Retrieved from http://www.businessweek.com/

Robbins, S. P., & Judge, T. A. (2011). *Organizational behavior* (14th ed.). Upper Saddle River, NJ: Pearson/Prentice Hall.

Roger, H. (n.d). Peak oil and strategic resource wars: When the oil fields run dry—and they will—what will happen to the economies of petroleum producers? And what will that mean for the rest of us? The time to consider the potential scenarios and strategies is now. *The Futurist, 43*(5), 18. Retrieved from http://www.wfs.org/futurist

Savitz, A. W., & Weber, K. (2006). *The triple bottom line. How today's best-run companies are achieving economic, social, and environmental success—and how you can too.* San Francisco, CA: Jossey-Bass.

Scott, W. R., & Davis, G. F. (2007). *Organizations and organizing: Rational, natural, and open system perspectives.* Upper Saddle River, NJ: Pearson Prentice Hall.

Senge, P., Smith, B., Kruschwitz, N., Laur, J., & Schley, S. (2008). *The necessary revolution: How individuals and organizations are working together to create a sustainable world.* New York, NY: Doublday.

Sustainable Endowments Institute [SEI]. (2008). *The college sustainability report card 2009.* Retrieved from: www.greenreportcard.org

Terry, K. (2010, February 4). Health spending hits 17.3 percent of GDP in largest annual jump. *CBSNews.* Retrieved from http://www.cbsnews.com/8301–505123_162–43841117/health-spending-hits-173-percent-of-gdp-in-largest-annual-jump/

Thorne, D. M., Farrell, O. C., & Ferrell, L. (2010). *Business and society: A strategic approach to social responsibility.* Mason, OH: Cengage Learning.

Tukker, A., Cohen, M. J., Hubacek, K., & Mont, O. (2010). The impacts of household consumption and options for change. *Journal of Industrial Ecology, 14*(1), 13–30. doi:10.1111/j.1530–9290.2009.00208.x

The United Nations Framework Convention on Climate Change [UNFCCC]. (n.d.). *Kyoto protocol.* Retrieved from: http://unfccc.int/kyoto_protocol/items/2830.php

U.S. Debt Clock. (2012). *United States debt clock.* Retrieved from: http://usdebtclock.org/

Walker, D. M. (2010). *Comeback America: Turning the country around and restoring fiscal responsibility.* New York, NY: Random House.

World Economic Forum. (2011). *Water security: The water-food-energy-climate nexus.* World Economic Forum Water Initiative. Washington, DC: Author.

Wright, R. T., & Boorse, D. (2011). *Environmental science: Toward a sustainable future with MasteringEnvironmentalScience™* (11th ed.). Upper Saddle River, NJ: Prentice Hall.

Yukl, G. A. (2010). *Leadership in organizations* (7th ed.). Upper Saddle River, NJ: Pearson/Prentice Hall.

About the Authors

Dr. Elmer B. Hall

Dr. Elmer Hall helps individuals and organizations plan for success that sustainably balances wellness and wealth.

He holds several accredited degrees: a BA and MBA from the University of South Florida; and a Doctorate of International Business Administration (DIBA) from Nova Southeastern University. For 25 years, he has taught at the undergraduate and graduate levels (MBA and MIS) at several Florida universities. He is a Facilitator and Dissertation Mentor for the University of Phoenix. His "real" education, however, is from his personal entrepreneurial ventures and those of clients.

Dr. Elmer is the President of Strategic Business Planning Company (www.SBPlan.com), doing strategic consulting for startups and existing ventures. He has also been interim Sustainability Officer and chair of a business incubator. Major clients: IBM, Ryder, Florida Power & Light (NextEra Energy), and Burger King (Diageo).

Publications/Seminars are on survival/scenario, sustainability in business and education, innovation, economic development, patent planning and Delphi Method research. With Robert 'Bob' M. Hinkelman, Dr. Elmer authored *Perpetual Innovation™: A Guide to Strategic Planning, Patent Commercialization and Enduring Competitive Advantage* and the *Patent Primer.* SBP has developed the Commercialization of Patent Assets, COMPASS®, process for intellectual property (IP) management (www.IPplan.com).

Sustainability planning/Blog: http://www.SustainZine.com

To reach Dr. Elmer please e-mail: elmer@SBPlan.com

Dr. Edward F. Knab

Growing up on a rural Wisconsin farm significantly impacted Dr. Edward F. Knab's understanding of sustainable environments; he developed a sense of the importance of the natural environment. Dr. Knab received a BA degree from James Madison College at Michigan State University, an MBA degree from Pepperdine University, and a doctorate from University of Phoenix in Organizational Leadership.

Dr. Knab began his business career in Michigan helping companies globalize their enterprise. His professional associations moved him to California and from there travelled extensively in Asia and Europe developing sustainable global supply chains. Currently, Dr. Knab operates and international consulting business (Productivity Constructs, Inc.) and is a professor at Embry-Riddle Aeronautics University. Dr. Knab works closely with the Center of Aviation and Aerospace Leadership (CAAL) and can be contacted at ed@edwardknab.com

Refractive Thinking: Lessons Learned

Dr. Cheryl A. Lentz

A s *The Refractive Thinker® Doctoral Anthology* series moves forward, throughout this journey of volume VII, knowledge is not only power but offers a role of social responsibility for its possessor, particularly the doctoral scholar. "For everyone to whom much is given, of him shall much be required." —Luke 12:48 is the quote that began this volume summarizing the societal expectation of the scholar where there is indeed both power and expectation. With this knowing comes the responsibly to share what one has learned to improve life around them for the greater good. This commentary provides an in-depth analysis of this dynamic perspective as we continue to expand our definition of the elusive refractive thinker. This volume continues this mission of this power project of discovery.

Think of the refractive thinkers throughout history. Where might society be were it not for Einstein, Madame Curie, and Sir Isaac Newton? They were not content to settle for what *was;* instead, their intellectual curiosity led them on a path of discovery of what *could be.* What would society look like without the many inventions of Thomas Edison, Ben Franklin, and Leonardo da Vinci? Refractive thinkers did not invent nor discover with only the intent to help or keep to themselves. Instead, refractive thinkers shared and continue to share their brilliance with humanity with the hope to better themselves and society.

With this hope of improving tomorrow, the doctoral scholars of volume VII offer their knowledge within the same vein. We have learned about social responsibility of the doctoral scholar, the empowerment of rural women, the influence of women leaders and entrepreneurs, generational conflict between nurses, the value of innovative leadership practices, succession planning in municipal governments, federal employees and instructors serving the public trust, ethics in sports, stakeholder theory, the impacts of technology, and sustainability.

Who is a Refractive Thinker®?

First, let us begin our discussion with the concept of *refractive thinking* itself. This concept emerged when I concluded the concept of critical thinking was incomplete. Having taught this for more than 10 years, there is more than simply an either or dichotomy where if thinking is *inside* the box, and critical thinking is *outside* the box. What then is beyond this approach? Who are those among us that think beyond this dichotomy? Enter the refractive thinker.

A refractive thinker is someone that is insatiable with his or her curiosity. They are not satisfied within current conventional parameters or the prevailing wisdom. They are frustrated by provincial thinking or analysis. They do not follow the crowd. Instead, the crowd follows *them.* They ask questions as they continue to dig deep in their pursuit of knowledge and understanding. They do not excel within the constraints of only an either/or option where many believe there are only two options: *in the box* or *out of the box* boundaries. Instead of merely preferring to color outside of the lines, they prefer to redefine the very rules that constrain the lines themselves, questioning the very structure itself.

Refractive thinkers are often those individuals innovating new business models, those who make new scientific discoveries, and those who offer never before held theories to try explaining existing or new phenomenon. They are the explorers of thoughts, those who are willing to ask the right questions that often take them—and those following them—in new and unchartered waters. The refractive thinker is comfortable with limitless boundaries and the suspensions of rules. Refractive thinkers are the pioneers such as Sir Isaac Newton, Albert Einstein, Benjamin Franklin, Leonardo da Vinci, Mohandas Gandhi, and Madame Curie to name but a few. They are those that not only ask *why,* but *why not* or *what else?*

The quest of the refractive thinker is to think *beyond* boundaries, to learn to tolerate ambiguity without form, to believe in the process and allow the shape to evolve on its own. A refractive thinker learns that sometimes there are no rules where they learn to take *perceived* limitations away, and offer permission to allow *the situation* to dictates its form, where our creativity generates an expansive array of new ideas. Refractive thinkers understand that we cannot put new ideas into old constructs (Senge, 1990).

What are the Benefits to Refractive Thinking?

Individuals within either academia or the business landscape seem to find comfort with what they currently regard as truth. To reiterate, refractive thinking is *beyond perceived* limits of the proverbial box.

The design looks toward existing issues and opportunities while suspending judgment, freeing one's mind to be limitless. Refractive thinking goes beyond the rules, simply existing where one suspends and resists any type of confinement, labels, or parameters of any kind. This free thinking without any convention at all is something that few truly can obtain.

Einstein was one of the rare few who could think beyond that had not been previously considered. He strove to decipher behavior in a way that did not follow conventional wisdom. Initially, few could grasp the radically different concepts Einstein put forth. Much like during the time of Sir Isaac Newton or perhaps even further, when the earth was believed to once be flat, these pioneers represent the ideals of refractive thinking.

Descartes offers the often quoted phrase: *"I think therefore I am."* Allow me to expand this view by adding "I critically think *to be,* I refractively think *to change the world*" (Lentz, 2009). My goal is to help adult learners develop their critical thinking skills to see what is already there through a slightly different lens. This new perspective enables them to learn to question everything they see-and to have their curiosity drive them to question, *why.*

Refractive thinking embraces the post modernism guise of being able to hold divergent points of view and theory *simultaneously.* It builds a foundation of duality. Society is uncomfortable with simultaneous duality—the thought that two divergent boundaries can exist and both can be correct—*from their point of view* is challenging to wrap one's arms around. Dealing within not only duality but also multiplicity of meaning is where refractive thinking exists, expands, and offers a new contemplation of thought. The goal is to be able to simply exist within a modality of asking *why* and *why not,* to suggest *what if?* The goal is to build the capacity to understanding limitlessness.

What is it that prevents most people from achieving this state? Why is it easier to cling to the safety of the confines of the proverbial box allowing only the dichotomy of opposites, or either or extremes? Instead, why not break this cycle of fear and simply stop? Perhaps the solution is not a box *at all.* Instead, this free form is fluid and dynamic. Can we exist without having to clearly define the parameters of that existence? This is the quest of the refractive thinker®—to discover the yet unknown and to realize that one cannot put new ideas into old constructs (Senge, 1990).

Index

Federal, 125–133, 197, 199, 200, 222

G
Generation X, 49, 59
GSA, 111, 112

H
Halo effect, 35, 36, 40
Higher education, 5, 182, 183, 185–190,
Holistic, 15, 23, 116, 203, 208
Human Growth Hormone, 137
Human resources, 93

I
Instructors, 111, 113, 114–132, 183, 222
Integrated, 15, 190, 203, 205, 207, 208, 210–212
Intellectual freedom, 188, 193
Intellectual property, 188, 193
Internet, 121, 129, 145, 181, 183, 185, 187–193
Internet-sharing sites, 187, 188, 193
Irresponsibility, 22, 197–203, 209, 213

J
Justification, 152, 154

K
Knowledge transfer, 91

L
Leadership comes softly, 6
Level 5 leaders, 211, 212

M
Mentoring, 184
Metacognition, 3, 4
Metacognitive experience, 3
Metacognitive knowledge, 3
Metacognitive skills, 3, 4
Models, 73, 81, 82, 140, 143, 145, 156, 189, 204, 205, 222
Municipal government, 91–95, 99, 102, 105, 222

O
Online learning, 182
Organization structure, 174
Organizational governance, 172

P
Pebble-in-the-Pond, 7
Pedagogy, 5, 191
Perception, 54, 58, 59, 60, 62, 69, 73, 76, 96–98, 114, 117–120, 123, 124, 128, 130, 131, 140, 144, 149, 150, 151, 152, 155, 156, 172
Planning, 7, 40, 48, 79, 91–97, 99–102, 104–106, 197, 205–208, 210–212, 222

The Refractive Thinker®

and

Pensiero Press

Dr. Cheryl A. Lentz, managing editor of The Lentz Leadership Institute, explains the unique benefits of the books for readers:

"They celebrate the diffusion of innovative refractive thinking through the writings of these doctoral scholars as they dare to think differently in search of new applications and understandings of research methodology. Unlike most academic books that merely define research, The Refractive Thinker® offers unique applications of research methodologies from the perspective of multiple authors—each offering a chapter based on their specific expertise."

Other Volumes of *The Refractive Thinker*®

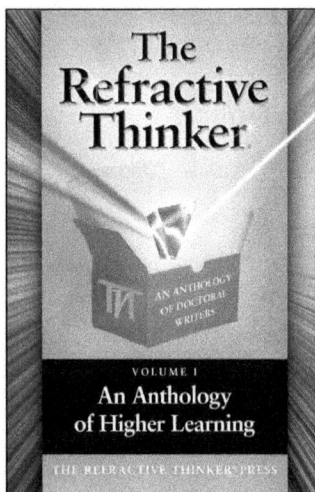

The Refractive Thinker®: Volume I: An Anthology of Higher Learning

The title of this book, *The Refractive Thinker®*, was chosen intentionally to highlight the ability of these doctoral scholars to bend thought, to converge its very essence on the ability to obliquely pass through the perspective of another. The goal is to ask and ponder the right questions; to dare to think differently, to find new applications within unique and cutting-edge dimensions, ultimately to lead where others may follow or to risk forging perhaps an entirely new path.

For more information, please visit our website: www.refractivethinker.com

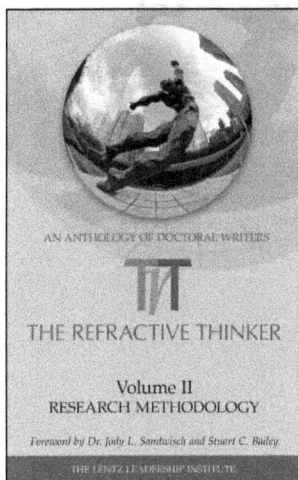

The Refractive Thinker®: Volume II: Research Methodology

The authors within these pages are on a mission to change the world, never satisfied or quite content with what is or asking *why,* instead these authors intentionally strive to push and test the limits to ask *why not. The Refractive Thinker®* is an intimate expression of who we are—the ability to think beyond the traditional boundaries of thinking and critical thinking. Instead of mere reflection and evaluation, one challenges the very boundaries of the constructs itself.

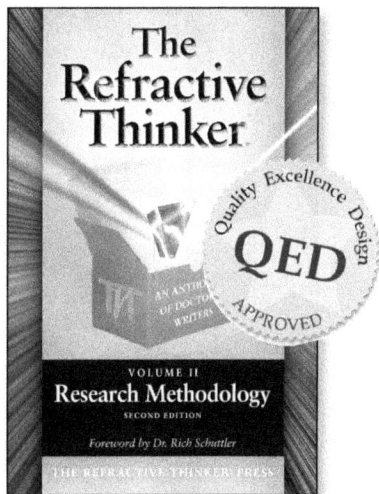

The Refractive Thinker®: Volume II: Research Methodology, 2nd Edition

Chosen as Finalist, Education/Academic category The USA "Best Books 2011" Awards, sponsored by USA Book News

As in Volume I, the authors within these pages are on a mission to change the world, never satisfied or quite content with what is or asking *why,* instead these authors intentionally strive to push and test the limits to ask *why not. The Refractive Thinker®* is an intimate expression of who we are—the ability to think beyond the traditional boundaries of thinking and critical thinking. Instead of mere reflection and evaluation, one challenges the very boundaries of the constructs itself.

For more information, please visit our website: www.refractivethinker.com

The Refractive Thinker®: Volume III:
Change Management

This next offering in the series shares yet another glimpse into the scholarly works of these authors, specifically on the topic of change management. In addition to exploring various aspects of change management, the purpose of *The Refractive Thinker®* is also to serve the tenets of leadership. Leadership is not simply a concept outside of the self, but comes from within, defining our very essence; where the search to define leadership becomes our personal journey, not yet a finite destination.

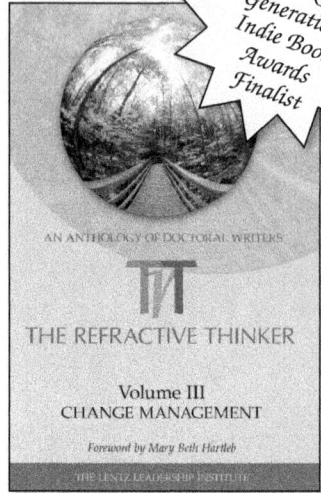

AN ANTHOLOGY OF DOCTORAL WRITERS

TT

THE REFRACTIVE THINKER

Volume III
CHANGE MANAGEMENT

Foreword by Mary Beth Hartleb

THE LENTZ LEADERSHIP INSTITUTE

2010 Next Generation Indie Book Awards Finalist

2011 Next Generation Indie Book Awards Finalist

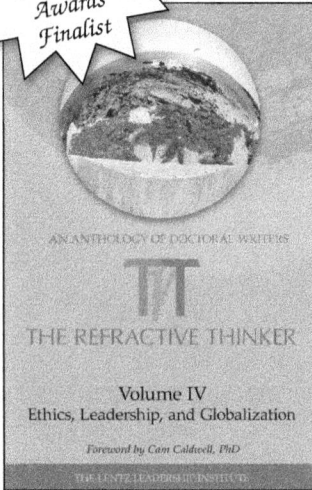

AN ANTHOLOGY OF DOCTORAL WRITERS

TT

THE REFRACTIVE THINKER

Volume IV
Ethics, Leadership, and Globalization

Foreword by Cam Caldwell, PhD

THE LENTZ LEADERSHIP INSTITUTE

The Refractive Thinker®: Volume IV:
Ethics, Leadership, and Globalization

The purpose of this volume is to highlight the scholarly works of these authors on the topics of ethics, leadership, and concerns within the global landscape of business. Join us as we venture forward to showcase the authors of Volume IV, and continue to celebrate the accomplishments of these doctoral scholars affiliated with many phenomenal institutions of higher learning.

Axiom 2011 Bronze Medal • Business Ethics
AXIOM

For more information, please visit our website: www.refractivethinker.com

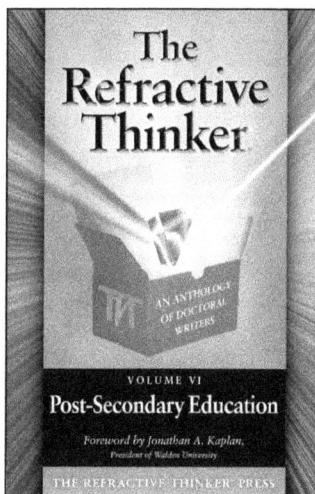

JOURNEY OUTSIDE THE GOLDEN PALACE

DR. CHERYL LENTZ

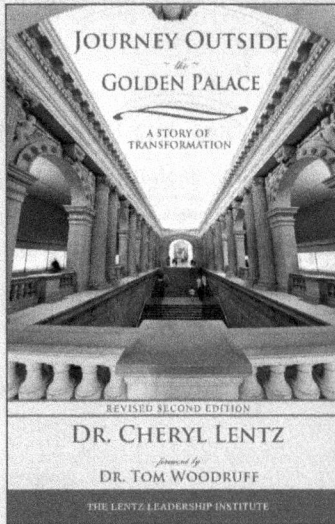

Come take a mythical journey with Henry from *The Village of Yore* and the many colorful characters of The Golden Palace on their quest to unlock the palatial gates of corporate Ivory Towers. This allegorical tale demonstrates the lessons learned when leaders in organizations fail to serve the needs of their stakeholders. Come join us in a journey toward understanding the elegant simplicity of effective leadership, unlocking the secrets to The Golden Palace Theory of Management along the way.

This revised second edition offers a companion workbook for discussion, reflection, and refractive thinking. The purpose of this workbook is to more closely examine each character and their leadership qualities. Take a leap of faith and follow us on our journey. Perhaps you may recognize some old friends on your travels.

Pensiero Press PUBLISHES LANDMARK BOOK ON THE CHANGING ADULT EDUCATION ARENA

2011 Next Generation Indie Book Awards Finalist

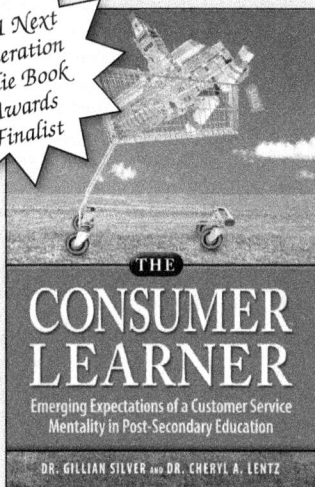

THE CONSUMER LEARNER
Emerging Expectations of a Customer Service Mentality in Post-Secondary Education

DR. GILLIAN SILVER AND DR. CHERYL A. LENTZ

PENSIERO PRESS WINS FINALIST AWARD

May 12, 2012, Las Vegas, NV—*The Consumer Learner* has been named a Finalist in the Education/Academic category of the 2012 Next Generational Indie Book Awards!

Anyone who has entered a college classroom in the last 5 years has recognized a clear transformation in the context of higher education. A dynamic revolution in practice and delivery is underway, and the implications of change are ripe for analysis.

Administrators are increasingly charged with revenue production and institutional leadership. Faculty are experimenting with new andragogical models and advances in interactive technology. Students are embracing new modalities as they strive to make curriculum immediately transferable into industry. *The Consumer Learner: Emergence and Expectations of a Customer Service Mentality in Post-Secondary Education* examines the new reality and emerging patterns shaping the experiences of these three diverse, yet interconnected, constituencies.

This book provides a distinctive approach to the transformation of the higher education culture within the U.S. Authors Dr. Gillian Silver and Dr. Cheryl Lentz, noted content experts, professors and curriculum/program developers, explain that the contents will initiate an intensive dialogue about the implications and impacts on administrative structure, faculty practice, and learner outcomes. According to Dr. Lentz, "This is a frank, encompassing work that has the capacity to ignite a national dialogue. We think the review will give voice to the significance of this evolving environment. The voices of experience leading this change will emerge."

Follow the authors on the Web: ww.consumerlearner.com and Blog: www.consumerlearner.com/wordpress/

Available through Pensiero Press, a division of the The Lentz Leadership Institute. $24.95 (HARDCOVER)

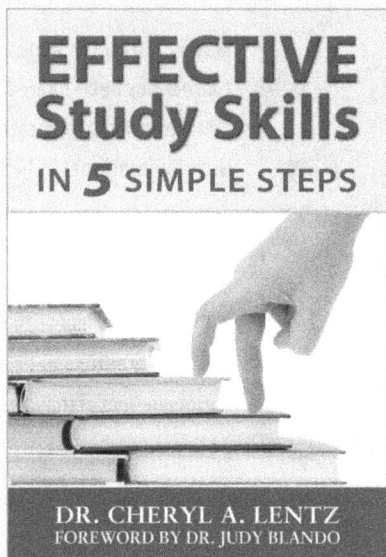

EFFECTIVE
Study Skills
IN **5** SIMPLE STEPS

Dr. Cheryl Lentz has compiled the valuable information she gives in her blog in one easy-to-use handbook. The study tips are designed to help any student improve learning and understanding, and ultimately earn higher grades. The handbook is not so large that it requires long hours of reading, as is the case with many books on the subject. The information is written in a manner to help a learner "see" and "practice" proven study techniques. Effective study skills must be practiced to for improvement to occur.

PUBLICATIONS ORDER FORM

Please send the following books:

❏ *The Refractive Thinker®: Volume I: An Anthology of Higher Learning*

❏ *The Refractive Thinker®: Volume II: Research Methodology*

❏ *The Refractive Thinker®: Volume II: Research Methodology, 2nd Edition*

❏ *The Refractive Thinker®: Volume III: Change Management*

❏ *The Refractive Thinker®: Volume IV: Ethics, Leadership, and Globalization*

❏ *The Refractive Thinker®: Volume V: Strategy in Innovation*

❏ *The Refractive Thinker®: Volume VI: Post-Secondary Education*

Please contact the Refractive Thinker® Press for book prices, e-book prices, and shipping.
Individual e-chapters available by author: $3.95 (plus applicable tax). www.refractivethinker.com

❏ *The Consumer Learner: Emergence and Expectations of a Customer Service Mentality in Post-Secondary Education*

❏ *Effective Study Skills in 5 Simple Steps*

❏ *Journey Outside the Golden Palace*

Please send more FREE information:

❏ Speaking engagements   ❏ Educational seminars   ❏ Consulting

Join our Mailing List

Name: _____

Address:_____

City: _____ State:_____ Zip: _____

Telephone: _____ Email:_____

Sales tax: NV Residents please add 8.1% sales tax

Shipping: *Please see our website for shipping rates.*

Please mail or e-mail form to:

The Refractive Thinker® Press/
  Pensiero Press
9065 Big Plantation Ave.
Las Vegas, NV 89143-5440 USA
E-mail: orders@lentzleadership.com

Yes, I would like to participate in:

❏ **Doctoral Volume**(s) for a specific university or organization:

Name: _____

Contact Person: _____

Telephone: _____ E-mail: _____

❏ **Specialized Volume**(s) Business or Themed:

Name: _____

Contact Person: _____

Telephone: _____ E-mail: _____

Please mail or e-mail form to:

The Refractive Thinker® Press
9065 Big Plantation Ave.
Las Vegas, NV 89143-5440 USA

E-mail: orders@lentzleadership.com
www.refractivethinker.com